182

Houses are much more than physical structures. This is obvious when we think about what makes a house a home. Like the people they contain, houses are dynamic entities which are often thought to be born, mature, grow old and die.

The essays in this collection reveal some of the different ways in which houses stand for social groups, and represent the surrounding world. They focus on the relations between buildings, the people who live in them, and the ideas they represent. Inspired by Lévi-Strauss's recent writings, the contributors critically assess Lévi-Strauss's notion of the 'house society' in various Southeast Asian and South American cultures. In their introduction, the editors place Lévi-Strauss's latest theories in a broad anthropological context. They demonstrate how an analysis of the house can bring together areas of social life which anthropology has tended to separate. Their innovative approach stresses kinship as a process of lived relationships, and links the anthropology of the house to the anthropology of the body.

The volume bridges the disciplines of anthropology and architecture, and marks a major step in our understanding of the relation between material culture and sociality. It will appeal to anthropologists, architects, social historians, archaeologists and social geographers.

ABOUT THE HOUSE

ABOUT THE HOUSE
LÉVI-STRAUSS AND BEYOND

Edited by

Janet Carsten

University of Edinburgh

and

Stephen Hugh-Jones

University of Cambridge

Published by the Press Syndicate of the University of Cambridge
The Pitt Building, Trumpington Street, Cambridge CB2 1RP
40 West 20th Street, New York, NY 10011–4211, USA
10 Stamford Road, Oakleigh, Melbourne 3166, Australia

© Cambridge University Press 1995

First published 1995

Printed in Great Britain at the University Press, Cambridge

A catalogue record for this book is available from the British Library

Library of Congress cataloguing in publication data
About the house: Lévi-Strauss and beyond / edited by Janet Carsten
and Stephen Hugh-Jones
    p.   cm.
  ISBN 0 521 47421 3 (hardback). – ISBN 0 521 47953 9 (pbk.)
  1. Dwellings – Social aspects. 2. Dwellings – Asia, Southeastern.
3. Dwellings – South America. 4. Kinship – Asia, Southeastern.
5. Indians of South America – Kinship. I. Carsten, Janet. II. Hugh-
Jones, Stephen, 1945–
GN414.A24   1995
307.3′36–dc20   94–26899
                                                 CIP

ISBN 0 521 47421 3 hardback
ISBN 0 521 47953 3 paperback

To Claude Lévi-Strauss

CONTENTS

Contents

ILLUSTRATIONS

CONTRIBUTORS

MAURICE BLOCH is a Professor of Social Anthropology at the London School of Economics. His most recent book is *From Prey into Hunter* (1992).

JANET CARSTEN is a Lecturer in Anthropology at the University of Edinburgh, and is the author of a number of articles on Malaysia.

THOMAS GIBSON is an Associate Professor of Anthropology at the University of Rochester. He is the author of *Sacrifice and Sharing in the Philippine Highlands* (1986).

SIGNE HOWELL is a Professor of Social Anthropology at the University of Oslo. She is the author of *Society and Cosmos* (1984) and *Societies at Peace* (1989).

STEPHEN HUGH-JONES is a Lecturer in Social Anthropology at the University of Cambridge. He is the author of *The Palm and the Pleiades* and joint editor of *Barter, Exchange, and Value* (1992).

MONICA JANOWSKI holds a Research Fellowship at the University of Cambridge and is the author of several articles on the Kelabit of Sarawak.

VANESSA LEA is a Lecturer in Anthropology at UNICAMP University, São Paulo and is the author of several articles on the Mẽbengokre of Central Brazil.

SUSAN McKINNON is an Associate Professor of Anthropology at the University of Virginia. She is the author of *From a Shattered Sun* (1991).

PETER RIVIÈRE is a Lecturer in Social Anthropology at the University of Oxford. He is the author of *Marriage among the Trio* (1969) and *Individual and Society in Guiana* (1984).

ROXANA WATERSON is a Senior Lecturer in the Department of Sociology, National University of Singapore. She is the author of *The Living House* (1990).

INTRODUCTION: ABOUT THE HOUSE – LEVI-STRAUSS AND
1   BEYOND

Janet Carsten and Stephen Hugh-Jones

House images move in two directions: they are in us as much as
we are in them.
(Gaston Bachelard 1964: xxxiii)

THE ESSAYS IN THIS COLLECTION are concerned with
houses, but not simply with houses as physical structures. They focus
instead on the interrelations between buildings, people and ideas,
using ethnographic case studies to reveal some of the different ways in
which houses come to stand for social groups and represent the world
around them. Places in which the to and fro of life unfolds, built,
modified, moved or abandoned in accord with the changing
circumstances of their inhabitants, houses have dynamic, processual
characteristics encapsulated in the word 'dwelling'. These characteristics, shared by buildings and the groups and categories they
represent, are also reflected in the chapters that follow.

Inspired by Lévi-Strauss's writings on 'house societies' and based
on a workshop held in Cambridge in the spring of 1990[1], our book
has two interconnected aims. We take a sympathetic but critical look
at Lévi-Strauss's ideas of the house as a specific form of social
organization, testing its utility against empirical cases drawn from
Southeast Asia and lowland South America. Forms of social organization in these two areas show both striking parallels and marked
contrasts and each has a key role in Lévi-Strauss's studies of kinship,
South America representing the earliest phase and Southeast Asia the
most recent.[2]

Through case studies, set in a comparative context, illustrating the
linkages between buildings, groups and categories, we also seek to go
beyond Lévi-Strauss's concept of 'house societies', the problematic

aspects of which are discussed below and in the chapters that follow. Though each explores different facets of the house, taken together our essays suggest that the real value of Lévi-Strauss's idea lies not so much in the creation of a new, unwieldy social type to complement or nuance already threadbare categories of traditional kinship theory but rather in providing a jumping-off point allowing a move beyond them towards a more holistic anthropology of architecture which might take its theoretical place alongside the anthropology of the body. We seek to develop an 'alternative language of the house', one not based on the assumed priority of kinship or economy but which enables us to escape some of the constraints of conventional analysis of these areas, and to bring together aspects of the house previously treated separately. Seeing houses 'in the round' enables us to focus on the links between their architectural, social and symbolic significance. Before discussing Lévi-Strauss's concept of house societies, we begin with a brief exploration of the potential but often neglected significance of architecture in anthropological analysis.

The house and the body are intimately linked. The house is an extension of the person; like an extra skin, carapace or second layer of clothes, it serves as much to reveal and display as it does to hide and protect. House, body and mind are in continuous interaction, the physical structure, furnishing, social conventions and mental images of the house at once enabling, moulding, informing and constraining the activities and ideas which unfold within its bounds. A ready-made environment fashioned by a previous generation and lived in long before it becomes an object of thought, the house is a prime agent of socialization. Littlejohn's (1960) article on the Temne house was an innovative exploration of the link between body and house, and between the house and the experience and activities of those who dwell in it. Bourdieu, in turn, describes the house as 'the principle locus for the objectification of generative schemes' (1977: 89) and compares it to a book in which is inscribed a vision and structure of society and the world. Moving in ordered space, the body 'reads' the house which serves as a mnemonic for the embodied person. Through habit and inhabiting, each person builds up a practical mastery of the fundamental schemes of their culture. Bourdieu's classic paper on the Kabyle house (1990 [1977]) prefigures the development of his concept of habitus, and the dialectical interaction between body and house plays a key role in his analysis of the logic of practice.

As our essays will show, houses are frequently thought of as bodies, sharing with them a common anatomy and a common life history. If people construct houses and make them in their own image, so also do they use these houses and house-images to construct themselves as individuals and as groups. At some level or other, the notion that houses are people is one of the universals of architecture. If the house is an extension of the person, it is also an extension of the self. As Bachelard reminds us, the space of the house is inhabited not just in daily life but also in the imagination. It is a 'topography of our intimate being', a 'felicitous space' with protective and comforting associations, a rich and varied poetic image which 'emerges into the consciousness as a direct product of the heart, soul, and being of man, apprehended in his actuality' (1964: xxxii, xxxi, xiv). Western children's drawings of houses with two windows and a door – two eyes and a mouth – underline this projection of the self in the house but there are surprisingly few anthropological explorations of this identity between house and self in non-Western societies.[3] The space that surrounds a house is also an extension of the personal space of its occupants. In Andean countries, implicit rules concerning the approach of visitors – whether they remain at the gate or enter yard, patio, porch or house – reflect social distance from household members in a manner reminiscent of Hall's (1959) discussion of proxemics.

Intimately linked both physically and conceptually, the body and the house are the loci for dense webs of signification and affect and serve as basic cognitive models used to structure, think and experience the world. Yet if the body has long been a focus of anthropological research which has revitalized the study of kinship and had a major impact on other disciplines, the same cannot be said for the house. As Humphrey observes, 'architecture has been curiously neglected by academic anthropology' (1988: 16). Although the interconnections between the material, social and symbolic aspects of houses are explored in several regional ethnographies,[4] her comment that 'dwellings tend to be thought of as "cases" of symbolism or cosmology rather than a subject in their own right' (1988: 16) still holds. Indeed, much of the more comparative and theoretical work on the anthropology of architecture has been done not by anthropologists but by architects and art historians.[5]

One reason for this neglect is that houses get taken for granted. Like our bodies, the houses in which we live are so commonplace, so familiar, so much a part of the way things are, that we often hardly seem to notice them. It is only under exceptional circumstances – house-moving, wars, fires, family rows, lost jobs or no money – that we are forcibly reminded of the house's central role and fundamental significance. Anthropological field research is another such exceptional circumstance. To enter another culture is to stand nervously in front of an alien house and to step inside a world of unfamiliar objects and strange people, a maze of spatial conventions whose invisible lines get easily scuffed and trampled by ignorant foreign feet. But these first, revealing, architectural impressions, reinforced by the painful process of learning who is who, who and what lives where, and what to do where and when, soon fade into the background to become merely the context and environment for the increasingly abstract and wordy conversation of ethnographic research. In time, for both anthropologists and their hosts, much of what houses are and imply becomes something that goes without saying (see also Bloch 1993a).

Institutional divisions and specializations also underlie anthropology's neglect of architecture – what might have been a more holistic anthropology of the house has been fragmented between various sub-disciplines and theoretical traditions. Family and household are basic units of analysis in studies of demography and kinship; economic anthropology deals with the physical and mental activities implied by the notion of 'housekeeping', treating the household as a basic unit of production and consumption;[6] cultural ecologists deal with subsistence as an adaptation to an environment whose architecture, the result of human activities and perceptions, is often masked by the term 'natural'. We have not considered here the relationship between the house and the landscape in which it is situated. Ingold (pers. comm.) suggests a homology between the relations body : house : landscape, and organism : dwelling : environment. The former set emphasizes form, the latter function. This provokes the further question of where each entity in the sets begins and ends.

On the other hand, architectural works focused on the more material aspects of dwellings typically say much about environmental conditions, resources, technology, techniques of construction and types of building, and about the spatial organization, symbolism and aesthetic values of buildings, but they often say relatively little about the social organization of the people who live inside.[7]

4

Despite this fragmentation, several recent works, written from quite different perspectives, have in common a more holistic focus on the house, a focus which implicitly evokes the pioneering works of Morgan (1965) and Mauss (1979). Hodder (1990) and Wilson (1989) give houses pride of place for an understanding of the development of human society in an archaeological or evolutionary frame, emphasizing the theoretical significance of domestication as an intellectual, political and sociological process which has both temporal and logical precedence over the more technical aspects of the Neolithic revolution. Ingold (n.d.) draws on Heidegger's (1971) insight that dwelling as being in the world is logically prior to and circumscribes the activity of building, to challenge Wilson's distinction between societies with and without architecture and the more general distinction between human culture and a given, neutral and objective 'nature' (see also Guidoni 1975, Egenter 1992). Authors such as Cuisenier (1991), Gudeman and Rivera (1990), Kuper (1982a; 1993) and Sabean (1990) all give weight to the house as a crucial practical and conceptual unit in the economies, kinship systems and political organization of widely different societies. Finally, both Wilson (1989: 58) and Bourdieu (1977: 89) stress the significance of the house as instrument of thought, especially in societies without writing.

According to Gudeman and Rivera, throughout much of rural Latin America, 'material practices are organised through the house, and the lexicon for them comes from the vocabulary for the physical dwelling: the house as shelter is a metaphor for the house as economy' (1990: 2). They stress that this ancient house model was brought from Europe at the time of the conquest but evidence from the Andean world (Arnold 1992, Gose 1992) suggests that it would have also struck a chord with indigenous ideas. Furthermore, though they say little about social and ceremonial ties beyond the household, these Andean data also show that where houses are concerned, economy, wider social interaction and ritual are not always easily disentangled.

The house economy, aimed more at balance and survival than at increase and profit, is opposed physically and conceptually to the corporation, modelled on the body and the domain to which neo-classical economic theory applies. Gudeman and Rivera note that, under the spell of Maine's one-sided emphasis, anthropologists have largely failed to see the potential significance of this dialectical relation between house and corporation. 'The onlooker can only wonder how the history of descent theory might have appeared had theorists of the 1940s, instead of exporting their own market experience, used a model of the home and the hearth, as Evans-Pritchard's own foundational work suggested' (1990: 183–4).

Despite this early ethnographic insight, it was Lévi-Strauss, following local imagery from native North America and matching it up with historical data from medieval Europe, who first drew attention to the potential theoretical significance of the house, who saw in house societies a specific and widespread social type, and who emphasized the significance of the indigenous category of house in the study of systems of social organization which appeared to make no sense when seen in terms of the categories of conventional kinship analysis. It is to his work that we now turn.

LEVI-STRAUSS AND SOCIETES A MAISON

Lévi-Strauss's writings on the house (1979, 1983a, 1983b, 1984, 1987, 1991) take their inspiration from the noble houses of medieval Europe. He first uses the notion of the house as a social group in a re-analysis of Boas's ethnography of the Kwakiutl whose principal grouping, a subdivision of the tribe, seemed to have both patrilineal and matrilineal characteristics. Finding that it fitted none of the conventional kinship categories of gens, sept, clan or sib, Boas admitted defeat and opted for the indigenous term *numayma*. (Lévi-Strauss 1983a: 163–70).

Lévi-Strauss makes a connection between Boas's problem and that of Kroeber in describing the social organization of the Californian Yurok. He argues that the Yurok house, which Kroeber had taken to be a mere building, was a central feature of their social organization and bore a striking resemblance to the *numayma*. Yurok houses were perpetual establishments whose names, taken from their location, decorations or ceremonial function, were used in turn by the house owners (1983a: 170–6).

Noting the similarity between these institutions and European noble houses, Lévi-Strauss points out that 'in order to recognise the house, it would have been necessary for ethnologists to look towards history' (1983a: 174). All these institutions are defined in similar terms as 'a moral person[8] holding an estate made up of material and immaterial wealth which perpetuates itself through the transmission of its name down a real or imaginary line, considered legitimate as long as this continuity can express itself in the language of kinship or of affinity, and, most often, of both' (1983a: 174).

Like their more exotic counterparts, European noble houses combined agnatic and uterine principles of succession as well as sometimes adopting in heirs, often through marriage. Their wealth consisted of both tangible property and less tangible names, titles and prerogatives, and their continuity was based on both kinship and marriage alliances. Alliances could be both endogamous (to keep the house from losing wealth) and exogamous (to accrue further property or status). The bringing together of 'antagonistic principles' – alliance, descent, endogamy, exogamy – was governed by political considerations and is a central feature of the house in these societies (1983a: 174–84).[9]

Our contributors pick up this definition in their discussions of Lévi-Strauss's work, analyzing its usefulness in the context of their own ethnographic studies. Before placing his notion of house in the context of his earlier work on kinship and examining some of the problems it raises, we underline some of the key points in the definition just quoted.

Lévi-Strauss stresses that the house as a grouping endures through time, continuity being assured not simply through succession and replacement of its human resources but also through holding on to fixed or movable property and through the transmission of the names, titles and prerogatives which are integral to its existence and identity. The importance of such ritualistic property is brought out in several of the cases examined here. McKinnon and Howell discuss the significance of heirlooms as encapsulating the enduring quality of the house amongst the Tanimbarese and Lio of island Southeast Asia whilst, for the Central Brazilian Mēbengokre and Northwest Amazonian Tukanoans, Lea and Hugh-Jones underline the centrality of names, titles and mythologically sanctioned rights to make and use ceremonial ornaments.

The diacritical, status-marking significance of such property appears to imply that the constituent units of society, the houses, are necessarily hierarchically ranked. However Lévi-Strauss himself is somewhat elusive on this point, and it is not entirely clear whether he considers that this is always the case (see Lévi-Strauss 1983a: 181;

Waterson this volume). Although working in quite different traditions, Hodder (1990) and Wilson (1988) also stress the role of houses as vehicles for rank; we return to the issue of hierarchy below.

Lévi-Strauss draws attention to the fact that, as a social institution, the house combines together a series of opposing principles or social forms such as filiation/residence, patri-/matri-lineal descent, hyper-gamy/hypogamy, close/distant marriage, which traditional kinship theory often treats as being mutually exclusive. In this context, the house takes on a crucial significance for, according to Lévi-Strauss, it 'reunites' or 'transcends' these incompatible principles. He writes: 'The whole function of noble houses, be they European or exotic, implies a fusion of categories which are elsewhere held to be in correlation with and opposition to each other, but are henceforth treated as inter-changeable: descent can substitute for affinity, and affinity for descent' (1983a: 187). The house thus gives an appearance of unity to opposing principles made equivalent to each other.

Though descent ('filiation'[10]) and alliance are equally important and mutually substitutable, Lévi-Strauss, characteristically, empha-sizes the centrality of alliance. The spouses are at once the centre of a family but also the focus of tension between their respective families of origin, particularly over residence. In 'house-based societies', where neither descent, property nor residence taken alone are criteria for the constitution of groups, alliance is both a source of antagonism and the principle of a rather brittle unity, the house as name, concept or building providing an image or demonstration of the unity achieved. In earlier writings, Lévi-Strauss had argued that native models could act as 'secondary rationalisations' of a different, underlying and largely unconscious social structure (see Lévi-Strauss 1963 [1956]). As it is close to native idioms, the notion of the house might, at first sight, suggest a less sceptical view. However, Lévi-Strauss cites the elaborate architectural constructions of the Indonesian Batak and Atoni to illustrate his argument that the house is an example of Marx's notion of fetishism. 'Transfixing' an unstable union, trans-cending the opposition between wife-givers and wife-takers and between descent and alliance, the house as institution is an illusory objectification of the unstable relation of alliance to which it lends solidity (1987: 155). It is given a further illusory quality by the fact that, underlying an institution apparently founded on kinship principles, economic and political considerations steer marriage choices, inheritance and succession, helping to determine the house's form and destiny.

If Lévi-Strauss himself provides no single, extended account of his theory of house societies nor sets it firmly in the context of his earlier works, it appears to represent at once a less deterministic, rule-bound version of his structuralism, a continuation of the general theory of kinship first outlined in his *Elementary Structures of Kinship* (1969 [1949]), and an extension of this theory to cognatic or bilateral kinship systems. Although here we situate Lévi-Strauss's theory of house societies in the context of his earlier work on kinship, we would also stress the extent to which it represents a new departure in this thinking. He moves away from a theory in which genealogy is primary, to one where it is displaced by other symbols and to a consideration of systems in which the criteria of wealth, power and status, normally associated with literate and class-based societies, begin to play an increasingly important role in the constitution of social groupings.

In his earlier work, Lévi-Strauss made a crucial distinction between 'elementary' and 'complex structures'. Elementary structures are characterized by positive rules of marriage specifying the category of kin from which a spouse must be taken; at the level of the model at least, choice of spouse is based on kinship criteria alone. These positive marriage rules set up networks of marriage exchange which give shape and solidarity to the society concerned. Complex systems have negative marriage rules (the incest taboo) but lack positive rules. Instead, choice of spouse is determined by factors lying outside the realm of kinship such as wealth, power, class and personal attributes. In such systems social integration from political and economic institutions progressively displaces that provided by kinship, and although the fundamental and universal principles of reciprocity and exchange marriage are still assumed to operate, this is obscured by the many other factors at work.

The evolutionary cast of Lévi-Strauss's argument – that complex structures develop out of elementary ones – reappears in his arguments concerning house societies. These exist in a world still ordered and conceptualized in kinship terms but with economic and political interests making ever greater inroads even if they do not yet overstep 'ties of blood'. 'In order to express and propagate themselves, these interests must inevitably borrow the language of kinship, though it is foreign to them, for none other is available' (Lévi-Strauss 1983a: 186–7).

This, then, is a key feature of Lévi-Strauss's house-based societies: they constitute a hybrid, transitional form between kin-based and class-based social orders, 'a type of social structure hitherto associated with complex societies [but] also to be found in non-literate societies' (Lévi-Strauss 1987: 151). In their chapters, Gibson, McKinnon and Waterson all pick up this point, questioning whether the cases they analyze can be thought of in these terms. If our contributors would hesitate to take on this evolutionary framework, Waterson, in particular, calls for a closer examination of the role of the house where it is a prominent institution in societies undergoing major social transformation.

Lévi-Strauss links the transitional quality of houses as a social form with the claim that they 'subvert' the language of kinship (1987: 187) by using it to 'naturalize' rank differences and competition over wealth and power. This raises a number of questions. First, as noted above, Lévi-Strauss appears to consider the ranking of the basic units of these societies, the houses, in terms of their wealth, status or prestige, to be a common and perhaps intrinsic feature of their organization (see Lévi-Strauss 1983a: 181). Several of the cases considered here – the Brazilian Mẽbengokre, the Zafimaniry of Madagascar or the Malays of Langkawi – cannot be thought of as hierarchical societies.

To what extent, then, can such broadly egalitarian societies be considered as falling within Lévi-Strauss's rubric of 'sociétés à maison'? This question is central to Roxana Waterson's chapter. She argues that whilst Lévi-Strauss's examples are all more or less hierarchical, societies without marked stratification can still meet his basic criteria of continuity and the passing on of wealth (see also Sellato 1987a and b). In contrast to Macdonald, Guerreiro and Sellato, who try to refine and formalize Lévi-Strauss's criteria (see Macdonald ed. 1987), Waterson proposes a looser definition of 'house society' to cover cases in which the house has a dominant role as a focus of social organization, irrespective of whether the society in question is hierarchical or egalitarian. This of course raises the issue of the extent to which it is useful to take Lévi-Strauss's definition of house society as a strict category, an issue to which we return below.

Lévi-Strauss suggests that, as core institutions, the houses of high-ranking groups are linked to those of commoners, both bringing together a number of heterogeneous aspects. He notes that although the Geertzes (1975) are happy to define the aristocratic Balinese *dadia* as a 'house', they hesitate over how to define its village counterpart which combines aspects of lineage, caste, cultural association and faction. Once again, drawing parallels with medieval Europe, Lévi-Strauss underlines the link between the aristocratic and commoner institutions (1987: 158–9), although this link is never fully explored.[11]

Waterson, McKinnon and Hugh-Jones all explore the link between high- and low-ranking houses and examine how the house may serve to legitimize 'the enterprises of the great'. Waterson considers a range of Southeast Asian societies which she compares with the case of Japan which is also discussed by Lévi-Strauss. Drawing on the material of scholars of Japan, particularly Murakami (1984), Nakane (1970), Fukutake (1967) and Bachnik (1983), Waterson shows the value of seeing the *ie*, a multi-faceted institution penetrating every level of Japanese society and fitting awkwardly with the terms of conventional kinship analysis, in the terms of Lévi-Strauss suggested for the house. Murakami (1984) traces the development of the *ie* over several centuries. In feudal times it operated at both aristocratic and commoner levels but later became increasingly abstracted from its material manifestations as it was used as an instrument of political legitimation to naturalize imperial power. Murakami suggests that the present culture of Japanese industrial management might be seen as a final transformation of '*ie* society'.

Waterson, Gibson, McKinnon and Hugh-Jones all focus on the way that the house can act as a vehicle for the naturalization of rank differences – both through architectural elaboration of the houses of high-ranking groups and through the expression of hierarchical differences based on membership of ranked houses in an idiom of kinship, as Lévi-Strauss suggests. The correlation between rank and architectural elaboration is often striking; it applies not simply in the contrast between ranked and egalitarian societies but also within hierarchical societies when the buildings of high-ranking groups are compared to those of commoners. Contrast between the flimsy, impermanent dwellings of the egalitarian Buid (Gibson 1986) and those of Toraja or Nias nobles and chiefs (Waterson 1990) provides a vivid Southeast Asian example of the association between high rank and prestige architecture. In South America, the same contrast appears between the Tukanoans' carefully built and elaborately painted *malocas* and the unwalled huts of their Makú 'serfs' (see Hugh-Jones this volume).

Lévi-Strauss talks of the 'borrowing' and 'subversion' of the language of kinship in the pursuance of political and economic interests (1983a: 187) but nowhere discusses how the naturalization of status differences is achieved. In fact, a striking omission from his writing is any detailed attention to the most obvious feature of houses: their physical characteristics. The architectural features of houses are usually ignored and no consideration is given to the association of rank with architecture. This point is graphically illustrated in *The Way of the Masks* which contains Lévi-Strauss's original discussion of 'house societies'. The photographs of painted house fronts and elaborately carved house posts might be taken to suggest that, for Northwest Coast Indians, the houses' sociological significance is reflected in the care and attention lavished on buildings. Yet in all his discussion of the Kwakiutl *numayma* or 'house' Lévi-Strauss makes no mention of their architecture. There is more to this than a simple correlation. The chapters by Hugh-Jones and McKinnon both show that internal features of the house such as the division of space often serve as vehicles for the symbolic elaboration of systems of hierarchy which may mirror or transform those represented by the house as a whole (see also Cunningham 1964; C. Hugh-Jones 1979). At the same time, decorative elaboration of the house's external facade, sometimes taken to extreme proportions (see Forge 1973; Hodder 1990), may serve as a sign for the inhabitants' identity, wealth and powers and as a vehicle for the conspicuous display of mythologically sanctioned powers and prerogatives reminiscent of the heraldic devices of medieval houses. Referring briefly to the elaborate houses of the Atoni and Batak, Lévi-Strauss does invoke the fetishistic quality of buildings as illusory objectifications of unstable alliance. The usage is suggestive but, as our essays reveal, it comes nowhere near to doing justice to the complexity of the issues involved. The house is a representation not just of unity but also of various kinds of hierarchy and division.

Although Lévi-Strauss makes no explicit connection between them, his characterization of 'sociétés à maison' as transitional between elementary and complex structures brings to mind his previous discussion of Crow–Omaha systems or 'systems of semi-complex alliance' (Héritier 1981). Such systems have negative rules prohibiting marriage with a wide range of kin: when two individuals marry, rules come into play which prohibit further marriages between their respective clans for several generations. If the absence of positive rules is a 'complex' feature, the tendency to marry those kin who are not ruled out, in societies with relatively small populations, appears to result in patterns of marriage similar to those found in elementary systems with positive rules, for the range of potential marriage partners is strictly delineated. (Lévi-Strauss 1969: xxv–xliii). Significantly, in both West and Southern Africa, the descent groups associated with Omaha systems are often termed 'houses' by the people concerned. That Héritier (1981) rejects a clan or lineage model of Crow–Omaha systems and instead draws attention to their hitherto unrecognized cognatic features (see also Kuper 1982c) would be consistent with the cognatic features that Lévi-Strauss recognizes in house societies (see below).

Abandoning the study of Crow–Omaha systems to the more mathematically inclined (see Héritier 1981; Héritier-Augé and Copet-Rougier 1990), Lévi-Strauss turned instead to the study of myth, an area apparently better suited to accessing the deep structures of the human mind than systems of kinship and marriage exchange, constrained and contaminated as they are by extraneous demographic, economic and political factors. However, it is these same factors that play such an important role in his thinking about house societies, seemingly a move to a less deterministic version of structuralism.

Although others have shown its compatibility with non-unilineal or cognatic systems,[12] Lévi-Strauss's own formulation of alliance theory is heavily dependent on descent and descent theory – in elementary kinship structures, marriage exchanges are characterized as taking place between unilineal descent groups. There is, however, an important difference in the status of such groups when seen from the perspective of the two theories. In simple terms, if descent theory stresses 'within relations' and sees the 'between relations' of marriage as in some ways secondary, for alliance theory these 'between relations' are of primary significance and colour the significance of the groups as units of exchange. In the first instance, the social order is constituted through the groups, in the second through exchanges between them.

Given this, we may understand why Lévi-Strauss should begin a discussion of cognatic societies by casting doubts on the utility of his Anglo-Saxon colleagues' notion of 'corporacy' or 'corporate groups' (Lévi-Strauss 1987: 153–4). For him the emphasis is on moral persons, whilst for descent theorists the emphasis is more on legal persons or corporate groups which make up the social order, which endure through time, and whose jurally-equivalent members live together and share rights and duties with respect to political and economic resources.[13] In a legal idiom, this is a difference in emphasis between 'corporations sole' and 'corporations aggregate'.

If descent theory stems ultimately from Maine, alliance theory owes much to Mauss. He writes,

> in the systems of the past ... it is groups, and not individuals, which carry on exchange, make contracts, and are bound by obligations; the persons represented in the contracts are moral persons ... Further, what they exchange is not exclusively goods and wealth, real and personal property, and things of economic value. They exchange rather courtesies, entertainments, ritual, military assistance, women, children, dances and feasts. (Mauss, 1954: 3)

As we have seen, this Maussian emphasis on moral persons, on mixed material and immaterial property, and on the interplay between ritual prerogatives and political alliances, reappears in Lévi-Strauss's notion of the house.

Despite this difference, some features of the house idea might superficially appear to represent a rapprochement with the Anglo-Saxon position. The house has several features reminiscent of the Africanists' unilineal descent group. It is characterized as a property-holding unit which endures through time and whose members resort to the same 'legal fictions' reported for African lineages – adoption and transmission through daughters and in-married sons – to recruit heirs. A second set of features brings to mind the caveats of even Lévi-Strauss's more enthusiastic Anglo-Saxon colleagues with respect to the relative status of models and empirical facts in alliance theory. If the original models of marriage exchange in elementary structures were based exclusively on kinship criteria, where houses are concerned, tactical choices motivated by political, economic and prestige considerations, lead to a situation in which features such as hypergamy and hypogamy, exogamy and endogamy, enlarged or

14

restricted networks of marriage alliance, instead of being characteristic of the marriage practices of whole societies, become options
chosen to suit the convenience of different units in different
circumstances (Lévi-Strauss 1991: 435). Long ago, Leach (1951, 1954)
drew attention to the importance of just such options and 'contam-
inating' political and economic factors for an understanding of the
real-life marriage exchanges between lineages or lineage-segments in
an elementary kinship system, that of the Kachin of Highland Burma.

Given all this, one might ask, 'why are houses not lineages?'
Several different answers can be given. To begin with, Lévi-Strauss
first introduced the notion of house to deal with the problematic, non-
unilineal or bilateral features of the apparently unilineal, clan-like
Kwakiutl *numayma*. If the house is a lineage, it is 'a hybrid descent
group with a lot of awkward appendages' (McKinnon this volume:
173), a form of social organization halfway between unilineal and
cognatic systems (Lévi-Strauss 1991: 434). However, despite the
models, both Fortes's (1949) and Evans-Pritchard's (1951) ethnographies make clear that, in real life, such awkward appendages can
make classic descent groups equally problematic. As Goody reminds
us, 'though descent groups are unilineal, kinship is everywhere
bilateral'; 'a system of agnatic clans or lineages does not exclude the
active presence of bilateral kinship' (1983: 16, 122).

For Goody, the distinction between lineage and *lignage* or house is
not about the presence or absence of such ties with the 'other parent'
nor about legal fictions, for modes of reckoning are specific to different
contexts or functions – group membership, access to property, office,
rank, etc. The distinction has more to do with the fact that the lineal,
agnatic features of the aristocratic European house are linked with
diverging devolution and intimately connected with landed estates, an
emphasis on primogeniture and a quite different productive regime.
The house is a mainly agnatic line of filiation organized around a
narrow pedigree whilst the branching, segmented lineage is organized
round a genealogy. For Goody, then, lineage and *lignage* are associated
respectively, with Africa and Europe, specific social systems with
differing polities and modes of livelihood. For Lévi-Strauss however,
the house is to be found in a wide variety of different cultural contexts
– native North America, historical Europe, ancient Greece, feudal
Japan, island Indonesia, Melanesia, Polynesia, New Zealand, Madagascar and Africa are all mentioned.

A specific mention of the Gulf of Guinea (Lévi-Strauss 1991: 436) could be a subtle reference to the Tallensi and other West African groups whose own terms for 'lineage' typically mean 'house' (Fortes 1949: 10). If, in the ethnographic sources for the classic models for unilineal descent, native idioms glossed as 'patrilineage' turn out to be words for dwellings, this might suggest that a second answer to the question 'why are houses not lineages?' would simply be the question 'why are lineages not houses?'. From the native point of view that indeed is what they often are. The shortcuts to analysis provided by ready-made models of legal or mercantile corporate bodies seem at times to have blinded anthropologists to what they had seen and made them deaf to their informants' more domestic talk of homesteads, byres and compounds, houses, rooms and hearths.

Evans-Pritchard tells us that the Nuer, thinking more in terms of community (1940: 203), had difficulty in understanding his enquiries about lineages – for them lineages are 'hearths' or 'entrances to huts' (1940: 195). Tallensi and Nuer apart, similar house-idioms, modelling social systems whose precise rules of inheritance, succession and group membership are no less protean than the lineages they threaten to subvert, have been reported for the Jie, Turkana and other East African groups (Gulliver 1955; Gray and Gulliver 1964), for the Tio and other groups in Zaire (Vansina 1973), and amongst the Zulu and other Bantu groups of Southern Africa (Gluckman 1950: 193ff; Kuper 1982a).

Lineage theory has been under fire for some time now for not explaining as much as its original proponents claimed. In African lineage-based societies, kinship is created not only out of descent but also out of ties to land and locality, a point which native idioms underscore. Observing that lineages do not represent folk models and that nowhere do repetitive series of descent groups appear to organize vital political or economic activities, Kuper's (1982b, 1988) own sustained attack concludes that 'the lineage model, its predecessors and its analogues, have no value for anthropological analysis' (1982b: 92). The counterpart to this disenchantment with the lineage is a move, by Kuper and others, towards giving an explicit recognition to the fact that houses often lurk behind lineages and that African societies once apparently explained in terms of descent and lineages can also be fruitfully analyzed in terms of their houses (see also Littlejohn 1967 [1960]).

Building on his earlier demonstration of the economic, social, legal and symbolic significance of a generalized Southern Bantu folk model of the homestead (1982a), Kuper has recently suggested that the 'house' – the homestead and its segments, at once both physical entity and social grouping – provides an alternative model for under-standing the structure and historical development of the Zulu state, one preferable to older assumptions concerning hypothetical descent groups and supposed transitions from kinship to territory or 'blood' to 'soil' (Kuper 1993).

A third answer to the question posed above takes us away from descent theory towards cognatic systems, the awkward leftovers of both alliance and descent theory. Having begun with lineage-like Kwakiutl and European houses, Lévi-Strauss later turns his attention to Austronesia, hoping to illuminate the notoriously elusive character-istics of social organization in the bilateral societies of Southeast Asia. Lacking unilineal descent, with no obvious mode of ensuring group continuity, no rules for allocating rights over persons, no ordered systems of marriage exchange, indeed apparently with no very discernible social structure at all, cognatic systems posed severe problems for descent theorists and alliance theorists alike. If Lévi-Strauss's earlier writings (1949) ignored them entirely, Radcliffe-Brown concluded that the absence of unilineal descent meant an absence of structure making cognatic systems 'rare, not only in Africa but in the world at large' (1950: 43, 82).

Defining cognatic systems has also proved difficult for they seem more to lack features characteristic of other systems than to possess specific features of their own (see Murdock 1960). What makes analysis of these 'loosely structured' (Embree 1950) societies prob-lematic is the degree of flexibility in the application of rules, the role of choice over residence and other arrangements in the formation of social groupings, the importance of personal autonomy, and the way that persons, activities and groupings are continuously in the process of being constructed rather than defined in advance by pre-given structures.

In the absence of corporate descent groups or other clearly bounded social units, anthropologists such as Freeman (1958, 1970) on the Iban and C. Geertz (1960) and H. Geertz (1961) on Java, focused on the individual and the household, echoing Murdock's (1960) criterion of the pre-eminence of small domestic groups in bilateral societies.

Problems in locating structural principles have led more recent analyses to concentrate on other organizational features such as ranking, residence (King 1978) or shared activity (Gibson 1986).

Lévi-Strauss's notion of the house might promise to integrate analytically the indigenous prominence of houses and the stress on individual autonomy and the processual aspects of personhood and activity that characterize Southeast Asian cognatic societies. Indeed, it is just such societies that appear, in Lévi-Strauss's discussion, to epitomise 'sociétés à maison' (1987: 153–5). Paradoxically, however, his discussion of them turns to the Atoni and Karo Batak (1987: 156–8), 'Eastern Indonesian' societies with symmetric alliance between lineal groupings.[14] As Carsten, Gibson and Howell all point out, there is some confusion over whether we are to consider the cognatic societies of Indonesia or those with descent groups and asymmetrical alliance as paradigmatic of his type.

Such quibbles would not, however, concern Lévi-Strauss who affirms that the house blurs the oppositions – unilineal, cognatic, alliance, descent – which anthropologists have used to classify forms of social organization. This is because 'in house societies, whilst the continuity of the *lignage*[15] is never forgotten, it combines with temporary or more permanent alliance between two or more *lignages* creating a *new type of social unit* in which the interlinkage of the *lignages* counts for as much or more than their continuity' (Lévi-Strauss 1991: 435, our gloss and emphasis). It is this which ultimately distinguishes houses both from the Africanists' lineages and from the lineages of Lévi-Strauss's own elementary structures. Depending on the relative weighting given to filiation and alliance, and to wealth, inheritance and status, houses can span a continuum from the more lineage-like to the entirely cognatic.

Instead of seeing its potential for a critique of other crumbling edifices, Lévi-Strauss would still see in the 'house' the discovery of a new social type to deal with societies which are neither lineage-based nor organized around clearly defined marriage rules. However, he then applies his model to societies which *are* organized around such rules, and it is also clear that the African societies once apparently explained in terms of descent and lineages might also be fruitfully analyzed in terms of their houses. In the end the problem is not one of discovering which societies are 'house societies' but of discovering which ones are not.

18

Our discussion and chapters would strongly suggest that the invention of a new category of 'house-based society' raises as many problems as it solves. While houses may receive indigenous emphasis in very many societies, their cultural and geographic diversity suggests that the 'type' will always be far too heterogeneous to constitute an analytic model. This can hardly be surprising if the notion of 'house society' simultaneously attempts to resolve the problems of both descent-group and alliance models whilst still relying upon them. If anthropologists have spent the last thirty years discovering that very few societies in fact conform to these models, that 'even the Nuer are not like *The Nuer*' (Kuper 1988: 201), it seems unlikely that the invention of a new category, reliant on the old, will provide a new basis for a synthetic theory of kinship.

The evolutionary tone of some of Lévi-Strauss's arguments, the idea that the development of class, capital and kingdoms all represent a progressive invasion and erosion of 'the old ties of blood' (Lévi-Strauss, 1983a: 186), points to a problem at the heart of his notion of house societies. This is the assumption, shared by descent theorists, that kinship is logically prior to forms of association based on residence, territory or 'soil' (see Kuper 1988) or other factors. There is, of course, abundant ethnographic evidence for the salience of relations founded on ties of blood and plenty too that kinship is frequently used as a language to talk about relations founded on common residence, property or political interests.[16] But this is not evidence for the ontological priority of 'blood' itself. 'Kinship' has several different sources. It is not just about sleeping together but also about living together, eating together and dying together, not just about bed but also about house, hearth and tomb, the last sometimes a monumental hypostasis of the house itself (see Bloch, 1971; Wilson 1988: 122ff; Hodder 1990).

Nor can we accept Lévi-Strauss's claim that, for peoples without writing, kinship is 'the only language available' (1987: 152). An alternative language is precisely that of the house. If the language of the house is 'about' kinship, it is no less 'about' economy and just as much about joint subsistence, production and consumption as it is about property. Crucially, this language is also about common spaces and about buildings which are palaces and temples as well as shelters and homes. Like the ramifications of words for house, home and hearth in Indo-European and other languages, (see Benveniste 1973

(1969)), the contributions to this volume demonstrate that these facets of the house are so closely intertwined that a focus on any one alone, be it kinship (Lévi-Strauss) or economy (Gudeman and Rivera), can only be partial.

While Lévi-Strauss's ideas about the house have proved very useful for thinking about the societies described here, it is also clear that the authors of this volume have found his own model, at once too specific and too general, to be constraining and have, in different ways, found it necessary to move beyond it. Insofar as he has focused attention on the house as a central feature of social organization, Lévi-Strauss has drawn attention to the importance of bringing together different aspects of an institution which many anthropologists have tended to consider in a rather fragmented manner. He has also reminded us of a sound anthropological principle: the priority of native categories.

Inasmuch as looking at particular societies through the house enables us to escape the constraints of conventional analytic categories, it is clear that there is much to be gained from his approach. This applies not just to the consideration of particular societies but to a comparison between them. In one way, this volume is testimony to the comparative potential of taking the house as a central institution. It has enabled us not only to compare cultures within one region but also to bring together areas as widely separated as South America and Southeast Asia within one framework. However there is a problem here, one also evident in previous attempts to apply Lévi-Strauss's ideas in a regional perspective (Macdonald (ed.) 1987). When something called a 'house society' becomes rigidly defined in an effort to come up with yet another analytic model, the usefulness of the approach is sharply diminished. As McKinnon notes in her chapter, the 'house society' is dogged by 'an unresolved tension between the dead weight of old kinship categories and the effort to transcend these in the face of the integrity of resistant social forms'.

For the authors of this volume, the significance of a focus on the house is that it brings together aspects of social life which have previously been ignored or treated separately. Crucially, we would consider architectural features of houses as an aspect of their importance as social units in both life and thought. Rather than seeing in the house the birth of a new analytic type, the anthropological child of alliance and descent, it is this holistic potential of viewing houses 'in the round' which we would emphasize. The relation between building and group is multifaceted and contextually determined, the house's role as a complex idiom for social groupings, as a vehicle to naturalize rank, and as a source of symbolic power being inseparable from the building itself. In this respect, although they do so in different ways and with different degrees of elaboration, the chapters in this book all represent a significant advance on Lévi-Strauss's own position. In the final sections of this introduction, focused more on the regions of Southeast Asia and South America, we look at the attempts that have been made to apply Lévi-Strauss's ideas and to move beyond them, exploring some of the physical characteristics of houses and linking these to the role that houses, like bodies, come to play as symbols of social groups, inscribing boundaries and hierarchies and giving them an aura of naturalness.

BEYOND LEVI-STRAUSS

The editors of this volume have both been impressed by the cultural significance of the house in the two regions, Southeast Asia and Amazonia, in which we do our research. In these areas the interconnections between group and living site, between house and household, and between domestic processes going on in the hearth and more general social processes in the society at large are very marked. We have also been struck by the fact that, for the people with whom we work, the house is a significant category, a focus of ritual elaboration and a point of reference in their own understanding of the world. In drawing together the cases discussed here, we aimed to extend the geographic scope of Lévi-Strauss's model, and to test his ideas in specific and detailed ethnographic contexts. While drawing on his formulations, we also sought to get beyond the limitations discussed above, to arrive at a more flexible approach which would pay more attention to the physical characteristics of buildings, and to see these as part of the social processes they contain.

The house in Southeast Asia[17]

The prominence of the house as kinship group, ritual entity and political unit in Austronesian societies emerges clearly in a number of recent ethnographic monographs, several of which draw explicitly on

Lévi-Strauss's model of house societies.[18] However, the centrality of the house was also brought out in earlier studies of societies in Southeast Asia which fitted awkwardly into the classic categories of kinship analysis. On the one hand, many Eastern Indonesian societies seemed to have descent groups but it was difficult to define these in terms of such labels as 'matrilineal', 'patrilineal' or 'double descent'. The composition of descent groups appeared irregular and marital alliances operated flexibly (see, for example, van Wouden 1935; Fox (ed.) 1980). In this context Fox (ed.) (1980: 12) notes the importance of the house as 'fundamental cultural category' designating 'a particular kind of social unit' which operates as a 'metaphor' for the descent group. On the other hand, in the cognatic societies of Western Indonesia, descent itself was not an important principle for group membership. Indeed, it was often difficult to discern bounded groups at all.

For the cognatic societies, authors such as Freeman (1958; 1970) on the Iban, C. Geertz (1960) and H. Geertz (1961) on Java and Firth (1966) on the Malays all emphasized the importance of the individual and the small domestic group. The focus of these studies was not the house but the *household*, a unit discussed in terms of membership, developmental cycle, decision-making, consumption, production and ritual. The kinship system was external to this unit and did not provide the organizing principles of these societies: individuals and households had considerable autonomy; social structure was 'flexible'; there was a lack of formal organization based either on kinship or on political groupings.

If such studies provided invaluable insight into the functioning of the household in cognatic societies, they sometimes failed to bring out the importance of the house as an indigenous category.[19] Nor was the household as a social unit necessarily linked to a description of the physical structure or spatial layout of the house. However, in the 1960s several articles discussed spatial organization and linked it to marriage rules and other social divisions in societies with descent groups and asymmetric alliance systems. Thus Cunningham (1964) associated the complex divisions of Atoni houses with their alliance system. Divisions between inner and outer, back and front, higher and lower areas, each a subdivision of a larger whole, were associated with different categories of person: men and women, kin and affine, wife-givers and wife-takers. The house could be seen as expressing the principles of unity and difference that were fundamental to the Atoni social order. In a similar manner, Tambiah (1969) linked the spatial organization of northern Thai houses to the classification of humans and animals.

If such articles[20] brought out the social and ritual significance of the Southeast Asian houses, despite a recognition of architecture's social context, their architectural emphasis sometimes seemed to eclipse the people who lived in them (Izikowitz and Sorensen 1982: 3).[21] Many of these papers focused on the house as a symbolic system. Cunningham (1964), and Forth (1981), writing on the Rindi house, explicitly described the house as a 'microcosm', expressing wider categories and principles in the symbolic universe (see Waterson 1990: 91–114). Ellen (1986), writing on the Eastern Indonesian Nuaulu, criticized the idea of the house as a symbolic microcosm, warning of the dangers of an overly rigid and static structuralist perspective in which 'the symbolic order is somehow frozen into the fabric' (1986: 4). He drew attention to the inter-penetrating levels of meaning of the various different kinds of order brought together in the house. Like Barnes (1980a), he also noted the contradictory expressions of symbolic meaning in the house and stressed its 'multiple significance'.

Ellen emphasizes how the house is an organic whole; in contrast, much analysis formalizes, divides and separates. House construction is ongoing and incomplete; in Indonesia the house must be 'planted' (Barnes 1974: 69; Ellen 1986: 26) and is widely conceived of as an animate being, an animation reflected in a spiritual essence and in the use of body imagery (see Kana 1980; Howe 1983).

Barnes (1974), Forth (1981) and Howe (1983) note the way that parts of the house in Kedang, Rindi and Bali are associated with parts of the body. Waterson (1990: 115–37) discusses how the vitality of houses is bound up with their spiritual essence or *semangat*,[22] which derives from several sources – from the trees used in building, from rituals which accompany construction, from body imagery, and from their occupants. The common 'life-essence' of people, houses and other entities emphasizes the unity of their animate qualities. Houses are not so much 'like' people as possessing the same qualities, products of the same processes. The animation of the house and its link to body imagery is not restricted to Southeast Asia and we take it up more generally below.

Ellen also drew attention to the significance of the Indonesian house as a political, as well as domestic and physical, unit, a point also clear from earlier studies elsewhere in the region. Thus, for example, in discussing the house's ritual significance, Turton (1978) brought out the link between domestic architecture and the wider polity in Southeast Asia. That the house constitutes a political and ritual entity as well as a domestic space has been underlined by Barraud (1979) for Tanebar-Evav, by Traube (1986) for the Mambai of East Timor, by Errington (1989) for Luwu in South Sulawesi, and by McKinnon (1991) for Tanimbar in the South Moluccas. As Waterson (1990: 71–2) notes, the fact that in many Southeast Asian societies there is a continuum between the dwelling house and public or religious buildings means that houses often combine 'public' and 'private', 'male' and 'female', 'sacred' and 'profane' aspects (see Carsten and Janowski this volume). And this has important implications when we consider the relationship between the house space and the encoding of rank and gender hierarchies (see also Waterson 1990: 167–98). We return to this theme in the following section.

Barraud (1979), Errington (1987; 1989), Waterson (1990: 138–66) and McKinnon (1991) all focus on the importance of the house as a kin group as well as politico-religious entity. In the societies they analyze, the house constitutes a perpetual entity combining these different aspects.[23] Most crucially, although the examples these authors discuss are very different, for all of them the model allows them to escape the 'strait-jacket of descent categories' (Waterson 1990: 166) which has often proved more of a hindrance than a help in the analysis of social forms in Southeast Asia.

Based on Lévi-Strauss's ideas, Errington's (1987) synthetic regional model distinguishes between the societies of 'Eastern Indonesia' with asymmetric alliance and those of the 'Centrist Archipelago' with cognatic kinship and endogamous marriage.[24] Following Lévi-Strauss (1963), she describes the former societies as underlain by a principle of 'concentric dualism' – that is, they cast a whole range of activities in dualistic forms. These societies have multiple houses with clear boundaries between them. In contrast, the societies of the Centrist Archipelago exhibit a strong centripetal tendency. Here, 'the "Houses" or social groupings tend either to coincide with the whole society, and hence be wishfully complete and autonomous as in the Indic States, or to be centred on an Ego or set of full siblings and to stretch indefinitely from that centre, with no clear boundaries' (1987: 405).

What is illuminated here is the way these two apparently different forms can be seen as transformations of each other. Both principles – that of dualism and that of centrism – are present in Eastern Indonesia *and* in the Centrist Archipelago. In the former case, the difference between brother and sister and their enforced separation at marriage ensures the whole system of exchange between houses; in the latter, cross-sex siblings epitomize unity and similarity. Here, the hierarchical states conceive themselves in an image of encompassment and unity which is often envisaged in terms of siblingship. Unity, however, is threatened by the outside: the centrist societies are shot through with dualism between 'us' and 'them'. As Errington puts it, 'Eastern Indonesia postulates unity but institutes fracture' (1987: 435), while the Centrist Archipelago 'institutionalises unity but is haunted by duality' (1987: 435).

Errington further distinguishes the centrist societies according to their degree of hierarchization, with the ranked Indic states at one end of a continuum and the more egalitarian groups on their periphery at the other. We have already discussed how the issue of hierarchy is central to Lévi-Strauss's model of the house society. It is explicitly explored in the collection edited by Charles Macdonald (1987) which seeks to test out Lévi-Strauss's ideas in a range of heterogeneous Southeast Asian societies. The authors in that collection suggest that only a small minority of the societies they consider can be thought of as house societies as defined by Lévi-Strauss, and that stratification is a necessary (but not sufficient) criterion to conform to this type. In societies which fit less well with the model, for example among the peasants of lowland Java (Headley 1987a; 1987b) or Malaysia (Carsten 1987a), the house appears in a 'fetishized' or 'phantasmagoric' form which can be linked to Lévi-Strauss's later formulations (1987: 155). Here Carsten and Headley suggest that the house is articulated in the idiom of siblingship. The authors in Macdonald (1987) confine themselves to a strict consideration of Lévi-Strauss's model, rather than broadening the criteria and adopting a looser definition as Waterson (this volume) suggests. In contrast, the recent collection edited by Fox (1993a) focuses on indigenous Austronesian notions of the house rather than on Lévi-Strauss's definitions, showing how the values of these societies can be discerned

25

from 'inside the house' (1993a: 2). Many features discussed by earlier authors are underlined and developed. The chapters by Fox and Sather bring out the ordered structure and orientation of Austronesian houses and Fox develops the idea of the house as having a 'ritual attractor' ((ed.) 1993a: 1) which encapsulates in concrete form the house as whole. Austronesian houses have certain defining features (posts, ladder, ridge-pole and hearth) and these often constitute the ritual attractor. Fox stresses a concern with origins, often expressed in a botanical idiom (see also Fox 1971). Finally, and perhaps most suggestively, he points out the interrelation between spatial and temporal categories. The house implicitly becomes a 'structure for remembering' (Fox (ed.) 1993a: 22–3).

In different ways the contributions of the authors of this volume bring out the themes we have discussed so far and enable us to push the analysis of the house further. In the context of Lévi-Strauss's model, Waterson considers a range of Southeast Asian societies as well as Japan and focuses on whether hierarchy is an intrinsic feature of the house society. In opting for a less strict application of his ideas, her approach accords with the other chapters on Austronesian societies which have a more specific ethnographic focus. Four of these focus on cognatic groups – the Zafimaniry of Madagascar (Bloch), the Kelabit of Sarawak (Janowski), the Malays of Langkawi (Carsten) and the Makassarese of South Sulawesi (Gibson). The Lio of Flores and the Tanimbarese of the South Moluccas discussed by Howell and McKinnon represent the hierarchical asymmetric alliance societies of Eastern Indonesia.

In their examples, Bloch and Janowski underline how the house is founded on marriage as Lévi-Strauss suggests. The married couple is the core of the house. Among the Zafimaniry the link between the process of making a house and that of making a marriage are closely intertwined – as a marriage grows and matures so too does the house. As a marriage emerges as stable and fertile from a transient relationship, so the house becomes stronger and firmer. From being a flimsy and impermanent dwelling, it gradually changes to a hardwood construction, 'acquiring bones', as the Zafimaniry say, until eventually, as a more permanent and beautifully carved building, it is a source of blessing for the descendants of its founding couple, a 'holy house'.

Janowski's chapter shows how the activities of the married couple, both in an everyday context and at ritual feasts, are central to the identity of the house and associated with different aspects of its architecture. In particular, the consumption of food which is associated with the senior married pair is a key facet of the hearth groups into which Kelabit longhouses are divided. Among the Kelabit (as among the Malays or the Zafimaniry), the undivided hearth is a central feature of the house. Men and women can be associated with different kinds of food. Janowski links this to a discussion of gender relations and the house. Her analysis alerts us to the subtle shifts between contexts: the house is at once a domestic entity associated with men and women as married couples, and a ritual entity, a prestige-holding unit, in which men and women are divided and have different associations.

Many of these associations also hold for the Malays of Langkawi where houses are also undivided commensal groups. Carsten shows how the importance of the house is not only domestic. At communal feasts, the whole community is imaged as an expanded house. This 'public' ritual identity is, however, one without much practical reality. Its importance lies in its symbolic power to counter the political and social division that underlies Langkawi people's experience in everyday life.

Carsten and Gibson also see marriage as fundamental to the house, but amongst the Malays and Makassarese marriage itself is thought of in terms of siblingship. In these cases the unity of the sibling group underlies the house as much as marriage. And here Carsten and Gibson draw attention to the centrality of siblingship to cognatic kinship in Southeast Asia and link this to the house. The process of marrying either occurs between kin who are already thought of as siblings, or turns previously unrelated people into siblings. In these examples, although houses are used as a symbolic device to represent social groups, they do not resolve an opposition between descent and alliance as Lévi-Strauss suggested. The house must be seen in terms of siblingship which is a more important principle than either alliance or descent.

Gibson shows how Makassarese rituals of house construction are linked to rituals of birth, marriage and death, and also to the ritual creation of the village realm. Architectural features of the house are linked both with notions of siblingship and with parts of the body. Whereas Carsten argues that, for Malays in Langkawi, relations between houses are perceived as equal, this is not the case for the Makassarese who were traditionally ranked as nobles, commoners and slaves. The rituals Gibson describes played up differences of rank between houses. Historically, Gibson argues, Lévi-Strauss's suggestions about what the house does are relevant. The Makassarese house may be seen as legitimating differences of, and competition over, wealth and power, which are expressed in the rituals in terms of innate rank.

The similarity of the themes which emerge from an examination of the house in the 'centrist' groups with those in the 'exchange archipelago' demonstrates how they can be seen as transformations of each other as Errington (1987) suggests. Indeed, the Lio of Flores, analyzed by Howell, bear out this point. Whilst the Lio themselves place emphasis on descent, on exogamy and on rank, their own account of their mythic past could be read as a portrayal of themselves in another mode – cognatic, endogamous and egalitarian. In the relationship between *kéda*, temple, and ceremonial house can be discerned that between the two types of society that Errington discusses. Carsten takes up Errington's suggestion in the concluding section of her paper, comparing the Langkawi house to a range of other Southeast Asian cases, and highlighting the problems of applying Lévi-Strauss's ideas to cognatic societies. Although explicitly an attempt to deal with these, his model might seem to fit more happily in the 'exchange archipelago'.

Howell addresses this question from the point of view of the Lio for whom the house is also a prominent social category. In some respects their named houses can be seen as functioning in the same way as the European noble houses discussed by Lévi-Strauss. However, the Lio also have named patrilineal descent groups between which prescriptive MBD/FZS marriage occurs. Howell is concerned to discover what the differences are between named houses and descent groups. She argues that ceremonial houses and families, lineages and clans, mutually constitute each other. Whereas descent groups regulate intergroup relations through marriages, births, death and control over property, ceremonial houses are concerned with intragroup relations and relations with the ancestors and deities. Each requires the other in order to fulfil these roles. At the same time, ceremonial houses are also predicated on the temple, *kéda*. Although similar in layout and construction, there are crucial differences between the two structures and what they represent. Above all, the *kéda* is not a building for humans but for deities. Howell argues that the priest-leaders of the ceremonial houses are the earthly transformations of the original inhabitants of the mythic *kéda*. The meaning of the ceremonial houses is created *between* the two buildings. The houses people live in, ceremonial houses and temples must all be seen in the context of each other.

Whereas those who analyze cognatic societies in this volume seem to feel Lévi-Strauss's suggestion might fit the Eastern Indonesian cases better, Howell reminds us that his model was in fact originally devised to deal with the cognatic cases. Where houses are prominent but descent is also important, as in the Lio case, Howell suggests that the house is doing something different from its cognatic counterpart. Amongst the Lio, where marriage alliances are not expressed as occurring between houses, but between agnatic descent groups, it is difficult to see the house as a master symbol, resolving the opposition between descent and alliance. Rather, an understanding of Lio society must take into account all the social groups mentioned.

McKinnon's discussion brings out the contradiction in Lévi-Strauss's model very clearly. As she points out, the house is at once an attempt to transcend the old categories of kinship, descent and alliance, but also premised upon them. But McKinnon puts this tension between kinship, and what she calls its 'objectification' in the house, to work. Her argument is that this opposition does not so much define two distinct types of society as a tension within a single society which is central to the realization of hierarchy. Her analysis shows how contrastive forms of affiliation, residence and marriage are central to the dynamics of Tanimbarese society.

Here permanent, named houses are distinguished from imperma-nent, unnamed ones. The hierarchical relation between the two is articulated through contrastive forms of marriage, affiliation and residence, and through the exchange of valuables which are appro-priate to their members. 'Rows' of named houses have enduring relations of matrilateral alliance through repeated marriages in which specific women are forgotten. In contrast, unnamed houses contract marriages along 'sisters and aunts pathways'. These alliance relations are thought of as impermanent, and the names of specific women are still remembered. The low status connotations of a potential incorporation of a husband into the house of his wife-givers can be averted through the gift of valuables to the wife-givers which establishes the patrifiliation of the husband and his children. If this is not achieved, the husband and his children are incorporated by the wife-givers, a subordination which results in the dissolution of the affinal relation between the two sides. Named houses are always attempting to convert the temporary hierarchy between wife-takers and wife-givers into the permanent hierarchy which is their hallmark.

McKinnon shows how the different forms of marriage imply a 'double movement'. One is a process of generalization of relations, and concentration of value which connects older brothers and members of named houses back to the past, anchoring the source of life. The other is a process of particularization of relations, and dispersal of value which expands along new pathways into the future. The two processes are integrated through the movement of women, mediated by the exchange of valuables. The two forms of marriage mutually imply each other. The continuity of alliance relations between rows of named houses is only made possible by the marriages with 'other women' of younger brothers and commoners of unnamed houses which open up new pathways and new sources of valuables. The articulation of the contrastive forms of affiliation, residence and marriage is productive of the hierarchical order of Tanimbarese society.

McKinnon's analysis demonstrates the way contrastive social forms, seen in terms of indigenous ideology rather than *a priori* categories of kinship analysis, are intrinsic to the internal dynamic of Tanimbar society. Although it is central to an understanding of this society, the house does not 'reunite' or 'transcend' oppositions in Lévi-Strauss's terms. Rather, it is the explicit articulation of these contrastive forms, governed by its own internal logic, which is the mark of a house society.

Architecture and spatial analysis in lowland South America

If the house as a social institution and salient native category has a firmly established place in Southeast Asian ethnography, the same cannot truly be said for lowland South America. Here categories such as Dravidian, Crow–Omaha, alliance, descent, lineages, kindreds and residence, dominant in the kinship theory applied to the region, have tended to overshadow recognition of the house as an institution or category in its own right. In his own writings on the house, Lévi-Strauss make no mention of the region presumably because the Amerindian societies there are typically characterized by positive marriage rules ordering regular systems of marriage alliance and would thus fall under his rubric of elementary structures of a relatively straightforward kind (see above). Often, as in the case of the Guyanese groups discussed in the chapter by Rivière, marriage alliances operate without even the presence of lineal groupings to provide some global coherence so that such systems might be said to represent the inner limits of elementary structures; in contrast, as we have indicated earlier, house societies might be said to represent a move beyond them.

There is however a rather different Americanist tradition, stemming in part from Lévi-Strauss's early writings on dual organization and the Bororo village (1973 [1955]; 1963 ([1956]), which represents a partial convergence towards the Southeast Asian work. It was this convergence, together with some striking similarities and contrasts between forms of social organization in the two regions, which initially suggested the potential of a cross-regional comparison. Lévi-Strauss's work on the Bororo had a seminal influence on anthropological explorations of the sociological and symbolic significance of architecture and spatial organization worldwide; it made the vocabulary of 'diametric' and 'concentric dualism' part of the common theoretical currency of anthropology, and found particular resonance amongst anthropologists working in Southeast Asia.

For South America, these writings, which linked together material forms, social arrangements and intellectual schema, transformed an earlier focus on the house as a mere item of material culture (see, for example, Roth 1924: 248–71) to create a general awareness of the spatial and architectural inscription of society and cosmology which has been one of the characteristic features of the ethnographic literature on the region. Outstanding examples of this genre include C. Hugh-Jones's (1979) demonstration of a structural model, based on the body and the communal house, whose spatio-temporal logic underlies and unifies the different domains of Barasana social life, and the collected works edited by Dreyfus (1972) and Caiuby Novaes (1983) dealing with territory, habitat and architecture.[25]

Lévi-Strauss's writings made clear that the cartwheel-like villages of the Bororo, bisected on an east–west axis and with a central men's house, represented diagrams of their society and the cosmos (see also Crocker 1985), and works by Nimuendajú (1971, 1983) suggested that this was also true of their Jê-speaking neighbours. These earlier works described Bororo and Northern Jê social structure in terms of unilineal descent but subsequent research by members of the Harvard–Central Brazil project[26] led to a rethinking of this characterization through a more culturally informed approach to kinship which included a consideration of spatial organization and ritual practices. It was argued that groupings with apparently 'matrilineal' features were better understood as epiphenomenal of a rule of uxorilocal post-marital residence combined with a system of name transmission in which men's names and social roles were typically transmitted between mothers' brothers and their sisters' sons. Similarly, the Crow- and Omaha-like features of Jê relationship terminologies were shown to be correlated not with matrilineal and patrilineal descent but with variations in the system of name transmission between different sub-groups. Both spatial symbolism and native conceptions of personhood were integral to this analysis for if names conferred social personae and served to recruit individuals to ceremonial groupings associated with the village centre, these were opposed to relations based on kinship and common substance and associated with domestic life and secular affairs on the village periphery.[27]

Lea's contribution gives a new twist to these developments and represents a return to a position closer to Lévi-Strauss's and Nimuendajú's original characterization. She argues that their focus on symbolic oppositions between the public and private spheres, between a ceremonial domain and men's house in the village centre and a domestic domain of households on the village circumference, has led anthropologists to treat these households as 'peripheral' or 'marginal' not simply in spatial terms but also in terms of value and thus to a failure to recognize the structural significance of matrilineage-like houses.

Mẽbengokre (Kayapó) households and dwellings are shown to be concrete expressions of more abstract houses, enduring property-owning groups each of which occupies a fixed place on the village circle. Each exogamous house owns a heritable patrimony made up of personal names and ritual prerogatives which constitute its distinct identity; ceremonies in the village centre dramatize these prerogatives and integrate the different houses into an organic whole. Individuals belong to the house of their mother. With uxorilocal residence men leave their natal households on marriage but transmit their names and ritual prerogatives back to their sisters' sons and own houses. Women remain in place and transmit their names to their brothers' daughters in other houses; these lent-out names return to the daughter's daughter and house of origin in the next generation. Lea points to similarities between Mẽbengokre houses and Bororo matrilineal clans (see J. C. Crocker 1977a, 1985) and suggests that references to 'longhouses', 'residential segments', 'domestic clusters', 'matrilines', 'matrilineages' and 'clans' amongst other Jê groups might also be seen in this light.

Whether or not Lea's provocative re-analysis will find favour with her colleagues, it opens up possibilities for wider comparison. Despite some striking cultural parallels between the Jê/Bororo of Central Brazil and Tukanoan-speaking groups in Northwest Amazonia, differences of analytic style amongst scholars working in the two regions combined with the apparent exclusivity of traditional categories of kinship have, if anything, tended to emphasize differences rather than to highlight points in common. Jê/Bororo nucleated villages, cognatic kinship, Crow/Omaha terminologies, emphasis on naming and absence of symmetric alliance all stand in contrast to the Tukanoans' dispersed communal houses, patrilineal descent groups, Dravidian terminologies and clear pattern of symmetric alliance.

Analysis of the symbolic significance of Tukanoan architecture and spatial divisions has often gone hand in hand with a rather uncritical acceptance of the established categories of conventional alliance and descent theory. Though Jackson (1975), Murphy (1979) and Shapiro (1987) have all noted that descent theory fits uneasily with the empirical data from Amazonia as a whole, the Tukanoans are usually seen as the one case to which it applies in a relatively straightforward manner. The chapter by Hugh-Jones argues that the different levels of patrilineal grouping – phratry, exogamous language group, sib/clan, sib-/clan-segment – found amongst the Barasana and neighbouring groups may be better rendered though the indigenous idiom of the house. This move takes more into account the Tukanoans' marked emphasis on houses not simply as buildings replete with cosmological symbolism but also as key points of reference in the mythological foundations of social structure, in local idioms for genealogy, and in collective rituals which represent and give substance to patrilineal groupings. Furthermore, whereas the observers' models focus upon descent, the actors focus more on the ownership and transmission of names, social persona, language and ritual prerogatives which constitute the identity and continuity of such groupings. Actors also stress ritual mechanisms which serve to abolish the genealogical and temporal space normally occupied by segmentary lineage systems (see Hugh-Jones 1977), and, instead of segmentation, seem more concerned with rank, hierarchical encompasssment and replication as characterizing relations within wider groupings.

This shift in emphasis from the 'neutral', global language of descent towards more local and culturally informed idioms has the added advantage of highlighting parallels between the Barasana and Mẽbengokre (or between the Tukanoans and Northern Jê). Mẽbengokre houses, associated with a rule of uxorilocal residence, own sets of personal names and ritual prerogatives which are passed from mother's brother to sister's son, from grandmother to granddaughter. The virilocal Barasana pass similar property from father to son, paternal grandfather to grandson. 'Matrilineal' Mẽbengokre houses, of roughly equal status, occupy fixed places on the village circumference and each is equidistant from a sacred centre. In contrast to this, the 'patrilineal' Tukanoan houses are dispersed along the banks of rivers in a linear hierarchy which ranks them relative to one another and to their closeness to a sacred source.

Conventional analysis of Tukanoan social structure in terms of unilineal descent has also tended to overshadow the significance of cognatic ties. Although the Barasana house serves as a predominantly masculine metaphor for hierarchically ordered clan-like groups, in other contexts it acts as a more feminine metaphor for egalitarian, cognatic ties between members of the same household and between different households in a local territorial grouping. This provides a link with the chapter by Rivière, a comparative overview of the architecture and social organization of the egalitarian, cognatic Carib-speaking groups of the Guianas where dwelling and settlement are usually coterminous with a community formed from an alliance-based, endogamous bilateral kindred. Despite variations in architecture and settlement patterns, the 'proper' Guianese house is a roundhouse which fulfils a set of spatial, social, ritual and symbolic specifications that are common to all the groups involved. Concentrically organized, the house's open centre is associated with men, with public, collective, community affairs and with visitors and ceremonial; it stands in contrast to the more particularistic and domestic associations of the family compartments and hearths on the periphery. This spatial organization also reflects fundamental social and cosmic distinctions: the house is both a model of the cosmos and a representation of the position of the community *vis-à-vis* outsiders. In relation to them, the house as a whole stands as centre to some further periphery.

Within the house, a contradiction between the ideal of autonomy, endogamy, and self-sufficiency and the demographic, practical and social needs for in-marriage, trade and wider relations is masked by the interchangeability and conflation between co-residence and kinship. This is consonant with Lévi-Strauss's suggestion that, in cognatic systems, the house serves to overcome such contradictions, but Rivière finds that, in this context, the notion of 'house society' adds little because 'the very nature of [Guianese] societies has always pushed ethnographers to look at them in terms of residential units' (p. 203). Most crucially there are no inherited ancestral possessions and no enduring social units which last beyond the lives of the leaders who build the houses with which communities are identified. The only enduring houses are the mountains, the dwellings of invisible spirit beings; human settlements are merely transitory evidence of these permanent houses. Such 'rock-houses' are also a feature of the Tukanoan landscape but here they represent the ancestral origin houses of enduring social groupings, the minimal units of which inhabit impressive painted longhouses.

Although analysis of this kind has a long way to go in comparison to the work on Southeast Asia, taken together, the chapters by Rivière, Lea and Hugh-Jones suggest that a focus on architecture, co-residence, the ownership and transmission of names and other ritual property, and on the house as a metaphor and category applied to social groupings, does have considerable potential as a basis for comparison of social organization in three different areas which have hitherto proved resistant to conceptual synthesis in terms of the categories of traditional kinship theory. Though a blanket category of 'house societies' would only confuse matters, features of the societies in these three regions can be ranged on a continuum. At one extreme lie the Guiana Caribs for whom the house is merely a group lasting only as long as the relatively unelaborated building in which it lives. At the other extreme are the spatially ordered households of Mẽbengokre circular villages, each a partial actualization of a transcendent village where every known house stands in its own fixed place on the village circumference. In between lie the Northwest Amazonian Tukanoans whose elaborate architecture provides the idiom and model for two complementary aspects of social organization each of which points towards features present in the regions at either end.

THE HOUSE AS PROCESS

In the first section of this introduction, we discussed anthropology's tendency to neglect architecture and offered some possible reasons for it. Using Lévi-Strauss's discussions of house societies as a springboard, we have also tried to indicate why a focus on the house as the basis and metaphor for various kinds of social groupings might play a more central role in social analysis. Of course this volume is not unique in arguing for a more holistic focus on the house. Apart from Lévi-Strauss's own earlier writings on the significance of spatial organization and later writings on the house itself, we have drawn attention to works by Hodder (1990), Wilson (1988) and others which have given theoretical priority to an analysis of the social correlates of architecture and to the processes of domestication.

We have also mentioned a number of more ethnographic works which pay particular attention to the various dimensions of houses as buildings, residences and subsistence units, as metaphors for various kinds of social units, as significant social categories and as symbolic media. Of these, the more theoretically oriented works by C. Hugh-Jones (1979) and Moore (1986) stand out for their attempts to integrate these different dimensions within a single analytical framework which links architectural analysis with studies of social organization. They are also notable for their emphasis on the dynamic, processual aspects of buildings and social groupings. It is to these aspects which we now turn.

Despite the historical element in Lévi-Strauss's analysis of house societies, his notion of the house often appears paradoxically static. The very language used to describe the house, how it 'solidifies' an unstable relation of alliance, or 'transfixes' irreconcilable oppositions, reveals a tendency, shared by others, to see the house in static terms. As against this, in different ways the contributions to this volume all underline the fact that houses are dynamic entities. Their vitality comes from a number of sources – most obviously from the people who live in them but also from the materials used in building, from life-giving rituals, or from the movement of the heavenly bodies which often determine their orientation.[28] But it is often expressed in much stronger terms. In the cultures that are examined here, houses are far from being merely static material structures. They have animate qualities; they are endowed with spirits or souls, and are imaged in terms of the human body. In going beyond Lévi-Strauss's formulations, we would place these qualities at the centre of an anthropology of the house which considers houses and their inhabitants as part of one process of living.

Notions of process, cycle and development are commonplace in the analysis of households and domestic groups but, in contrast to the people involved, the buildings are often portrayed as relatively fixed and permanent. The expression 'bricks and mortar', with its connotations of hardness, security and permanence, finds echoes in other parts of the world. The Amazonian Indians' ancestral stone houses in rocky outcrops towering above the forest, the massive stone tombs of the Merina (Bloch 1971), the monumental long-barrows of prehistoric Europe (Hodder 1990), the soaring houses of Toraja aristocrats (Waterson 1990), and the complexes of palace, temple, shrine and tomb which make up the fixed centres of Southeast Asian kingdoms (Wilson 1988: 157–9) are all vividly permanent constructions, quintessential houses which dominate and transform the landscape and stand in contrast to the more ephemeral structures in which ordinary people live out their lives. Some houses do indeed endure for a very long time but others are much more transient.

What we would stress here is the need to consider the house and its occupants within the same analytical framework. In much of the material discussed in this volume, the opposition between the permanent house and its impermanent occupants does not apply in a straightfoward way. We would argue against such an opposition from two points of view. With respect to the people, their kinship and social groups must be understood in processual terms; with respect to the buildings themselves, we would also stress their processual aspects. We will take each of these arguments in turn.

The argument that kinship is processual is hardly new. Several of our contributors stress the role of feeding, and thus of the hearth, in the active creation of kinship, whilst the fact that marriages are made and children born, that people change residence, and that domestic groups are established, decline and replace each other in time was the main thrust of Goody's (1958) collection on the developmental cycle. However, despite the emphasis on cycles, these are often presented as a series of stages or static images (see especially Fortes 1958: 4–5). Data from the cognatic groups of Southeast Asia strongly suggest that the emphasis should be placed not on the stages but rather on the process of transformation which gives rise to them.

This is most striking in the way that siblingship and marriage are presented as transformations and oppositions of each other. As Carsten and Gibson make clear, the married couple is thought of in terms of both affinity *and* siblingship. The Malays, Makassarese and other cognatic groups in Southeast Asia marry their kin and kinship here means extended siblingship. Marriage often occurs between cousins who call each other by sibling terms. But this also involves a tension – such marriage carries implications of incest. As if to avoid these uncomfortable associations, the marriage rituals often seem to create a formal category of affines. During the cycle of betrothal and marriage there is a striking degree of avoidance between the principal parties as well as a rather frenzied exchange of gifts through their intermediaries.

If the marriage rituals create affines, as soon as they are over these same affines are transformed into kin. Amongst the Malays, a new son- or daughter-in-law's incorporation into their affinal household is vividly expressed in a series of 'domestic' rituals. These include feeding and participating in domestic labour, and most striking of all, a ritual procession through the new house which begins through the kitchen (an entry normally only used by close family members). The process of transforming affinity into domestic kinship operates in exactly the same way when people marry non-relatives, and is one of many ways in which strangers or distant kin are brought closer (see McKinley 1981).

Married couples eventually produce new sibling sets in their children. These siblings are strongly associated with the unity of the house but are also differentiated by the order of their birth. This is often the basis of rank and hierarchy. On marriage, these siblings divide and occupy different houses to begin the cycle anew. Marriage between houses is transformed once again into siblingship within the house. In this way we can see how the house represents not only siblingship but also marriage. In a continuous two-way process, siblingship becomes affinity, and affinity becomes siblingship (see McKinley 1981, Waterson 1986, Errington 1987, Carsten 1991). The nature of this continuous process of transformation would be lost if it were represented simply as a series of stages.

There is a parallel here with the interplay between relations based on naming and relations based on bodily substance amongst the uxorilocal Jê groups discussed by Lea. Children get substance from their parents but their names and social personality come (usually) from their parents' cross-sex siblings. Siblings share common sub-stance but when they grow up, marry and live separately, these bonds progressively weaken as their own substance merges with that of their respective spouses. As they produce children of their own, they simultaneously transmit their names back to the children of their own cross-sex siblings.

Inasmuch as we stress the processual nature of kinship, more radically we would also stress the processual nature of the house. Buildings themselves are not static and many of our chapters pick up the theme of an interplay between permanence and impermanence. This is not simply the obvious point that houses must be built and maintained, get modified to fit the needs of their occupants, are extended and rebuilt, and ultimately decay and fall down. It is also to stress that such architectural processes are made to coincide, in various ways, with important events and processes in the lives of their occupants and are thought of in terms of them. In her chapter on Langkawi, Carsten stresses how houses are continuously under construction; in peasant Latin America, the conversion of surplus and savings from the annual round into building materials links the house as an ongoing project with the house as economy. Even more vividly, as Bloch shows, the Zafimaniry house hardens and matures together with the people who occupy it. House building is begun at the same time as a couple embarks on marriage and only completed when their first child is born. Likewise, Gibson's Makassarese compare house building to childbirth, a process completed only with the birth of three children. In Amazonia too, whilst ancestral stone houses are fixed and eternal, their pale reflections in the world of the living are in a constant state of flux. Houses undergo a rapid turnover and a constant reshuffling of their occupants, a process that coincides with the careers of the leaders who build them. When the leader dies the house dies with him.

Perhaps even more surprisingly, although we tend to think of people as mobile and houses as stationary, we are confronted here with cases in which houses actually move. At its simplest this is a matter of people rebuilding their house anew; for swidden cultivators, periodic relocation and rebuilding is a feature of life which militates against the development of truly permanent prestige architecture. More radically, in parts of Southeast Asia such as Langkawi, the house itself may be lifted up by a group of men so that it seems actually to acquire legs and to walk or run to a new site. This image of a walking house emphatically demonstrates its animate qualities. It also emphasizes the need for a unitary analysis of the house and the people who inhabit it. Houses only walk or run when their occupants change or require a larger site, perhaps as a result of a marriage or the birth of more children. The process of kinship and the process of the house are so thoroughly intertwined as to be one process.

Bourdieu (1990 [1970]), in his study of the Kabyle house, observed that when Berbers cross the threshold and move from the outside to the inside of the house, their whole world is reversed. However, the chapters by Carsten, Janowski and Hugh-Jones all suggest that this relation between interior and exterior is more than simply one of opposition and homology as Bourdieu (1990: 277) puts it; it is also one of movement. The continuous movement of goods and people between the inside and the outside, a movement sometimes represented as one through the orifices of the body (see also C. Hugh-Jones 1979), again attests to the processual and animate qualities of the house.

In the Kabyle case, the external world and the internal one are associated with men and women respectively, and they are in a hierarchical relation. The house is defined as it were from the outside, by men; women, on the inside, are subordinate to them. Movement inwards is intrinsically female movement; movement outwards, intrinsically male. Bourdieu sees '[t]he supremacy given to movement outwards ... [as] merely a form of the categorical refusal of nature, the inevitable origin of man's movement away from nature' (1990: 283). In the cases we consider here, however, the gendered associations of internal and external are more variable and more complex. In different contexts, the Malay, Tukanoan or Kelabit house can be associated with women, with women and men, or with men. As Bourdieu (1977) has himself argued, space comes to have meaning through particular practices. It has no fixed meaning outside these (see also Moore 1986). Depending on whether the Kelabit are eating a domestic meal or holding a formal feast, the associations of their hearths shift.

In both South America and Southeast Asia, houses can be simultaneously 'private' and 'public', associated with women or with men or both, and can provide models for the wider polity as well as being domestic entities. We should then be wary about describing the house as a structure of unchanging gendered oppositions. As Moore (1986) has forcefully argued, the meanings of what she would call 'spatial texts', which she sees as cultural representations, continuously shift and are reworked. Their relationship to particular ideologies are mutable both in differing historical conditions and with the interests of different actors. In an analysis that takes account of different power relations and of historical change, she shows how actors create and constitute meanings in their everyday practices.

As the cases studied here demonstrate, the opposition between inside and outside may not be perceived in gendered terms at all. It may be linked to oppositions based on other kinds of perceived social differences. Amongst the Makassarese, the Lio, the Tukanoans or the Mẽbengokre, inside or outside may be linked with siblingship or marriage, with descent or affinity, with unity or difference, with women or men, or with high rank or low. And this of course brings us back to the links between the house as a material entity, as a social group and as a symbolic category.

What all this suggests is that although anthropologists have tended to assume that buildings and the people they contain are entities of entirely different kinds, much of the material we discuss indicates that, in certain contexts at least, this distinction may be blurred: houses or settlements are spoken about as if they were people and people are likened to houses. At the simplest level, this analogy between houses and people is manifest in the mapping of anatomy onto architecture and architecture onto anatomy, a mapping widely reported in the literature and well illustrated in this volume.

CONCLUSION

The metaphorical associations between people and houses go well beyond a simple analogy of parts. It was with this in mind that we began this introduction with some remarks concerning the more general linkage between houses and bodies, between inhabiting and embodiment. The relation of people to houses is also one of contained to container so that the contrast between body and house can be made to relate to differences in scale and relations of encompassment between the individual and society or between levels of social grouping. Gudeman and Rivera's (1990) discussion of the house-model of the domestic economy provides one example. Here the house is opposed to the wider corporation on which it depends. If the house goes into business, it may be incorporated (Gudeman 1992); if it resists, it tends to be pushed ever further towards the margins of productivity. The Tukanoan mythology discussed in this volume provides another example in which body and house are presented as a series of nested boxes with the house mediating between the body and the cosmos, between the present and the past, and providing the ritual switch point between microcosm and macrocosm on which continued access to ancestral potency depends.

Given its living qualities and close association with the body, it comes as no surprise that natural processes normally associated with people, animals or plants may also apply to the house. Houses may be said to be born, to grow, to mature and die, to move and walk, to feed and be fed, and they may even be said to marry and copulate. Because shared consumption often provides the basic ideas about cohabitation and kinship – it is in this sense that both houses and their occupants are fed – the hearth itself may be the central image and focal point of the house.[29] As many of the contributions to this volume make clear, the hearth is as much a defining feature of the house as eating together is a defining feature of kinship. But the hearth is not just a symbolic centre; it is also instrumental in processes of transformation. It is in the hearth that the different elements that enter the house – meat and vegetable, kin and affine, the like and the unlike – may be said to be mixed and blended, veritably cooked together. Insofar as houses are continually transforming what passes through them, the hearth is both literally and figuratively the site where these transformations actually take place.[30]

That houses may be personified and bodies objectified in terms of the house brings us back to the question of the sources of the house's symbolic power. We would suggest that this can be linked to the constant two-way mapping that goes on between the body and its close, everyday environment. That people talk of houses as outer shells, skins or garments, that the Barasana link architectural features with facial paint and feather ornaments and that in Langkawi the house must be dressed suggests just this. Because both body and house constitute the most intimate everyday environment and often serve as analogies for each other, it may sometimes seem unclear which is serving as metaphor for which – house for body or body for house.

As McKinnon's contribution shows, whilst the social relations of high-ranking Tanimbarese may be said to be 'objectified' in houses and ancestral heirlooms, those between the social groups or houses of lower-ranking commoners are 'personified' and spoken of in terms of individuals and their bodies. The two versions always refer to each other so that a lower ranking house evokes the symbolic associations of the more elaborate high-ranking house and vice versa. In the yet more elaborated, hierarchical model, exemplified by peoples such as the Toraja and Bugis, the noble house or royal palace stands for the whole polity or group and encompasses all the commoner houses.

The chapters by Hugh-Jones and Lea offer further examples of such personification. The Tukanoan house, as both building and group, is clearly seen in bodily terms, a theme which reappears in the Xingú region (see Fénelon Costa and Botelho Malhano 1987: 51–5). The Xingúano circular villages and central men's houses call to mind those of the Mẽbengokre but, for the latter, it is the whole village rather than the individual house which provides a pervasive bodily metaphor for society. The Tukanoans and Mẽbengokre both stress access to ritual prerogatives and non-material wealth; it is tempting to relate the Tukanoans' greater emphasis on bodily imagery, especially the opposition between head and body, to their more overtly hierarchical system.

It would seem that body image serves as a vehicle to naturalize social hierarchy so that where hierarchical differences are important we also tend to find a greater elaboration of bodily imagery in the house. This use of body imagery to express and naturalize hierarchy may occur together with gender imagery. Houses may be weakly gendered and linked to siblings of both sexes. Or they may be strongly gendered and linked to sibling sets and lineages which, though conceived of in some circumstances as being predominantly male, themselves have a dual or androgynous aspect expressed in terms of a brother–sister pair. Once again this brings up the question of what symbolizes what. Does the house naturalize the hierarchization of gender or does gender serve to naturalize social ranking of which the house is a central component?

The answer to this question is clearly neither one nor the other but both. The hierarchization of differences between parts of the body, between genders, between houses and between ranks are all interconnected. It is this interconnectedness that makes it impossible to pick out any one and to give it priority over the others. Because each of these hierarchies assumes and implies all the others, they each gain added force and authority.

The source of the symbolic power of the house does not reside in the house as isolated entity, but in the multiple connections between the house and the people it contains. This is vividly brought out by the fact that a house without people in it is not a proper house. In English we might say it is not a home; in Barasana we would say it lacks a heart. Malays, like many other people, do not distinguish house from home; they take it for granted that a house contains people, minimally a woman or a married couple. Houses that are abandoned decay surprisingly rapidly and may be a source of anxiety, just as the people without houses who are a feature of present-day life in urban Britain give rise to another kind of alarm.

This brings us back to our starting point, that in the discrete analytical domains of anthropological analysis, the multifaceted character of the house tends to get lost. Though households figure in kinship theory and buildings are mentioned in the analysis of households, people tend to get detached from the houses in which they live and the house itself often gets hidden under the notion of 'residence' (see Rivière this volume). Conversely, although people and social groupings obviously play an important role in discussions of architecture, only rarely is the house's vital role in kinship systems fully appreciated, a role which involves the house not only as the building in which a group of people live but also as a social grouping and cultural concept in its own right.

The value of Lévi-Strauss's contribution lies precisely in his suggestion that these different aspects of the house might be brought together. But, in the end, because it is mainly offered as a contribution to a narrowly conceived theory of kinship and because he concentrates his attention almost exclusively on the house as a social grouping, Lévi-Strauss never fully explores the potential of his own argument. What many of the chapters in this volume could be taken to suggest is that the house has two sides. Insofar as it is a native category referring to a social group, the house, in Lévi-Strauss's sense, is largely a ritual construct which is related to ancestors, embodied in names, heirlooms and titles brought out and displayed in ritual contexts, and objectified in a temple or in a domestic dwelling which temporarily takes on this quality.

Some of the contributions to this volume reflect a tendency in anthropology, not limited to Lévi-Strauss, to focus on the ritual aspects of social life. But the house has another side. It is an ordinary group of people concerned with their day-to-day affairs, sharing consumption and living in the shared space of a domestic dwelling. It is out of these everyday activities, carried on without ritual, reflection or fuss and, significantly, often by women, that the house is built. This house, all too easily taken for granted, is one that anthropologists have tended to ignore. One conclusion we would emphasize is the need for further research on an anthropology of everyday life which might both balance, and eventually be incorporated into, studies of ritual and ideology (see also Bloch 1991).

We have shown the value of seeing houses together with the people who inhabit them as mutually implicated in the process of living. Houses have many aspects. None of these can be understood as static pre-given structures, whether these are of the material kind or mental projections of a structuralist sort. They are born, live, grow old, die and decay. Their complexity is often only partially rendered. If our attempt to do more than this here has only partly succeeded, we would argue that this is a more or less inevitable failing. One conclusion of our introduction might be that a single theory of the house is as fraught with difficulties as a single theory of the body. Houses, like bodies, are complex, multifaceted entities, particular aspects of which are given meaning by different people, in particular cultures, in particular contexts and particular historical conditions. These meanings constantly shift within cultures, and they have no inherent cross-cultural validity. However, although the meanings of the house may be specific, the processes by which these are generated, and which we have attempted to outline, are much more general.

We began by examining one global theory of the house. Our analysis might be said to add up to an exposition of the weaknesses in Lévi-Strauss's model. But the studies collected here also demonstrate the stengths of an alternative which his writings have encouraged us to pursue. That is, a strong, ethnographically-based view of the house understood in holistic terms which takes account of processes of living that may be said to be universal.

In their different ways, the chapters in this volume all attempt to integrate architecture, kinship and cultural categories as they are brought together in the house, exploring the different ways in which houses and people are connected. On the one hand, people and groups are objectified in buildings; on the other hand, houses as buildings are personified and animated both in thought and in life. At one extreme are the lifeless ancestral houses, mountains or tombs, frozen in time but vividly permanent; at the other extreme are those highly animated houses, in a constant state of changing but ultimately ephemeral. But in all of these, container and contained are related as parts of a continuous process of living.

2 HOUSES AND HIERARCHIES IN ISLAND SOUTHEAST ASIA

Roxana Waterson

For Southeast Asianists, Lévi-Strauss's concept of the 'house society' has been one of the most stimulating and provocative to emerge in recent years (Lévi-Strauss 1983a: 163–76, 1987). Yet, considering the startling scope of his idea, Lévi-Strauss's treatment of it in print is so brief as to leave many questions unanswered. In *The Way of the Masks*, he compares the Kwakiutl *numayma* to the noble houses of feudal Europe, while merely hinting that the category of 'house societies' might be extended to include Ancient Greece, feudal Japan, the Philippines, Indonesia, Melanesia and Polynesia. The more recent records of his lectures (1987) are scarcely more illuminating, being highly compressed summaries of lines of thought originally developed throughout whole lecture courses. Thus, as others observe (Macdonald (ed.) 1987), his various essays at defining the concept remain sufficiently vague as to leave room for continued debate about the application of his model in particular cases. Island Southeast Asia provides a fertile field in which to explore the many dimensions of this intriguing yet elusive concept. Not only do its impressive vernacular architectures already provide an obvious clue to the importance of houses in this region, but it abounds in examples of kinship systems whose ambiguities have puzzled anthropologists, but which might be resolved by seeing them as house-focused systems.

In my research on the Sa'dan Toraja of highland South Sulawesi, I found it impossible to grasp the workings of their cognatic kinship system without an understanding of houses as the focal points of the system (Waterson 1984, 1986). I have since attempted to demonstrate the central role of houses in other societies of island Southeast Asia (Waterson 1990). Others have likewise been exploring the idea of 'house societies' in the region (McKinnon 1983; Errington 1987; Macdonald (ed.) 1987). This is indicative perhaps of our own felt need for a new approach to some of the problems of Southeast Asian social organization. But should we be using this simply as a jumping-off point from which to examine indigenous concepts? Or is what is needed a rigorous refinement of Lévi-Strauss's definition, in order to decide exactly which societies may qualify as 'true' house societies and which must be excluded? Efforts to produce watertight typologies are generally doomed to failure; I believe it more rewarding to concentrate on the functioning of various principles which Lévi-Strauss perceives as characteristic of 'house societies'. His sweeping approach to such societies as 'variations on a theme' parallels his treatment of myths as variant sets; in this way we may be able to view Indonesian societies as transformations of each other, whose common feature is the importance of the house as a focus of social organization.[1] All the same, we need *some* form of limiting criteria to make the concept workable. I shall suggest that there are some irreducible features which must be present for a society meaningfully to be thought of as a 'house society'; but if we avoid attempting to apply an idealized model, we need not necessarily expect to find every principle at work in every instance. We also leave open the possibility that 'house ideology' can be made to serve different purposes.

In seeking to test the 'house society' concept further, three general questions arise: first, is the 'house' a salient, organizing category for the people themselves? A failure to begin with indigenous concepts is what led Kroeber to conclude, as Lévi-Strauss points out, that the Yurok of California had 'no society as such ... no social organization ... no authority', in the face of his own data which demonstrate clearly the centrality of houses as enduring named units of social organization, with important jural and ceremonial functions, whose owners even took their names from the house itself (Kroeber 1925; Lévi-Strauss 1983a: 171–3).[2] Secondly, how well can the 'house society' concept help in the analysis of kinship systems? Unless it makes sense of otherwise recalcitrant data in any given instance, there would seem little point in introducing the concept.[3] Thirdly (my chief concern in this paper), how critical a feature is the existence of a social hierarchy to the emergence of a 'house society'? Is an unstratified house society a possibility, or are they all, as Lévi-Strauss's main examples suggest, in the throes of a political transition in which the interests of those who seek to concentrate power must yet continue to 'borrow the language of kinship' in order to express themselves (Lévi-Strauss 1983a: 187)?

Another related question may be posed here, namely, whether a 'house society' ought properly to be one in which the 'house' is the *dominant* institution? Considering examples such as the tribes of the Northwest Coast discussed by Lévi-Strauss, this might appear as a reasonable condition to set, but other instances suggest the contrary. In feudal Europe, royal and noble houses co-existed with other powerful social institutions, such as the Church; while in the dense network of Balinese social life, the *dadia* competes with organizations dedicated to village, religious, agricultural and irrigation affairs, involving all the adult couples of the community.[4] If we are to call these 'house societies', then that is certainly not all there is to be said about them. Part of the problem lies in translation: what precisely is the force of the '*à*' in the phrase '*sociétés à maison*', variously translated as 'house societies' or 'societies with houses'? These two English renderings certainly carry different implications, the latter much weaker than the former. And for whom is the house important? Is it an institution of significance at all levels of a society, or a development only of the elite? As we shall see, the variations to be found in the role of the house are wider than we might suspect, and an examination of them should eventually help, if not to pin down the concept, at least to clarify its usefulness.

HOUSES AND HIERARCHY

I take as my starting point Lévi-Strauss's oft-cited definition of the house as 'a corporate body holding an estate made up of both material and immaterial wealth, which perpetuates itself through the transmission of its name, its goods and its titles down a real or imaginary line, considered legitimate as long as this continuity can express itself in the language of kinship or of affinity and, most often, of both' (Lévi-Strauss 1983a: 174). The key features of this definition are (i) the ideal of continuity; (ii) the passing down of some form of valued property (a name, land, titles, sacra, even supernatural powers); and (iii) the strategic exploitation of the 'language of kinship or affinity' (which includes extensive use of fictive relations when necessary to prevent the extinction of a 'house'). These, then, may be judged the irreducible aspects of the 'house' as a social phenomenon. But as Macdonald (1987a: 5) has observed, in subsequent writings Lévi-Strauss extends this apparently straightforward definition into more ambiguous areas when he speaks of the 'fetishization' of the house, and its role in uniting within itself, 'if only in an illusory form', such contradictions as the tension between alliance and descent (Lévi-Strauss 1987: 155).

The possibility of viewing the 'house' in ideological terms, rather than as a group or a building, renders conceivable the notion of a 'house society' existing in the absence of any actual house *structures*, as Ivanoff (1987) postulates for the Moken sea nomads of Thailand. Their boat-communities show some features of 'house societies' in their attachment to islands of origin, where they reside in the company of their ancestors during each year's monsoons, while celebrating significant rituals. This attachment creates a sense of social continuity for Moken sub-groups, so that the island symbolically performs the role of the 'house'. One might prefer to leave this comparison at the level of analogy, given that no indigenous Moken concept appears to correspond to the idea of the 'house'. But in another instance, that of Langkawi (Malaysia), the category 'house' is part of the indigenous framework, though applied very abstractly. Carsten (1987a) shows how the 'shadow' image of the Langkawi village community as 'house', which is given substance by being acted out at communal feasts, projects a unity intended to transcend the divisions between actual households and individuals. We are here confronted with the irony that actual houses may appear very flimsy, utilitarian structures – a feature which Errington (1989) also notes of the Buginese. These examples might be taken to illustrate one end of a continuum of 'house societies', where the 'house' appears at its most abstract and metaphorical. What is illuminated is, in the first case, a sense of location, and in the second, the articulation of social relationships.

Macdonald remarks on the 'audacity' of a schema which would unite under one classification such widely differing societies as the Iban, tribes of the Northwest Coast of North America, and feudal

Europe and Japan. Not only are they widely separated in space and time, but they appear to range from among the most egalitarian to the most hierarchical. Is it really possible that this one concept can encompass all of these realities? Most critically, does the passing on of names, goods and titles through houses necessarily imply some degree of social inequality in house societies? This might appear to be implied in Lévi-Strauss's writings, but it is nowhere specifically addressed by him. In *The Way of the Masks* he writes, for example, that the 'house', '[b]y gluing together real interests and mythical pedigrees ... procures for the enterprises of the great a starting point endowed with absolute value' (1983a: 187). But must we therefore conclude that only where such enterprises are under way is the 'house' to be found?

All the examples treated by Lévi-Strauss – from the tribes of the Northwest Coast, to Europe, Japan, Polynesia and Bali – are to a greater or lesser degree hierarchical systems. But there are obvious differences between the kind of social hierarchy present among the Kwakiutl, extraordinary in the degree of social differentiation which had developed between lineages on the basis of a hunting and gathering economy, and the stratification of a state system such as Tokugawa Japan or the feudal kingdoms of Europe. I propose that a society *need* not be highly stratified in order for the house to fulfil the basic criteria of continuity and the passing on of wealth – as the examples of the Iban (see below) and the Kayapó (Lea, this volume) indicate.[5] However, Lévi-Strauss's stress on both the material and immaterial nature of house wealth is highly significant and must lead us to consider the relation of 'houses' both to systems of economic stratification and to hierarchies of status, prestige or ritual power.

In regions as culturally diverse as Southeast Asia, how widely can Lévi-Strauss's concept be applied? Sellato (1987a) and Guerreiro (1987), both reviewing Borneo societies, and Macdonald (1987b), examining the Philippines, all conclude that only a small proportion of groups in these areas constitute fully-fledged 'house societies'. Guerreiro decides that a hereditary stratification system is an essential feature of a 'house society', but Sellato notes that in some egalitarian societies such as the Iban and Selako, longhouse apartments also form units which pass on heirloom wealth and are not supposed to die out. He concludes that, although the majority of Borneo groups are not really 'house societies', it is not exclusively to the stratified ones that the concept may be applied. Furthermore, although the longhouse as an institution may favour development of the 'house' concept, Borneo longhouse societies are not *necessarily* 'house societies'. The relation of apartment households to each other within a longhouse differs considerably from society to society. The degree of autonomy of the apartment and its right to secede from the longhouse varies; among the Kenyah and Kayan, for example, chiefs are powerful enough to prevent secession.[6] This creates a different kind of longhouse 'unity' than exists among the Iban, for example. And in other instances, there is little evidence of the longhouse functioning as a united entity in any circumstances.

The inclination to separate out the more 'feudal' types as more likely to be 'true' house societies is a movement contrary to Lévi-Strauss's original 'audacity' in grouping them with other types and I think requires careful examination. Any such separation would certainly exclude the Northwest Coast societies which were his starting point. Given the ambiguities of the Iban case, among others, one must also address the possibility that the features attributed by Lévi-Strauss to the 'house' could be distributed over more than one unit of the society: there are some contexts in which the household acts as a unity and others in which the entire longhouse, or even a group of longhouses, does so. In such a case, it is problematic to decide which one of these is the 'house' (Sellato 1987a: 44; Sather 1993).[7] Sellato (1987b: 196) proposes restricting the term 'house' to ordinary domestic units and using 'House' to describe dominant families in feudal systems. Thus, he would judge the Iban as having 'houses' but no 'Houses', while the sultanates of the southern Philippines and the kingdoms of feudal Europe have 'Houses' but no 'houses'. The problem is that he nowhere defines what he means by 'feudal'. Stratified societies like the Kenyah, although they have an aristocracy, can hardly be described as 'feudal' if our definition of feudalism is based on the features of medieval European society, and Sellato judges the apartment of a Kenyah chief to be a 'house', and not a 'House'. He sees as a feature of such stratified societies the way in which the noble 'house', at the same time as it stands opposed to the 'houses' of commoners, is part of a basically homogeneous structure and functions in just the same manner as commoners' 'houses'. As such, the noble house is also able to stand for the rest of the community. Thus, among the Kenyah, the chief in his specially grand apartment with its concentration of heirloom wealth both represents a concentration of political and supernatural power and, in relations with outsiders, stands for the rest of the longhouse and even a community of longhouses.

By contrast, in the sultanates of the southern Philippines (Maranao, Maguindanao and Tausug) described by Loyré (1987), the Royal House forms the dominant political institution in the society, binding together rulers, kin and followers (including slaves). The appropriateness of using the term 'feudal' for these systems would seem to be limited, though certain features might seem reminiscent, for example the claim of Maranao Princes to ultimate ownership of all their subjects' lands, in the name of God. However, other features such as the heavy dependence on slaves to perform all manner of economic tasks, including agriculture, does not accord with most definitions of feudalism. What is intriguing about Loyré's account is the different political histories of each of his three examples, though the noble 'House' plays a dominant role in all of them. Among the Tausug, a single sultan succeeded in concentrating all power in his own hands and establishing a centralized state; the Maguindanao had a bicephalous arrangement resulting from the splitting of the royal line into two; while for the Maranao, power was distributed among numerous sultans and noble rulers, their precise numbers varying at different periods but currently totalling forty-three. It is not unambiguously clear from Loyré's writing that commoner 'houses' are of no importance as an institution in these societies. But Sellato apparently dismisses the possibility of 'Houses' co-existing with 'houses' in more centralized societies. By contrast, I shall argue that the 'house' concept is open to ideological exploitation in a great range of social formations, and it is in fact quite possible to find examples where the 'house' is an important unit among both noble and commoner strata of society. While the 'house' can clearly be exploited for purposes of social differentiation, it can also – and still more powerfully – be used in the attempt to create a legitimating and apparently 'natural' unity in which the houses of rulers are conceived as 'encompassing' those of their followers.[8]

The above discussion inevitably raises the question of defining 'feudal' systems, for it is debatable whether the term can appropriately be applied in Southeast Asia at all. Ito and Reid (1975), for example, in a lucid analysis of seventeenth-century Aceh, conclude that although Aceh and some other Southeast Asian societies in this period showed *some* of the features classically associated with feudalism in Europe, there were crucial features of the latter which remain very different. What they see as significant is that a *transition* of similar magnitude as that from Antiquity to Feudalism appears to have taken place in Aceh at that time. Not all petty states are necessarily 'feudal', and in fact the only two examples of feudal systems on which all scholars seem to be agreed are medieval Europe and Japan.[9] Sellato's 'House'/'house' distinction may be a useful shorthand for thinking about the exact relations between aristocratic and commoner establishments, but it should not be used to try and categorize Southeast Asian societies into two groups, 'feudal' and otherwise. It is more significant to ask how many of the societies in which the 'house' appears as a dominant institution actually were undergoing some kind of political transition, and if they were, what exactly was the role of the 'house' in this process?

'HOUSE SOCIETIES' AND ISLAND SOUTHEAST ASIA

In island Southeast Asia, a number of common themes are prominent both in architectural styles, and in ways of talking about houses and relating to them. The wide distribution of these features, and the vocabularies used for discussing them, are strongly suggestive of shared Austronesian origins.[10] A consistent picture emerges of the house as a key social unit, functioning less as dwelling (it may even be unoccupied) than as origin-place, ritual site, holder of ritual offices and storage-place for heirlooms. Ancestors may be literally considered to be present in the house, or at least symbolically represented by supernaturally charged heirloom valuables stored away in attics. House idioms dominate as ways of expressing ideas about kinship.

Broad differences have often been noted between the typically cognatic systems of most of western Indonesia (such as Toraja), and the asymmetric alliance systems of eastern Indonesia. Yet in both these areas, one finds that the house is the focal institution. Toraja kinship is emphatically bilateral and there is no limiting factor, such as residence, restricting one's membership of origin-houses.[11] All individuals can potentially trace links with numerous origin-houses, the birthplaces of their parents, grandparents or more remote ancestors. Effectually, since these ties are principally demonstrated in a ritual context, ceremonial expenditure curtails active participation in too many houses. The aristocracy show the greatest concern with houses, genealogies and ritual display, but even ordinary people trace their ties to each other through houses.[12] There are no clearly bounded groups of kin 'belonging' to houses, but people remember their links with each other in terms of shared *houses* even when exact genealogical ties have been forgotten. The preferred way to express a relation between cousins is to say 'Our origin-houses join', or 'We are siblings within the origin-house'. Thinking about kinship is very ego-centred or (as Errington, following Freeman, would have it) sibling-centred (Errington 1987: 413), since terminology arranges people into generational layers. In this stratified society, commoners were also locked into relationships with politically dominant noble houses, to whom they were sometimes related by marriage.[13]

Tracing descent is of little concern to the Toraja except in particular circumstances: inheritance, contributing to the rebuilding of an origin-house, or choosing a tomb (*liang*). By contrast, the idea of descent has until recently been described as important in most eastern Indonesian systems. But currently here, too, ethnographers are rapidly moving away from descent, and even alliance, theory in favour of a concentration on the house as the organizing principle of kinship. The great merit of this development is that it brings us closer to indigenous categories, helping us to understand them in their own terms. It may ultimately provide the resolution to the 'tension' which Lévi-Strauss finds at the heart of the house, which may be the result of our own insistence on the primacy of these categories. Descent in these societies is not unilineal; affiliation with a house depends upon the type of marriage one's parents contracted, and upon residence, which can be changed. The individual may follow a variable path of changing allegiances during life, only coming to rest finally in the tomb. The question of loyalties, as expressed in residence, is in fact more likely to create a crisis in death than in life. In Toraja, as well as on Roti (Fox 1987: 175), it is quite possible during life to trace ties to, even to live in, a number of different houses, but you can only be buried in one place. Each Toraja origin-house has its own rock grave, while the Rotinese used to bury their dead in the floor of the house, their spirits being thought to take up residence in the attic. An individual's final allegiance is not decided until death. In Toraja, the bilateral tracing of descent enables each individual to claim links to many houses and consequently to their graves. In both Toraja and Roti, violent fights have been known to break out over a corpse, as relatives of the deceased person struggle to claim the honour of burial (Toraja) or of performing the mortuary rites (Roti), and the consequent incorporation of that person into their own group of beneficent ancestors.[14]

The common practice in eastern Indonesia of 'returning a child' to the house of whichever spouse changed residence at marriage creates subsidiary lines within some houses. Among the Atoni, these are thought of as 'female' lines within an overarching 'male' line. In the second generation after its formation, this line can marry back into the principal 'male' line. If the overarching 'male' line becomes weakened, a powerful wife-taker may try to *give* a wife and thus reverse the flow of women, and consequently the relation of superiority/inferiority which exists between wife-givers and wife-takers. Houses here play a key role as the *exchanging* units in marriage systems, but the tracing either of 'descent' or 'alliance' relations becomes extremely complicated. It is hard even to say who is an affine, where marriage partners are so frequently already related through houses (Fox 1993b).

Although the relation of exchange involves a hierarchical marking of one party (wife-givers) as superior, not all eastern Indonesian societies had fixed hereditary ranking systems. The question of what we mean by 'hierarchy' is one which has generated much anthropological debate. Dumont for example considers hierarchical principles at an abstract level and claims to have been misunderstood by those who interpret hierarchy as having something to do with actual inequalities embedded in systems of social stratification. Following his example, several ethnographers have managed to discuss hierarchical relations within the symbolic systems of Indonesian societies without any reference to economic or power relations, or their implications for individuals in the system (Barnes *et al.* 1985). Unsatisfying as this approach may be, it must be recognized that eastern Indonesian groups differ considerably in the degree of social stratification that they exhibit, though in their symbolic universes the complementary yet hierarchical arrangement of paired categories is an almost obsessive theme. Since some of these societies do seem to me to be extremely house-oriented, I conclude that societies do not have to be highly stratified nor to approach some version of 'feudalism' before we can think of them as 'house societies'.

Within the Indonesian archipelago, we find types of social organization ranging from foraging groups to shifting cultivators, to settled agriculturalists with petty chiefdoms like the Toraja, to centralized states of historically differing sizes and degrees of power. Rank systems also differ. Among the Toba Batak of Sumatra, the Kei islands or the Tanimbarese, instead of an overall ranking system cutting right through the society, we find only a ranking of houses within a particular community, based upon seniority or closeness to a founding ancestor. Each Toba clan or lineage, for example, traditionally dominated others within the villages which its own members had founded, while occupying a subordinate role in other villages where they were not the founders – for example, where members resided with their wife-givers. In Tanimbar, rank may be lost over time as 'branch' houses become further removed from core origin-houses, or through debt and clientage (McKinnon 1983: 276–80). For the Mambai of East Timor, the ranking of houses seems to develop organically out of the 'branching' process, explained in the pervasive Austronesian imagery of 'trunk' and 'tip'. New 'tip' houses branch off from older, ancestral 'trunk' houses, as in myth the ancestors 'cut a slip' from the central pillar of the first house and spread out to found new settlements, 'planting' their cuttings on the sites where they built new houses (Traube 1986: 168).

Such systems contrast with those like the Sa'dan Toraja, who have a hereditary ranking system of nobles, commoners and (former) slaves, within which aristocrats were the major owners of irrigated rice land and enjoyed at times considerable claims upon the labour and produce of their followers. Among the societies of eastern Indonesia, some – like the Sumbanese, Savunese or the Tetum of Timor – also have hereditary ranking systems in which aristocrats traditionally presided (both politically and ritually) over district communities or domains. At the end of the continuum we find centralized state systems, organized around a court where hierarchy and the etiquette of rank assumed still greater importance. In a number of petty states, the ideology of the 'house' retains a central place, while in the more heavily Indicized ones, the cosmological function was partly taken over by monumental building projects in stone.

The built environment provides one of the major means by which people construct for themselves a sense of place, but it is not essential. Foraging groups have no use for such investments of energy and their sense of location embraces the whole environment. Shifting agriculture, too, imposes certain limitations on the impulse to build elaborately, as fields over time become inconveniently remote from settlements and the latter will sooner or later have to be moved. Fox notes, with regard to the Atoni, that both Schulte Nordholt and Cunningham worked in Insana, a princely domain close to the border with the generally much more hierarchical and house-oriented Tetum people. The picture they present of the centrality of the house in Atoni organization is much diluted in other areas of Atoni country. Being shifting cultivators, who make a practice of moving their settlements every two generations or so, the Atoni rarely build houses in a manner sufficiently permanent to last very long as origin-places. Their profound sense of place is instead encoded in oral traditions describing the journeys of a descent-group founder from place to place, this individual representing his descendants as they spread and established new settlements. In most Atoni regions, then, house 'ideology' is largely a monopoly of the aristocracy, irrelevant to ordinary people.[15]

In stratified societies, the house offers itself to the aristocracy as a vivid means of differentiating themselves from commoners. Larger, taller houses with more decoration serve to embody and display their wealth, status and power (often, too, their ritual superiority, by the addition of emblems signifying that certain great feasts have been held). It is therefore no surprise to find baroque elaborations of the 'house' in societies like the Toraja, where the towering, richly carved houses of ruling nobles are a dominating presence in each community – nor to discover that aristocrats are the ones who cultivate long genealogical memories. In the late nineteenth century, some Toraja nobles, developing expansionist ambitions, allied themselves with Bugis mercenaries seeking to control the coffee trade out of the highlands. They raided remoter districts for slaves and seized large tracts of land from weaker neighbours.[16] Architecture has undoubtedly played its part in the process of aggrandisement. Kis-Jovak, Schefold *et al.* (1988) trace the historical development of the Toraja *tongkonan*, whose present form is actually recent (Plate 1). The oldest houses still standing are small, plain and massively built. But later styles have grown progressively upward and outward, culminating in today's version with its tall, slender piles, highly exaggerated curve to the roof, and richness of coloured woodcarving, pushing the traditional

58

Plate 1   Origin house (*tongkonan*) of a Toraja noble family, Ulusalu district, Tana Toraja, 1977. Traditionally the nobility reserved to themselves the right to build these great houses with their elaborately carved and painted facades. Photo: Roxana Waterson.

construction method to its limits and progressively reducing the proportion of habitable space inside the building even as the symbolic messages about social status conveyed by the exterior become more and more impressive. A similar kind of development can be detected in South Nias architecture during the nineteenth century (Feldman 1984) and, I would argue, a parallel process of appropriation of cosmology by the ruling elite, as they attempted to make their own houses a more and more elaborate microcosm. In the case of nineteenth-century Sumba, the aristocracy increased their power through control of a profitable trade in horses and cattle, as well as controlling the creation of wealth in the form of textiles, made only by aristocratic women. In different ways in all these societies, the 'house' provided an effective instrument in legitimating the 'enterprises of the great'.

THE HOUSE AND IMAGES OF POWER

Relations between houses in these different house societies may perhaps be characterized in various ways – as exchanging, branching, or encompassing. The image of the 'encompassing' house can be more or less hierarchical. The Langkawi community as a kind of 'phantom' house (Carsten 1987a) serves a rather egalitarian purpose, though it would be interesting to know how it articulates (if at all) with other images of the house in the wider society, such as those held by Malay royalty or nobility. Again, to the extent that longhouse unity exists among the Iban (chiefly in ritual and warfare, but also in the sense that the *bilek* as a functioning unit must be predicated upon the existence of other, similar units within the longhouse), the longhouse 'encompasses', for the Iban, in a rather egalitarian way.

The 'branching' image – which, in Southeast Asia, often forms part of more elaborate botanical metaphors of relationships between 'trunk' and 'tip' – is a crucial one for expressing hierarchy, and is one of the ways in which status may be shed over time as power remains concentrated in older origin-houses. This is essentially the process which H. and C. Geertz (1975: 124) call the 'principle of sinking status' in their discussion of the Balinese *dadia*. 'Encompassing' images may be combined with those of 'branching', as in some of the small kingdoms of island Southeast Asia where there is an attempt to make the ruler's house stand for all houses in the realm. This appears to apply in Luwu', where the palace of the Datu (basically a much enlarged version of the timber house of the rest of the population) represents the immobile and encompassing hegemonic centre of a concentric political space (Errington 1987: 436). The idea is made more real by the belief in the ability of noble rulers to concentrate spiritual power in themselves and thus protect their followers (Errington 1983: 547). The possession of sacred heirlooms (stored in the attic of the house or palace) was another vital attribute of power.[17]

The Atoni ruler in his palace at the 'root' or 'navel' of the kingdom provides another example of the 'encompassing' house (Schulte Nordholt 1980: 241; Cunningham 1964: 54). Similarly, the Minangkabau *raja* dwelt in a large timber palace at Pagarruyung, in the heart of Minangkabau territory. He had almost no political power and principally fulfilled a sacred, symbolic role as representative of the unity of the Minangkabau world (P. E. de Josselin de Jong 1951: 108). At least in the case of Luwu' and Minangkabau, this concentration of power at the centre in no way implies that the 'house' ceases to be a relevant category for ordinary people. Instead, we may perhaps imagine a pyramid of houses and branch houses, the greatest of which lies at the centre and conceptually encompasses the rest.

The question of whether state systems should be thought of as having 'Houses', 'houses' or both can now be more closely considered. As noted earlier, Sellato proposes that the Philippine sultanates, as well as the feudal systems of Europe, were characterized by having 'Houses' as a noble institution only. Lévi-Strauss on the other hand seems to suggest, in his discussion of the Balinese *dadia*, that in both Bali and Europe, 'Houses' and 'houses' were inextricably interlinked. He writes that in Europe, 'family solidarity provided a model, albeit fictitious' for 'more or less durable social formations of diverse natures and origins – communes, commercial or religious associations, guilds, brotherhoods, etc.' (1987: 158). Reproaching anthropologists for failing to make use of historical data, he continues:

The difficulties of the Geertzes in dealing with the institution called *dadia* in Bali has seemed especially revealing to us. When they encounter it in an aristocratic context, the word 'house' comes spontaneously and with justification to their pen; but in the village context they no longer know what definition to choose, and hesitate inconclusively between lineage, caste, cultural association and faction. It is 'a little of all of these, and even sometimes a political party', as Boon acutely comments. Was it not the peculiarity of the house, as described by historians of medieval Europe, to bring together all these aspects? And did not the houses also come into being and fade away? (Lévi-Strauss 1987: 158)

It is clear from the writings of H. and C. Geertz and of Boon that the *dadia* is a significant institution at both commoner and aristocratic levels. H. and C. Geertz (1975: 61) for example note that 'Villages containing only a few commoner castes of nearly equal rank seem especially liable ... to develop strong *dadia* organization, because the struggle for local eminence in such communities tends to be keen'. Writing of the aristocracy, Geertz (1980) makes it clear that politics consisted essentially of struggles within and between *dadia*, since these were the only integral power blocs in the political cosmos. He observes that the *dadia* provided 'a familistic framework within which political maneuver could take place' (1980: 33); clearly, no description of it as a purely kinship institution would be complete. An interesting passage details some of the forms of immaterial wealth which served to set one house apart from another:

The various houses were called either *puri* or *jero*, depending upon their rank. The core-line house was usually referred to as 'the great puri' (*puri gdé*); the 'closer', 'more recent' noble houses as '*puri* such-and-such', the name itself being more or less arbitrary; and the (genealogically) more distant houses as '*jero* such-and-such'. A great many other symbols of relative status were employed to give this formal structure an explicit cultural expression: subtle title differences among heads (and members) of the various houses; elaborate etiquette prescribing customs of deference among houses, including highly developed differential language use; precise inter-dining, seating, precedence, and marriage rules; enormously detailed sumptuary regulations for the layout, types of buildings, and decorations permitted in the house's 'palace', as well as for the proper dress of its inhabitants; meticulously defined ritual rights and obligations, perhaps the most notable of which centered on cremation and death. And so on to an absolutely astonishing degree of invidious distinction. (Geertz 1980: 32)

As for the picture in Europe, I believe it must be much more complicated than Lévi-Strauss's utterances would suggest. When he speaks of Europe, he is in many places talking about France; no doubt even within its borders there are differences in how far the peasant household operated as a 'house'. In the case of England, it would appear much more likely that aristocratic 'Houses' existed in the absence of any corresponding commoner institution, for the small size and mobility of English households, and the tendency towards economic individualism, have been characteristic since at least the sixteenth century (Laslett 1972; Macfarlane 1978). On the European continent, Goody remarks that: 'The importance of "houses" [such as the *lignage* of medieval Tuscany] ... based on patrifiliation and linked to property and office, is undeniable, especially among the aristocracy' (Goody 1983: 238) – which leaves open the possibility of 'houses' existing among lower social strata. An excellent picture of the 'house' as a peasant institution in Portugal is given by Pina-Cabral (1986), but one may hope that more work on Europe will clarify the picture further.

THE CASE OF JAPAN

Lévi-Strauss had also proposed Japan as a 'house society', and for comparative purposes I shall take it as my concluding example. As a highly stratified society, with a powerful centralized bureaucracy developing in the Tokugawa period, feudal Japan represents one extreme of the continuum of 'house societies' which we have examined here. Writings on the institution of the *ie*, often translated as 'household', and described by Nakane (1970: 4) as 'a concept which penetrates every nook and cranny of Japanese society', indubitably suggest that it may be regarded as a 'house' in Lévi-Strauss's sense. Fukutake (1967: 40) observes that 'like the English word "house" the Japanese *ie* means both the physical house as well as the continuing family – as in "the House of Windsor"', and he adds that it is also 'a feature very much bound up with the establishment of feudalism in Japan', while Nakane (1970: 4–5) notes that 'the human relationships within this household group are thought of as more important than all other human relationships'. An important fact about *ie* organization is that it has been a fundamental feature of peasant social life, peasants having formed over 80 per cent of the population in Tokugawa Japan.[18] Murakami (1984) goes so far as to characterize Japanese civilization as '*Ie* Society'.

A penetrating analysis of the multi-faceted nature of the *ie* is provided by Bachnik (1983). She observes that the word itself

has two clearly-understood senses: that of a socioreligious group, which includes the *ie* history and its ancestors; and that of the group enterprise, including the property and physical house. The household has been a production-oriented group, organised around agriculture, mercantile pursuits or craft production in pre-modern times. At present many households in Japan are involved in part-time agriculture as well as small businesses ... The successor succeeds to the *office* of headship in the *ie*, and the property, although now legally separated from succession to office, has traditionally been transmitted as part of the office. The duties of the office include responsibility for the ancestor ritual of the *ie*, heading the *ie*-group, representing it to the community and managing the *ie*-enterprise. (Bachnik 1983: 161)

Although Bachnik makes no reference to Lévi-Strauss's analysis, we are instantly reminded of it when she reveals that the *ie* is a phenomenon which has repeatedly, but only inadequately, been explained by ethnographers as a kinship institution. Insisting upon analyzing it instead in its own terms, she demonstrates that, although kinship relations certainly exist within the *ie*, they are not essential for its continuity and represent merely one recruitment option by which this continuity may be assured. Although male primogeniture is the 'preferred' form of inheritance, numerous strategies of adoption (of sons or sons-in-law, women or men, close relatives or non-kin, in childhood or at marriage) are recognized (Bachnik 1983: 163; Norbeck 1954: 53). No distinction is drawn by members of the *ie* between consanguineal and 'fictive' kin, so that the latter category cannot help to explain the incorporation of non-kin, even servants, as members. Moreover it is not uncommon for the eldest son to be passed over in favour of an adoptee, and there are some parts of Japan where sons may be passed over in favour of daughters (Bachnik 1983: 163). Recruitment for succession, therefore, 'is a political decision and should not be viewed as an internal dynamic of the *ie*'. In pre-modern times there may even have been a greater pragmatic use of kinship than is common today.

It seems clear that the *ie* institution operated at the level of both peasant 'houses' and aristocratic 'Houses'. Murakami talks about the *ie* in the broadest sense, referring not just to single households but to the network of stem and branch houses, with their retainers, which some other authors have termed the *dozoku* or *dozokudan*. Fukutake describes the *dozoku* as a patrilineal kinship group consisting of a 'stem family' and group of 'branch families' linked by mutually recognized genealogical relationships. Again, it is clear that this kinship model does not account for all facts about the *dozoku*. Upper-class families with large landholdings were the ones most easily able to found branch *ie* which they endowed with property, and the subordinate relation of the 'branch' to the 'stem' formed a model for patron–client relations. These relations were highly strategic in nature.[19] Just as adoption provides a mechanism for recruiting unrelated members into the *ie*, even households which originally had no relationship with the *dozoku* could be absorbed into it as 'commended' branch families. In time, an original stem family might go into decline and be challenged by a powerful branch family which could break away and set up its own *dozoku* (Fukutake 1967: 65).

According to Murakami, a feature of early feudal Japan was the predominance of *ie* organization. In the twelfth century, samurai *ie* developed especially in frontier areas far from the capital, where there was scope for the expansion of agriculture. Each warrior lord and his retainers formed a kind of agro-military unit having considerable autonomy. The result was a society in which power was highly decentralized and which was therefore prone to 'vertical' division. This fragmentation of power is a key feature in which Japanese feudalism parallels that of medieval Europe. By the sixteenth century, as larger lords or *daimyo* began successfully to concentrate power in their own hands, they made attempts at a hierarchical integration of the *ie* of their kinsmen and followers as 'branches' of their own 'stem' line. Murakami calls this type of organization the 'meta-*ie*'. With greater centralization of power in the Tokugawa period, the ideology of the *ie* was stretched still further to provide legitimation for the new government. Ieyasu, the first Tokugawa shogun, visualized the structure of his government as a great federation of 'meta-*ie*'. Murakami writes that 'the primary ideological foundation of the Tokugawa Bakufu [government] was the analogy to the *ie* and its solidarity'; but on this national scale, the analogy was already overstretched to the point of frailty: 'There is quite a bit of evidence that the average *samurai*, let alone the farmers, regarded the *daimyo* as their real "lord" but

65

the *shogun* was too remote to be an object of their loyalty ... The *ie*-type organization on a national scale was obviously beyond the optimal size' (Murakami 1984: 331). This account, though in some respects speculative, is of particular interest because it illustrates that over time the *ie*, from being a concrete organizational unit, began increasingly to be exploited as an abstract concept which could be utilized in the search for political legitimation.

During the nineteenth century, ideological exploitation of the conceptual relation between 'stem' and 'branch' houses was taken to a final extreme. After the Meiji Restoration of 1868, and the abolition of the *samurai* class, conservative ideologues sought for a means of binding the mass of the population in more direct loyalty to the Emperor. They chose to do this through the old household-centred practice of ancestor-worship, attempting to conflate imperial loyalty and filial piety. They asserted that all Japanese were ultimately related to each other, being descended ultimately from the imperial house, and they cast this relation as follows:

The connection between the Imperial House and its subjects is thus: one forms the main house and the others form the branch house, so that from ancient times we have worshipped the founder of the Imperial House and the heavenly gods. Our relationship to this house is sincerely founded on repaying our debt of gratitude to our ancestors. (Caiger 1968, cited in Smith 1983: 32)

Moreover, the subjects of the emperor were described as his children, using a word (*sekishi*) which literally means 'infants'. Thus all subjects could be depicted as sharing the same kind of dependent genealogical relation to the Emperor, their houses being joined to his House. 'House ideology' at this point has become still more of an abstraction, being manipulated in a highly centralized political system to provide a 'naturalizing' and legitimizing rhetoric in support of imperial power. The incorporation of principles of *ie* organization (eternal continuity of the *ie*, autonomy of individual *ie*, 'achievement' orientation, strong stress on group loyalty) into the 'Japanese management system' which developed from the 1920s with the drive for industrialization, represents one final and perhaps unexpected transformation of the '*Ie* Society' in modern times (Murakami 1984: 356–7).

CONCLUSION

I have attempted to pursue the concept of the 'house society' through Indonesia, drawing comparisons with other areas of island Southeast Asia, including Borneo, Malaysia and the Philippines. I have also tried to broaden the perspective by making comparisons with some of Lévi-Strauss's major examples, such as Japan. Within island Southeast Asia, we find the house playing a dominant role as a focus of organization in a number of societies which have both very different kinship systems, and differing forms of social hierarchy and stratification. Examples range from highly egalitarian groups like the Iban, to state systems like those of the Bugis and Balinese. It seems impossible, therefore, to limit the application of the 'house' concept only to a part of this continuum, in spite of the suggestions of some authors that hierarchy be taken as an essential feature of a 'house society'. Still less is it useful, I have suggested, to try to draw a clear distinction between 'feudal' and other types of society, given the problems of applying this label in Southeast Asia. It is not only in petty state systems that we find the 'house' developing as a fully-fledged institution, as Lévi-Strauss's own chief examples, drawn from the Pacific Northwest Coast, would themselves imply.

However, Lévi-Strauss's writings about the house do raise the very interesting question of the ways in which the 'house', as institution and ideology, can be harnessed to the 'enterprises of the great' in societies which are in the throes of a political transition towards a greater concentration of power in the hands of a few, with a shift from kinship-based to more complex political, economic and religious structures of organization; where, as Lévi-Strauss puts it, 'political and economic interests, on the verge of invading the social field, have not yet overstepped the "old ties of blood"' (Lévi-Strauss 1983a: 186). Some Indonesian 'house societies' may well have been quite stable politically over long periods, but there is evidence that in other cases (such as Nias, Toraja and Sumba) the aristocracy were indeed in the process of expanding their power at the time of Dutch intervention, and that they were using the house (as institution, as ideology, or simply as architecture) to promote this endeavour. The house seems to have retained a similar prominence in the organization of states such as the Buginese and Balinese. We need to understand the role that the house has played in these social transformations. I see no reason to dismiss this concern as 'evolutionist' (Gibson, this volume), for I do not myself see any necessity to assume a unilineal path of development here, or any one moment at which kinship-based organization must give way to other types of structure. For that matter, one can think of plenty of modern nation-states in which kinship relations continue to play a critical role in politics (the Philippines, Iraq or Pakistan, to mention only a few). Murakami's analysis of the Japanese *ie*, too, indicates that 'house' ideology was utilized as a legitimating device over several centuries of historical development in Japan, during which time political organization changed a great deal.

If anything, the picture that emerges is one in which the 'house' appears at its most abstract at the extreme ends of the continuum of social differentiation, as in the examples of the Moken boat nomads on the one hand, and late imperial Japan on the other. The 'house' concept here becomes little more than analogy, in the hands either of the anthropologist or of an élite attempting to exploit it for political ends. Between these extremes we can situate many of the Indonesian societies in which the literal dominance of the house, as a physical structure and a grouping of kin, is inescapably obvious. These are not the most stratified societies, nor those most closely approaching a 'feudal' form of organization – some of them have strong notions of hierarchy, but no hereditary social classes or ranks. But in certain of them, at least, we can witness the utilization of the 'house' as an instrument of legitimation for 'the enterprises of the great'. Just how far 'house' ideology can be stretched to serve these ends is illustrated by the case of Japan.

If, finally, I have not exactly helped to refine and restrict the concept of 'house society', this is because the house appears and reappears in so many different transformations. Rather than struggling to decide how closely these fit with Lévi-Strauss's model, we must first move closer to understanding Southeast Asian 'house' systems in their own terms. The principles involved may be worked out in different ways within a variety of kinship and political structures, but always with certain recurring features which I have suggested may be taken as minimum criteria for the concept to be meaningfully applied. Some may conclude that this very broadness makes the concept too all-embracing and unwieldy to be a truly incisive tool of investigation; but in giving us a fresh stimulus to examine social organization in the archipelago and beyond, it has so far only begun to yield its rewards.

THE RESURRECTION OF THE HOUSE AMONGST THE ZAFIMANIRY OF MADAGASCAR

3

Maurice Bloch

T‍HE ZAFIMANIRY ARE A GROUP of Malagasy swidden cultivators living in high-altitude montane forest. In terms of general culture they are fairly close to the neighbouring Betsileo or even the Merina. Their political history has been characterized by their determined attempts to avoid various forms of centralized government, attempts which on the whole have been fairly successful.

The only period when the Zafimaniry suffered tight government control followed the Madagascar-wide anti-colonial revolt of 1947 when the French army probably killed at least 80,000 people. The best detailed study of this revolt remains Jacques Tronchon's *L'Insurrection Malgache de 1947* (1974), but it would not be appropriate for the purposes of this chapter to give a general account of the events here.

The revolt affected the Zafimaniry particularly badly. This is largely because of their geographic position. The largest contingent of the rebel army had grouped on the coast to the east of them and then marched up to the central plateau in order to attack the larger towns in the centre of Madagascar. They chose to do this through the least accessible parts of the east coast forest in order to avoid detection and that meant through Zafimaniry country. The rebels and what they had to say was mostly well received by the Zafimaniry although I think very few Zafimaniry actually joined them. Nonetheless it is significant that to this day no Zafimaniry I know ever refers to the rebels of 1947 by the normal Malagasy word for 'rebel', which in their dialect has negative connotations, but they use instead another term with positive connotations.[1]

It was not the passage of the rebels through their villages which had such terrible effects on the Zafimaniry but the revenge of the French as they regained control of the situation and pushed the defeated Malagasy back the way they had come.

Because the village where I recently did field work, like most other Zafimaniry villages, had welcomed the rebels, the administration of the time deemed it should be punished. For this purpose, the French attempted to take the whole population to one of a number of concentration camps. In fact most of the villagers managed to escape in the forest leaving only three sick or crippled persons behind. The army force-marched these remaining captives to the concentration camp five miles away with such brutality that all three died before getting there.

The French then burnt the village so that nothing was left above ground and the villagers stayed in hiding in the forest for two and a half years,[2] living in low grass shelters, and eating by hunting and gathering and by rescuing what crops they could from their abandoned swiddens. Even after the withdrawal of the troops they were afraid to return, in part because the initial repression was succeeded by a bout of the recurrent colonial enthusiasm for ecology which, as usual, had the declared aim of preserving the forest from slash and burn agriculture but which was also intended to keep the people in the concentration camps, now renamed 'new villages'. However, even when this policy was abandoned, the people in the village were unsure of the government's intentions and they stayed in hiding, watching the site of their village gradually becoming engulfed by vegetation, but not daring to return.

In order to comprehend the circumstances of this return, which is what this chapter is about, it is necessary to understand Zafimaniry concepts of the house. However, even before turning to this topic something also needs to be said about Zafimaniry Catholicism since it too has a minor but significant role to play in the story.

The history of the Catholic Church in the part of Zafimaniry country with which I am concerned here goes back, as far as I can work out, to the early thirties, when, as a result of an epidemic, several closely related villages all became converted. Immediately the church sent a priest to the area, the first of a series continuing to the present day. This first priest greatly influenced certain people, especially the family with whom I shall be concerned. The influence of the church today is less than it was in 1947, but it is still very great for some people, though much less for others. However, even for those most involved in the church, Catholic belief and practice is, and has always been, only an *added* element on top of traditional religious beliefs and practices of a non-Christian character. Foremost among these traditional beliefs and practices are those concerning ancestors. These seem to remain almost totally unaffected by equally strongly held Christian beliefs.[3]

I now turn to the theme of this volume and to Zafimaniry ideas concerning the house. This is a topic that has an importance for them which cannot be exaggerated.

In considering Zafimaniry notions of the house some of the ideas of Lévi-Strauss concerning house-based societies are very helpful, although others are clearly not applicable. Firstly, grouped under the label are some very different systems so that house-based societies cannot, and probably should not, be clearly contrasted with other types of societies as Lévi-Strauss would have us do. Secondly, because the association Lévi-Strauss sees between an emphasis on the house and hierarchy is actually reversed in Madagascar (Lévi-Strauss 1979, part 2, ch.2). The Zafimaniry who are, one could say, obsessed with the house are non-stratified,[4] while the Merina who have always stressed hierarchy (Bloch 1977) have an anti-house ideology, and instead stress the tomb (Bloch 1986).[5]

For Madagascar the most valuable part of Lévi-Strauss's theory is the close association he sees between the symbolism of the house as a building and the centrality of monogamous marriage in both the symbolism and the organization of kinship. For Lévi-Strauss, in fact, the house is the 'objectification of a relationship' (1984: 195) which is marriage. As a result, he argues, in house-based societies, instead of alliance occurring *between* units, marriage actually forms the *core* of the unit, a unit which is identified with the material house. Lévi-Strauss in fact applies his theory specifically to the Merina (1984: 226) in a way which is highly perceptive but which, because of the inadequacy of his sources, is also rather confusing in its treatment of the relations between the house and the tomb. But the notion of the house as the core of the marital unit is one which if anything applies even better to the case of the Zafimaniry.

71

These ideas have proved particularly fruitful in Southeast Asia and Japan where we find, it seems to me, two different types of house-based societies. On the one hand, we have what used to be called stem family systems of which the Japanese *Ie* or the Iban *Bilek* are classic examples, and where one married pair alone succeeds another in the house, replacing each other with the passage of time. On the other hand we have systems where houses permanently associated with a founding couple become a ritual focus for descendants. The Northern Thai 'core house'[6] and the Zafimaniry houses are examples of this latter type.

Zafimaniry marriage and house creation are both very long-drawn-out processes, not surprisingly since the two are merely two sides of the same thing. Marriage without a house is a contradiction in terms, simply because the Zafimaniry notion which I choose to translate as 'marriage' is distinguished from other forms of sexual union precisely by the existence of a house. This is reflected in the fact that the normal way of asking the question corresponding to our 'are you married?' is phrased, literally, to mean 'Have you obtained a house with a hearth?'[7]

The process which leads to marriage begins, however, before the construction of the house. The beginning of this process is the sexual affection and intercourse which occurs between very young people indeed. The Zafimaniry seem to want to place particular stress on the chaotic, fluid and fickle character of this type of relationship, largely, I feel, to contrast it with the stability and immobility ultimately achieved by a successful union represented by the house. Ideally, out of chaotic promiscuity will emerge a more stable monogamous relationship based on mutual affection and this will lead to the partners establishing a house with a hearth.

In fact, there is often much less spontaneity than would appear in the creation of stable marriages, for the parents of the couple may have arranged a marriage between them while they were still only babies. If so, however, this agreement will be kept secret and the couple will merely be subtly encouraged towards each other by their parents, in the hope that they will begin the marriage process seemingly on their own initiative.[8] The reason why this strategy is often successful is that the parents of such a couple go out of their way to patch up the relationship between the two when it threatens to break up, while on the other hand they may actually secretly encourage the demise of other liaisons.

72

The rationale behind this rather strange way of going about arranged marriages is the very great importance that the Zafimaniry attach to individual attraction in sexual relations, especially among the young. This is because sexual attraction and mutual affection are believed to be linked to the important concept of compatibility, as they understood it.

The notion of compatibility in marriage is crucial for the Zafimaniry. This is well shown by the fact that they attribute the barrenness of a couple not so much to a deficiency in the woman, as the Merina and other groups usually do, but rather to a problem in the mutual compatibility of the two spouses. We can also, I believe, get a glimpse of the Zafimaniry notion of compatibility from the fact that of the most common words used by the Zafimaniry for sexual intercourse one means 'becoming one', or 'uniting', and the other means literally 'to twin'. Zafimaniry houses are often decorated with a sculpted bird placed on the apex of the roof which is explained by them, and in contrast to the meaning of such birds in other parts of Madagascar (Beaujard 1983, ch.3), as being a sign of domestic peace since if the spouses quarrelled the birds would be frightened and fly away.

The Zafimaniry concept of compatibility does not, however, correspond to stereotypic European ideas of marital love. First of all, it is thought of as being largely due to astrological causes. Most different to the western notion, however, is the fact that compatibility is not demonstrated principally by the spouses getting on well together, it is proved above all by the fertility of the union. Two spouses, however devoted to each other, who have only one child or none at all are seen as incompatible.[9] Because this fruitful compatibility grows with the production of descendants it is something to be sought and gained, largely by trial and error, but when gradually established it leads to stability which in turn leads to fertility.

Whenever a boy and girl are clearly attracted to each other and are having intercourse more regularly with each other than with anybody else, either they or their parents (depending on the part played in the relationship by the sort of parental strategy I mentioned above) may want to transform the relationship into something more permanent, something for which the English word 'marriage' offers a loose translation.

The first step along this path is the *recognition*, by the parents of the girl, of the fact that she is having sexual intercourse with a particular boy. This recognition process usually only takes place when the Zafimaniry consider a girl to be mature, in some cases this may mean she is little more than twelve, but usually this occurs when she is around fifteen.

This recognition needs to be understood partly in terms of the very strong taboo which forbids adjacent generations from having knowledge of each others' sexual activity, especially if the representatives of these adjacent generations are of different sexes.

The first stage in this revelation occurs when the mother of the boy tells the mother of the girl of their children's liaison and when, in turn, the mother of the girl tells the father. This process is called *tapa sofina*, or the breaking of the ear, because first the girl's mother and then the girl's father have their ears 'broken' by having to take cognisance of their daughter's sexual activity and thereby break the taboo.

After the 'breaking of the ear' the girl may, from time to time, spend the night at her husband's house and need not any more take too elaborate precautions of secrecy.

After the *tapa sofina* comes the *tapa maso* which means the breaking of the eyes. This involves a major ritual where the family of the boy visits the family of the girl and acts on his behalf. It seems the only absolutely essential ritual of marriage. The central part of the ritual is when the bride and groom appear together shamefaced in front of her parents, thereby making public, especially to her father, their sexual relation. In return for the breaking of the taboo (another word for *tapa maso* is *ala fady*:[10] the removal of the taboo) the groom gives a small sum of money to the girl's parents. Then the parents of the girl will bless the boy and the parents of the boy will bless the girl. After that the girl may have sexual relations in her own house. The 'appearance' of the couple together will then be repeated in a minor way when the new spouses together visit the houses of a variety of senior relatives of both the groom and bride.

Ideally the *tapa maso* should be followed by yet another ritual called the *fananbarana* or 'making evident'. In many ways this ought to be the most important marriage ritual; it should involve many people and requires a big feast. However, precisely because of this it is almost never done nowadays and I have never seen it. It should occur at the house of the bride and involves the husband giving a formal acknowledgement of his sonhood to his parents-in-law and later the bride doing the same for her parents-in-law at their house.[11] The *fananbarana* involves a declaration by both sides of their familial taboos so that both spouses will know what not to do so as not to endanger each other, by, for example, the wife using a pot in which a food tabooed to the husband has been cooked, or by the husband bringing into the house an animal tabooed to the wife.

Most important, however, is the fact that the ritual should end with the bride being given cooking and eating implements by her parents. She will then take these implements back to her husband's village. Her *trousseau* thus consists essentially of the cooking implements which will furnish the hearth of her marital home. The most important items of this *trousseau* are a cooking pot, a wooden plate and a large stirring spoon.

I think it is clear from the names of the rituals as well as from the way that they are carried out that underlying them is the idea of the union emerging into view. This is also what we see when we look at the house as a building. Before the *tapa maso* or immediately after it the young man will have started to build a house, or rather the framework for a house. The house will be situated near his parents' house, though in an inferior position, which usually means to the south and lower. It will be a very simple house, but it will have a hearth consisting of three stones in a wooden frame and three posts. One is the central post. This is the so-called 'hot post' because it is near the hearth and it will be the largest piece of wood in the house and will consist of a particular hardwood said to be the hardest of all woods. There will also be two 'cold posts', at either end of the house, which, like the hot post, support the ridge pole. These two should be somewhat less massive than the 'hot post' and made of the next hardest wood. At this stage, for the most part the house will be made of flimsy, woven, flattened-out bamboos and reed mats which let in light and sound. It will probably have doors and windows also made of flimsy material.[12]

Before the house can be lived in, and that especially means cooking and having sex in it, it will have to be blessed in an important ritual of blessing carried out by the elders of the families of both the parents of the groom and the bride.

The ritual of blessing the new house starts with cooking second-year taro on the hearth. This will be the first occasion that the cooking and eating implements brought by the bride are used and also the first time that a fire is lit in the hearth. Once the taro has been thoroughly cooked it is distributed to everyone present and used for the blessing. This blessing takes the form of the most senior elder present rubbing the cooked taro on the three posts in turn and, while doing this, calling on God and the ancestors to bring children, crops, wealth and money to the family that will live in the house.

To understand the significance of this action it is necessary to turn to Zafimaniry ideas concerning taro. Taro has central importance to them because they rightly stress that it is the food that one can always rely on, because it is not attacked by pests or bad weather like other crops. It can even be relied on in years when, for political or climatic reasons, it has not been possible to plant. This is because it stays in the ground for a long time, up to six years, and it even multiplies of its own accord underground, like naturalizing daffodils. Taro is, and is recognized to be, a guarantee of survival, a fact spelled out by the elder in his prayer as he rubs taro on the posts. Indeed the Zafimaniry repeatedly told me that, were it not for taro, they could not have survived when they were hiding from the French, and I believe them. So the rubbing of second-year taro on to the central posts ensures the continuity and successful survival of the future inhabitants of the house.

But there is more to the action of rubbing the taro on the posts. In a way that is so obvious that it only rarely gets mentioned, the house posts are associated with the man of the couple. They are what he must put up, and the man's place in the house is traditionally sitting leaning against the central hot post. The woman, on the other hand, is associated with the activity of the hearth and the furniture of the hearth, the cooking pot, the serving plate and the big stirring spoon. As we saw, a marriage is 'made clear' by the bringing of these items by the woman to the house built by the man. Therefore the consummation of the marriage, not sexually but (in the fullest and most literal sense) domestically, is the conjunction of cooking pot and house post brought about by a life-sustaining vegetable: taro.

However, neither the marriage nor the house is completed by the ritual of the inauguration of the house. A marriage of compatible people needs children and so the practices surrounding childbirth are the continuation of the process. Here I only note those aspects related to the house.

The birth of the first child in a way strengthens the marriage and in a way weakens it. It strengthens the marriage in that, as a direct result, the spouses become terminologically related through tekno-nymy. This links the two parents since henceforth they have the name of their child in common.

The marriage is weakened, however, by the movements of the mother. When a woman who is pregnant for the first time is approaching the time to give birth, she will leave her husband's parents' house (or her husband's house if the couple already lives independently) and go back to her natal house, whether this be in another village or in her own village. After the birth she will remain for a number of months in what might be called a hyper-house, that is a house within a house, built on the bed where she has the child. The child will be associated with the mother's parents' house because the normal birth ritual, which is done a few days after birth, will be held there. The central section of this ritual makes a crucial material association between the child and the house, and does this in two ways: firstly, by putting some of the soot of the hearth of the house on the forehead of the child and secondly by burying the placenta, thought of as a twin as in other Southeast Asian cultures, between the 'hot post' and the hearth.

In theory at least, after a few months the mother will return to her husband's house, but in fact this never happens smoothly. For her to do that she has to be courted again not only by her husband but also by her husband's family in a repeat of the *fananbarana* in order to convince her to go home. If this is successful she will probably obtain quite a few new clothes and renewed promises to be treated with great consideration by the family of her husband. Very often, however, the husband will not be successful in getting his wife and child back at this stage.

Exactly the same performance will be repeated after the birth of the second child. It is usually only after the birth of the third child that the process is reversed in that the mother remains in her house and the mother's mother comes to the house of the couple. Then the child is marked on the forehead with the soot of its own parents' hearth and its 'twin' is buried there.

Only when children are born into it are the initial stages of marriage or of house creation complete – the two ways of putting the matter merely refer to two aspects of the same process. However, it is not merely the fact that the house is producing descendants which matters, but the fact that the couple of the house can nurture and nourish these children and grandchildren, which marks fruitfulness. As a result the agricultural work of the parents, something that they do together in a way that is often rhetorically stressed and which supplies basic starch foods for the upkeep of the family, is also seen as part of the necessary process for the successful growth of the marriage.

But the house is also changing materially as a result of a different but linked form of conjugal work. When first built, the house is highly permeable to the outside. This permeability means that one can see in when one looks through the roughly woven bamboo, and neighbours are continually looking in; one can also speak from the outside to people in the house as though no partition existed. However, this flimsy permeability diminishes with time. The Zafimaniry say that the house will then be gradually acquiring 'bones'. This refers to the massive wooden planks that will, little by little, replace the woven bamboo. Ultimately the house will look a little like a Canadian log cabin, except that the wood is vertical.

The work of getting this wood and preparing it for the house is typically a task that a man does with his wife's brother's help. The wife's brother is in Zafimaniry kinship terminology called *vady lahy* by male *ego*. This term literally means 'male wife'. The act of building up the house, 'hardening it with bones', as the Zafimaniry say, therefore also involves a semi-ritualized cooperation of a quasi-marital pair. The continuing building is thus also a joint enterprise of spouses.

Two aspects of this 'house hardening' give us further insights in to the Zafimaniry understanding of marriage. First of all the wood that is used in such house building is not only particularly hard, it must also have what the Zafimaniry call *teza*. This refers to the darker, impacted, inner core of some woods which gradually appears in older trees and which ultimately forms the greater part of it. For the Zafimaniry the *teza* of trees is like the bones of humans, but a bone which continues to grow and thereby transcends the mortality of the bodies of people. The word *teza* also forms the root of the Malagasy verb for 'to remain'. Thus the marriage, by being made with the *teza* of wood, is made to last, and last beyond the mortality of its human initiators. Secondly, the hardening of the house also involves the beginning of the decorative low-relief carving which the Zafimaniry put everywhere on the hardwoods which constitute the house, but especially on doors, windows and, above all, on the central posts. What these decorations are about, according to my informants, is 'giving honour to the *teza* of the wood'.[13] This process of decorative carving, which has made the Zafimaniry famous throughout Madagascar and beyond, will continue as the house continues to harden. Zafimaniry houses therefore seem a perfect example of how the aesthetics and architecture of house building become the objectification and fetishization of a social relation in the way postulated by Lévi-Strauss.

With time, therefore, the house hardens and becomes more and more beautifully decorated. When this process has really advanced, and if everything has gone well, the children of the couple will themselves have begun the process of marriage and the family will be enlarging. The girls will, to a certain extent, have left, but, as we saw, only to a certain extent since they will return to have their children in their parents' house. More importantly, they will return with their husbands and children to seek blessing for any major enterprise from the woman's parents.

The sons, on the other hand, will be building their own houses near that of their parents but they, with their wives and children, will, like the daughters, also seek blessings from their parents.

What this means is that, at certain times, grown-up sons and daughters still consider the house of their parents as their own. They will behave there just as though they had never left and they will share in the tasks that maintain the house. In particular they, together with their spouses (including their male spouses) will contribute to the hardening and decorating of the parental house. The same will be true of grandchildren, great-grandchildren and so on.

I think it is therefore right to consider these further stages of house construction as the continuation of the process of marriage, a process which began weakly with the 'breaking of the ear' but which now stands evident and beautiful in the form of a proud building.

As the parents get older and less able to work, the marriage pattern of the children changes slightly. The last son, as he marries, instead of moving out of his parents' house, will instead divide it with a partition so that the parents can live to the north and his own family to the south. With time, this young family will look after the parents more and more until their death. When that occurs the family of the younger son will take over the house completely.

Plate 2   Zafimaniry houses with a 'holy house' to the right of the picture.

To say this, though, is somewhat misleading in that the couple who takes over the house are, in theory, only caretakers of the house of the original founders, whose marriage house it is and remains. However when this founding couple dies, their descendants gradually come to feel that they are present as the conjoined house itself rather than as two individual people. It is at this point that the house will increasingly be referred to as a 'holy house' (Plate 2).

A holy house is a house where one goes for blessing from God and the ancestors. This is the answer that I would be given every time I asked: 'What is a holy house?' And when I asked 'How do you know which holy house you go to to ask for a blessing'? the answer was: 'It is the house of one's forebears which has successfully produced offspring.'

Holy houses are the growing fulfilment of the marriages of one's forebears which have been fruitful. The Zafimaniry do not think of this process of marriage and house growth as ending with the death of the original couple, so long as the children of the couple, and their children and so on, continue to reproduce and multiply, so that the original marriage continues to grow and harden. Or rather, it is the holy house which grows and hardens as descendants and their affines continue to make it of ever harder wood, more and more decorated, and as they replace any bits that might have been damaged or rotted. A person who is acting morally will only build up a holy house and will never diminish it. It is for this reason that no one who needs to repair a holy house in a way which requires some preliminary dismantlement of damaged parts can do so without offering a sacrifice of atonement to the original founding couple, even though the intention of the work is clearly to strengthen and beautify the house.

As the anthropology textbooks used to say: marriage is a process, but this process continues much longer among the Zafimaniry than the books envisaged, since it continues long after the death of the pair. A marriage, that is a house, is still growing perhaps a hundred years after it started.[14]

The image of being descended from a successful marriage which has hardened into a holy house is perhaps nowhere more vivid than in the phrase that the Zafimaniry use to describe everything they inherit from forebears, whether it be rights to clear land in a particular territory, recipes for medicines, or direct inheritance of beehives and reed beds. The term is *loha lambo* which literally means 'the head of a wild boar' but which actually refers to the apex of the house. In this phrase we seem to have the blessings of the ancestors descending onto the descendants from the apex of their house.

The source of this blessing is said to be the success of the process begun by the original marriage; obtaining a house with a hearth, joining the central post and the implements of the hearth, hardening the house, and then producing, feeding and nurturing the numerous descendants who come to the original house for blessing. Being blessed in a holy house, therefore, is putting oneself under the protection of that fertile compatibility of the spouses which still flows there.

This is made clear at all the meetings and blessings which take place in the holy house. At each of these occasions, speeches and requests are addressed to the central post, and a meal cooked on the hearth with the original pot, spoon and dish must be prepared and eaten. All parts of the holy house, but especially the central post and an ancestral cooking pot and stirring spoon, must be treated with great reverence and are surrounded by many taboos. Any breach of these taboos is seen as an attack against the body of the founding couple, as is often said quite explicitly during such requests for blessing.[15] It is through these blessings that the original fruitful marriage in its hardened form as the conjoined house post and furniture of the hearth, through its continuing fetishized life,[16] still produces its descendants, still nurtures and guides them, still feeds them.

In theory, of course, any one person has a whole set of holy houses, since one holds them both on one's own side and on that of one's spouse, besides belonging to all the houses of one's parents, grand-parents and more distant ancestors.

In fact the operative holy houses from which one gets blessing are much more restricted because usually one has only two lines of ascendants as a result of the preferential moiety exchange marriage system of the Zafimaniry[17] and because one usually only concerns oneself with two houses in either line.

One set of these is the houses of one's own parents and parents-in-law and these are visualized more in terms of people rather than buildings; at least while this parental generation is still alive, one speaks in terms of getting blessing from them as people, and not from their houses.

The other set of holy houses is the houses of the founders of the lines of one's own family and of that of one's spouse in a particular locality. This means that these holy houses are the foundation houses of villages, since a village is best seen as the result of one or two marriages/houses which have produced many children/marriages/houses.

These holy houses of founders of communities are the ritual centres of their villages. In fact, symbolically they can be said to encompass the village in many ways, and one goes to such houses before any major enterprise to get blessing. They are also the place where all family rituals will take place and where the descendants will meet to discuss important matters and settle disputes. They are the source of blessing of the village.

So when, in 1947, the French burnt down the village they were not just burning the wooden cabins which the foreign soldiers saw, they were burning all the holy houses of the village and the founding holy house in particular; they were burning down the blessing which came from that original marital compatibility. And the villagers who could not stop the desecration were failing their ancestors by their weakness.[18]

As a result the fear of returning to the village was not only a fear of what the government might do, but also a fear of the ancestors' punishment for the destruction of the house which they should have been continuing to build and beautify.

But they did return, and this is how, more or less in the words in which, with great emotion, I was told the story.

While the villagers were still hiding, uncertain whether to return, the father of the head of the village, died in hiding on a Friday. This was wrong because one should, if at all possible, die in the holy house or, if not, be brought back there.[19] Furthermore, although a devout Catholic, he died without being able to say any prayers. And so his children did not know what to do. They tied the corpse up, as is usually done, and finally on the Sunday with great hesitation they decided to take it back to the grass spot where the founders' holy house once stood and they placed his body on the place of the hot post. As soon as they did this he revived for a moment, said a 'Hail Mary' and then finally died and was buried.

The villagers felt that this meant that they could return and they began to drift back and to rebuild the houses, but they kept on falling ill, in particular the only and newborn son of the man who had brought back the corpse. His father went from diviner to diviner but none could find a medicine to cure him. Finally, he went to a spirit medium who asked him to come back the next morning. The next morning, he asked him to come back on the morning after that when the same happened once again. Then the spirit medium told him that in a dream that he had seen the man's father, the one who had died in the forest, and that he had told him to tell his son that he should cook a mixture of three leaves on the hearth of the holy house and then pour some of the broth where the posts had been and feed it to the baby.

They did so. The baby recovered and so did the whole village. The original marriage was reconstructed, the ritual of house foundation had been alluded to and almost repeated, and the holy house had been resurrected. The village was rebuilt.

83

THE HEARTH-GROUP, THE CONJUGAL COUPLE AND THE SYMBOLISM OF THE RICE MEAL AMONG THE KELABIT OF SARAWAK

4

Monica Janowski

LÉVI-STRAUSS (1983a, 1983b, 1987) looks at two aspects of what he terms 'house-based societies'. In the chapter on 'The social organization of the Kwakiutl' in *The Way of the Masks* (1983a) he takes a historical approach to his subject and looks in particular at European noble houses. Here he places a good deal of emphasis on the way in which the 'house' perpetuates itself from generation to generation and discusses the house as 'a corporate body holding an estate . . . which perpetuates itself . . . down a real or imaginary line . . .' (1983a: 174).

In his later lectures on 'The concept of house' and 'On Indonesia', published in *Anthropology and Myth* in 1987, Lévi-Strauss is more interested in the way that the 'house' enables antagonistic principles to be resolved. He appears to be arguing that there is one core antagonism, resolved in the house, to which all others may be reduced. This is between descent and alliance. The conjugal couple, which he describes as 'the true kernel of the family, and more generally, of the kindred' (1987: 155) appears to symbolize, for Lévi-Strauss, the focal importance of alliance. He seems to be arguing that the achievement of alliance is what the house is about. Through the conjugal couple, and the house which symbolizes their union, this is made possible.

Discussions of the applicability of Lévi-Strauss's model of the 'house-based society' to particular societies in Southeast Asia (in particular in many of the papers in Macdonald (ed.) 1987) have concentrated on a consideration of whether or not what may be called houses in these societies actually do have a corporate nature. Rather than attempting to answer this question, I want to look at the other aspect of Lévi-Strauss's discussion of 'house-based societies', that relating to the resolution of antagonisms. I would like to look more closely at the conjugal couple, at the relationship that it has with what may be called the house, and to consider what may be said to be resolved through the conjugal couple and through the house.[1]

While Lévi-Strauss focuses on the husband and wife as representatives of groups which must come to an agreement as well as coming together, I want to look at the individual members of the couple, differentiated by gender. I propose to look at how this difference is handled and at how it relates to the house. In doing this, I will use data on the Kelabit, a cognatic tribal group in Sarawak, East Malaysia.

The Kelabit cannot be said to have alliance relations between corporate groups which persist over time. In each generation, the configuration of relationships between people is remade by marriage. This, of course, happens in all societies; but it may be perceived as happening in the context of the continuing existence of some unchanging entity down the generations. This continued existence is based on an ideology which expresses the mode in which the entity can be perpetuated, such as patrilineality or matrilineality. In such a situation, the different configurations of real-life relationships are seen by members of the society concerned to be simply varying expressions of the same, unchanging thing. Lévi-Strauss is suggesting that the house fulfils this function in house-based societies, including those of Southeast Asia. However, I would argue that the house for the Kelabit does not fulfil this function, and that the couple does not represent a relationship between groups which persists over time. The Kelabit do say that virilocality is preferable to uxorilocality; but in practice there appears to be an approximately equal incidence of the two — as is common in Sarawak — and it does not appear to be of much significance which occurs. Virilocality and uxorilocality are not modes of perpetuation of a corporate group. The significance of the couple is not that it is the expression at a specific point in time of a longer-lasting entity.

I think that Lévi-Strauss is right to insist on the importance of the conjugal couple in Southeast Asia, and to link the couple with something which may be described as the house in the region. He is also, I think, right in saying that the couple resolves something through its existence. But, for the Kelabit, what is resolved is not the relationship between descent and alliance, nor is the resolution which is achieved about the necessity to bring about alliance. It is rather about the need to negotiate the relationship between the man and the woman as representatives of two genders.

Among the Kelabit, the issue being 'dealt with' through the medium of the house is one that exists within the group rather than being one between groups, as Lévi-Strauss would have it. Other contributors to this volume (Bloch, Carsten, Gibson) present data on other cognatic, 'centrist' groups (see Errington 1989: 207–16; 1990 for a discussion of the term 'centrist') in Southeast Asia which suggest a similar focus on the interior constitution of the group rather than on relations between groups. This inward-directed focus tends actually to represent the group as self-perpetuating, and to play down the importance of alliance between groups.

THE KELABIT AND THEIR ENVIRONMENT

The Kelabit are a group of some 5,000 people (Ko 1987: 35) whose homeland is at the headwaters of the Baram river in Sarawak, East Malaysia, on the island of Borneo. They live in an area of fairly flat, relatively inaccessible tableland at about 3,000–3,500 feet above sea level, characterized by a cooler climate, slower rivers and more successful cultivation of rice than is the case in the middle reaches of the Baram and other rivers in Sarawak. The Kelabit traditionally practised both wet and dry cultivation of rice; traditional Kelabit wet cultivation of rice did not involve the creation of permanent fields and thus both techniques of rice cultivation might be described as 'shifting'. Nowadays they are investing a good deal of energy in creating permanent wet rice fields more similar to the classic *sawah* of Java and Bali.

The Kelabit Highlands is predominantly an area of primary forest, interspersed with settlements surrounded by rice fields and areas of secondary forest. Both primary and secondary forest are of great significance to the Kelabit. Traditionally, the forest supplied all the protein food – meat, fish and foods such as insect larvae – eaten on an everyday basis, a very large proportion of vegetables, and all of the materials used for such things as building and crafts.

The Kelabit living in the Highlands are now mostly resident in the area around Bario, where the only government-administered airstrip is located; during the confrontation with Indonesia, the majority of the Kelabit were resettled in the Bario area. I did my fieldwork, however, in Pa' Dalih, an outlying community of about 120 individuals located in the southern part of the Kelabit Highlands some six to twelve hours' walk from the Bario area. Whilst some imported food is eaten in the Bario area, in Pa' Dalih, apart from rice, the forest continues to provide practically all non-cultivated foods.

THE IMPORTANCE OF RICE

Despite the importance of the forest as a source of food, the cultivation of rice (*pade* in its unhusked form, *bra* in its husked but uncooked form) is the axis around which life revolves for the Kelabit. Success in rice growing is traditionally equivalent to success in life. This is widely true of Borneo tribal groups which have adopted rice cultivation. The only group which has actually moved away from rice cultivation is the Melanau, and even they buy rice as a prestige food (Morris 1953). For Borneo rice-growers, to be forced to rely on starches other than rice (i.e. tubers or sago) is unprestigious and a mark of poverty (Whittier 1973: 95; Metcalf 1974: 34, 1989: 113, note 37). For the Kelabit, to be able to eat rice produced by one's own co-resident family group or hearth-group (see below), rather than eating rice produced by others, is vitally important to the maintenance of prestige, described as 'goodness'. To eat rice is the mark of a fully human being; to take responsibility for the cultivation, processing and cooking of rice, and to provide rice meals for children and other dependants (who may be said to be symbolic children), may be said to be the mark of the fully adult human being. It is this status which is the basis of prestige, as I will show.

The cultivation and consumption of rice structures Kelabit society. Through the consumption of the rice meal, rice delineates the basic unit of society, the hearth-group which is replicated symbolically at higher levels in the longhouse community and in the whole of the social universe to include all Kelabit.[2] These levels, like the base-level hearth-group, are defined through the joint consumption of rice meals.

THE KELABIT LONGHOUSE AND HEARTH-GROUP

Like many other Borneo peoples, the Kelabit live in longhouses; the terms for such houses, *ruma' kadang* or *ruma' rawir*, can be literally glossed as 'long house'. The longhouse is divided up in two cross-cutting senses: into the areas built by different 'households' – I shall return to a discussion of the Kelabit term for this group in a moment – and into two major lengthways divisions, the *dalim* or 'room' containing the hearth at which meals are cooked, and the *tawa'* or 'gallery'. This division is broadly equivalent to that which exists in many other Borneo groups, where longhouses are divided into a more private area, where the hearth is (or was situated in the past), and a more public area, where guests are received. In the past Kelabit houses were similarly divided into two halves (see Figs 4.1 and 4.2) but today these two halves are located in two separate, parallel buildings, joined by walkways, one for each household or hearth-group (see Fig. 4.3).

There are three terms for the Kelabit 'household' or hearth-group: *lobang ruma'*, *ruma'* and *tetal*. The term *ruma'* describes the physical place of the household: in the literature on other Borneo groups, similar entities are referred as 'apartments'. In particular, *ruma'* is used to refer to the part of the apartment which contains the hearth. The term *lobang ruma'* is used to describe the group of people inhabiting this apartment as a physical space and means literally 'that which is contained within the cavity of the *ruma'*. The term *tetal*, which may be used to describe the people of the household, literally means 'hearth' (see Fig. 4.4).

The fact that the term *ruma'* is used both to describe the longhouse and to describe the part of the longhouse belonging to one household reflects the fact that, as mentioned above, they may be seen as equivalent entities. Because of the ambiguity involved in the term *ruma'*, and also because I have been told by Kelabit that the term *tetal* or hearth is the one which most truly reflects the basic nature of the

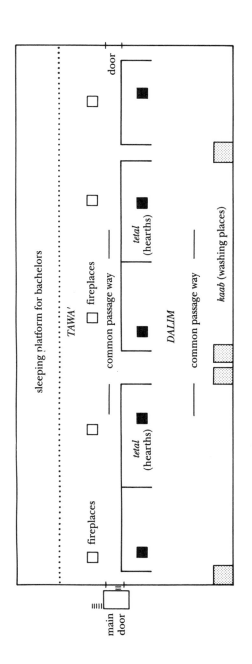

Fig. 4.1 Kelabit longhouse, pre-1945.

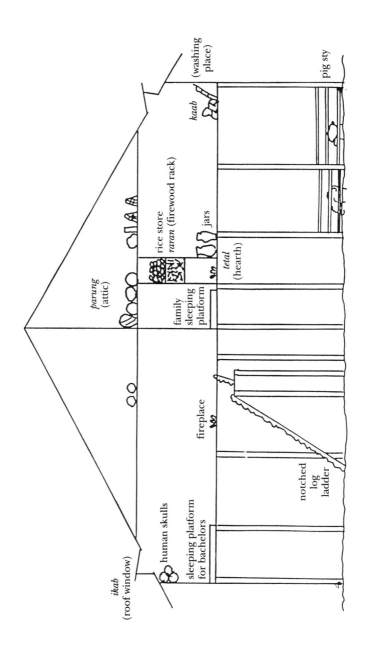

Fig. 4.2   Cross-section of a Kelabit longhouse, pre-1945.

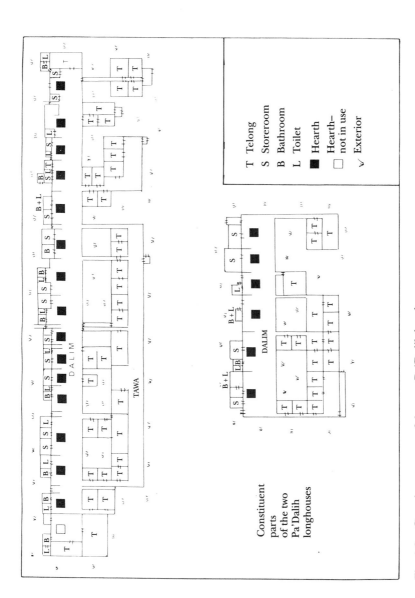

Fig. 4.3   Constituent parts of the two Pa'Dalih longhouses.

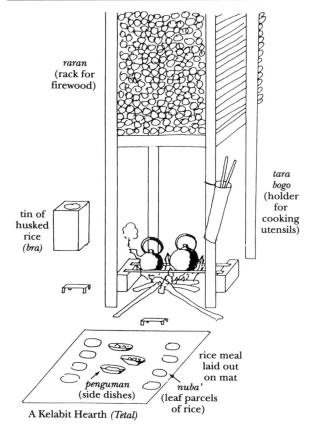

raran
(rack for
firewood)

tara
bogo
(holder
for
cooking
utensils)

tin of
husked
rice
(bra)

rice meal
laid out
on mat

penguman
(side dishes)

nuba'
(leaf parcels
of rice)

A Kelabit Hearth *(Tetal)*

Fig. 4.4   A Kelabit hearth *(tetal)*.

household as focused on the hearth, I shall use the term hearth-group to describe the household. I shall argue that the hearth itself is one of the core symbols associated with the nature of the house. The hearth is what makes a house possible and therefore may be seen actually to constitute the house.

The hearth-group's apartment includes a portion of the *dalim* and a portion of the *tawa'*. The term *dalim* means 'inside', as well as 'deep' and 'true'. The *dalim* is the core of the apartment. Its focus is the hearth where rice meals are cooked and next to which they are eaten by the hearth-group. Only the area around the hearth itself is truly private and it is not intruded upon by members of other hearth-groups except by invitation; other parts of the apartment, including the washing areas and bathrooms adjacent to the *dalim* and the *tawa'*, are freely entered and used by anyone.

Although the parts of the *dalim* built by the different hearth-groups are only separated by very low walls extending a few feet from the outside wall, the conceptual division between hearth-areas belonging to different hearth-groups is very definite. The gallery or *tawa'*, on the other hand, is a long, undivided area. Although each hearth-group builds their own portion of the gallery, it is used freely by all and sundry without regard for who built which part. The Kelabit define the *tawa'* in explicitly negative terms as 'not-*dalim*', i.e. not inside, rather than giving it a positive identity of its own. It is the place of those who are not inside; the young, on an everyday basis, and visitors. In the past, it was used predominantly in the evening. Fires were made on it (at which, however, only snacks, not rice meals, could be cooked) and groups of individuals belonging to different hearth-groups gathered to socialize. Now that fires are no longer built on the *tawa'* (in order not to dirty modern possessions stored in the adjacent *telong* compartments used for sleeping and storage), such groups meet in the *dalim*, by one of the hearths as it is too cold to sit around in the evening without a fire.

The hearth is closely associated with the preparation and consumption of the rice meal. While snack foods, including maize, root crops and meat (eaten on its own, roasted) could in the past be cooked on the fires in the *tawa'*, rice, as well as vegetables and meat (in this context boiled) to be eaten with the rice meal, may only be cooked at the hearth in the *dalim*.

For the Kelabit, the cooking and eating of rice meals represents what it means to belong to one hearth-group (as in Langkawi, these activities are equivalent to being of one house – see Carsten 1987a; this volume). The rice belonging to a particular hearth-group is always cooked at its own hearth and hearth-group members practically always eat their rice meals by their own hearth. Not only will they strongly resist eating rice belonging to another hearth-group, but they are extremely unwilling even to eat their own rice by another hearth-group's hearth. It is very important that rice meals be shared and eaten together at their own hearth by co-members of that hearth. This applies particularly to the morning and evening rice meals, when everyone belonging to the longhouse who is not away on a visit to another longhouse or who is not spending the night at their field house is present.

If possible, midday rice meals should also be eaten at the hearth in the longhouse. At lunch time, when co-operative work groups are often in the middle of a day's work in the fields of a particular hearth-group, individuals prefer to return to the longhouse to eat their midday meal separately at their separate hearths since, if possible, they prefer to eat at their hearth rather than in the fields. They take back a side dish prepared by the hearth-group sponsoring the work and this they eat at their own hearth along with their own rice. If the longhouse is too far away (more than about ten minutes' walk) then the workers eat in a field house, usually the one belonging to the hearth-group whose fields are being worked. But even here, though the rice meal is shared by people, mostly 'big people', from different hearth-groups, they arrange themselves in such a way that they appear to replicate the hearth-groups to which they belong. Turning inwards to face each other in a semi-circle, husband, wife and any dependants pile up the packets of rice they have brought with them and share them out along with side dishes supplied by the group for whom they are working.

THE COUPLE AND THE SYMBOLIC UTILIZATION OF GENDER

I would suggest that the two key symbols that are important in the ideological construction of the Kelabit house are the focal conjugal couple – termed *lun merar*, or 'big people', full social adults – and the hearth. The focal couple has a close relationship with the hearth and with the rice meal which is prepared and eaten there by members of that couple's hearth-group. However, this relationship is not a straightforward one.

I would suggest that, in the Kelabit context, gender and the conjugal couple can be viewed from two different perspectives. From one of these, the conjunction of the two genders is emphasized whilst, from the other, the distinction between them is played up. The conjunction of the two genders, in the form of the focal couple or 'big people', is highlighted when they are contrasted with the *anak adi'* or junior members of the household, the children and young adults who as yet lack children, all of whom are referred to by the same term. The conjugal couple, as an undivided entity, is associated with rice, with the hearth and with the 'inside' of the hearth-group, whilst the *anak adi'* or 'young people' have an eminently peripheral, 'outside' character associated with the extended gallery. Furthermore, in the conjugal couple or 'big people', the two genders are clearly combined whilst amongst those who are not yet 'big people', they remain separate and distinct.

The hearth area is closely associated with the 'big people', who ideally spend the majority of their time there when they are in the longhouse. The growing of rice for cooking and consumption at the hearth is the job of the couple working together; the longer they have been married the more time they spend together and the more time they spend on rice cultivation. Although *anak adi'* belong to a hearth-group (usually that of their parents), they are much less closely anchored to it than are the 'big people'. They spend most of their time with their peer group and wander around a good deal within the longhouse. Rather than spending their time by the hearth, they spend it in sleeping or in storage rooms allocated to one of their number. Such rooms, called *telong*, are conceptually part of the *tawa'* or are, at least, distinct from the *dalim*. They are thus associated with areas which are not the hearth, that is with what is not 'inside'. Among the young, the two genders come together only for social purposes, never for economically productive purposes and in theory not for reproductive purposes either. Outside the longhouse, young people spend most of their time in activities unconnected with rice-growing, and in separate gender groups. Young men hunt, and young girls pick cultivated vegetables and gather wild ones. However, girls are drawn into rice cultivation and processing earlier than young men; I shall return to the significance of this below.

In contrast to the merging of the male and female aspects of the conjugal couple discussed above, in other contexts these two aspects of the couple stand out as being separate, something which becomes explicit only at naming feasts, *irau pekaa ngadan*. On an everyday level this separation may be perceptible but it is pushed below the surface of explicit discourse. Seen from this perspective, there is an association between women and rice – hinted at by the earlier involvement of young women with rice-growing mentioned above – and between men and the forest and meat.

I return below to this emphasis on a separation between male and female. I want first of all to deal with what may be seen as the more explicit perspective from which there is emphasis on the undivided nature of the couple and their association with rice-growing and the hearth.

THE FOCAL COUPLE, THE HEARTH AND RICE

The transition from *anak adi'* to *lun merar*, from being a young person to being a 'big person' or adult, is associated with two things: the relationship of a couple to the growing of rice, and the birth of children and grandchildren. With a deepening association with rice-growing, an individual gradually becomes a full adult. Without children, however, an individual is not treated as a full adult, regardless of marriage or of his or her involvement in rice-growing. With the birth of their first child, the young parents are gradually drawn more and more into rice-growing and into co-operation with each other; they are criticized if they resist this. A new name is given to the young couple at the naming feast, shortly after the birth of the first child, and this marks the beginning of the transition. The peak of adulthood is reached at the entrance into grandparenthood, which is again marked by the taking of a new name at a naming feast held 'for' a real or classificatory grandchild, and at which the child's parents take parental names. Although a hearth-group may be made up of more than one couple, i.e. a husband and wife living together with a married child and in-married spouse, one of these is always dominant over the other. Which one acts as the focal couple, the couple with whom decision-making rests, depends on their relative age and strength. To begin with the senior pair are dominant and it is the duty of the junior pair to help them in rice-growing; as they gradually age and give up their own active role in rice-growing, the junior pair take over. All other individuals in the hearth-group, even if they are involved in rice-growing, are considered dependants without the right, or even the ability, to make decisions.

It is not proper for there to be two active, fully proficient, rice-growing couples in one hearth-group. Normally, this does not seem to occur; by the time the younger couple, now in their forties, reaches full proficiency in rice-growing, the elder couple retires from an active role. However, if it does happen, the two couples will cultivate rice separately, although in the one case of this kind in Pa' Dalih, they pooled their rice. I was, however, told that they should not really pool their rice nor should they share a hearth. Separate cultivation of rice should mean separate households.

The focal couple is responsible for the provision of the rice meal for other, dependant members of the hearth-group. The provision of the rice meal may be seen as the practical and symbolic equivalent of the biological reproduction of the hearth-group in the form of children and, as has been noted, the production and provision of rice and the reproduction of children are both essential to the status of full adult or 'big person'. If the hearth-group regularly fails to produce sufficient rice, it does not run the risk of starving; no Kelabit would be allowed to go hungry by fellow members of the longhouse. Its 'big people' do, however, run the risk of losing their status. This happens if they reach the point of being unable to maintain a separate hearth-group and become the dependants of the focal couple of another hearth-group. This would, in the past (before the Second World War), have meant their becoming slaves (demulun). Being a 'big person' means being able to maintain a separate hearth-group.

The way in which the rice meal is eaten is indicative of its symbolic importance. Rice meals, especially when taken in the longhouse, are eaten quite quickly and in silence. This is not a time for social communication. There is a heaviness, a seriousness in the air. Such rice meals are eaten three times a day, each hearth-group forming a semi-circle turned inwards to face the hearth itself. Eating rice together indicates joint membership of the same hearth-group and makes a statement about responsibility – on the part of the 'big people' – and about dependency – on the part of the young and old (and, in the past, of slaves as well).

Rice is very explicitly owned and it is owned by the hearth-group. Transactions involving rice are fraught with insinuations. Rice cannot be given away without the implication that the 'big people' of the recipient hearth-group are in need of rice, that they are unable to grow enough to provide for their own people. Rice-growing labour cannot be given away either, without creating a debt; debts created in the co-operative labour groups which are the core of the production of rice are carefully repaid. Where labour for rice cultivation is donated to a hearth-group this threatens the status of its 'big people' just as the receipt of rice as a gift would. Even the sale of rice is problematic because to buy rice implies that you are short of it. Those who could afford to buy rice do not do so. I know of no instances of rice being sold to other Kelabit.

ADULTHOOD AND PRESTIGE

One can equate the prestige of the 'big person' who is able to maintain a separate hearth-group with the prestige of people of high status. The same term, 'good people', *lun doo*, is used to describe those who are able to maintain a separate hearth-group and those who are prestigious in society. The prestige, characteristic of *lun doo*, is the very nature of what it is to be a true human being.[3] It derives from the production of rice and the provision of rice meals for other people who are dependants: the more dependants provided for the better in terms of the generation of prestige. Thus there is considerable eagerness to provide rice meals for others but an extreme reluctance to accept them.

Focal couples of successful separate hearth-groups provide these prestige-generating rice meals every day; at a higher level, the 'really good people', *lun doo to'oh*, sometimes referred to in the literature on the Kelabit as 'aristocrats', provide such meals at naming feasts where the whole Kelabit population is fed a rice meal by the host hearth-group. At present, by far the most important kind of feast is the naming feast; in the past very important feasts were also held at the secondary funerals of 'really good people' but these are no longer held since the Kelabit converted to Christianity in the 1950s.[4] Rice meals at naming feasts generate not only the status of 'really good person' but that of full adult as well; all couples hold a feast at the birth of their first co-resident grandchild and this confirms that they are now full *lun merar* or 'big people'.

Symbolically, the rice meal at naming feasts may be said to be making the statement that the whole Kelabit population is equivalent to one hearth-group and that all those present are the dependants of the host hearth-group. This is why it is generative of prestige in the same way and of the same kind as that generated by the everyday rice meal, and explains why the same term (*lun doo*) may be used both for the focal couple of the hearth-group and for people of high status in society at large. The status of 'good person' is achieved to varying degrees; characteristic of the Kelabit system of prestige differentiation is a lack of clear distinctions between named 'strata'.

Although naming feasts are held for all young couples, and are hosted by the focal couple of the hearth-group to which they belong, normally the parents of either the young husband or the young wife, there is a lot of variation in the scale involved. The difference lies in the number of people who attend as well as in the provision for the guests. It is prestigious to have as many guests as possible. The symbolic hearth-group which is generated through the meal held at the naming feast varies in size according to the number of guests and the larger it is the better in terms of prestige. Thus different naming feasts make very different statements about the prestige of the hosts. This creates the basis for the system of prestige differentiation.[5]

Thus both the base-level hearth-group and a higher-level symbolic hearth-group are brought into being and prestige is generated, through the holding of rice meals. It is through the rice meal, whether the everyday rice meal or the rice meal held at feasts, that the nature of the hearth-group is stated.

THE TWO COMPONENTS OF THE RICE MEAL: RICE AND WILD FOODS

The rice meal consists of two complementary components. One is rice;[6] the other is the foods which are eaten with rice. These consist, at everyday rice meals, of any combination of meat, fish, other protein foods, and vegetables.

Foods eaten with rice are either wild or are, in important respects, treated as though they were wild. They are derived from plants and animals which are said to 'live on their own' (*mulun sebulang*), in other words, without human help. Rice, on the other hand, cannot, the Kelabit say, live unless humans help it do so. This is the basic distinction between the two components of the rice meal.

While rice, as discussed above, is owned, foods eaten with rice at the everyday rice meal – meat from wild animals, wild vegetables and cultivated vegetables – are not treated as though they belong to the person who obtains them by hunting, gathering or collecting or who planted them. Such foods are shared between hearth-groups quite freely in both their raw and cooked states; this applies both to those foods which are to be eaten at the rice meal and to those to be eaten as snacks between meals. Unlike transactions involving rice, this kind of sharing does not create any indebtedness.

The two components of the rice meal have different status on an everyday level. The rice meal is described as just that – *kuman nuba'*, 'eating rice'. At everyday rice meals, the wild foods which are eaten are not accorded any value, and are freely given away. The situation is different, as we shall see, at *irau* feasts.

THE OTHER PERSPECTIVE ON GENDER: THE SEPARATE ASSOCIATIONS OF MALE AND FEMALE

At that point I want to go back to the two perspectives that I mentioned above. From one of these, the couple is an undivided whole and opposed, as 'inside', to the 'outside' represented by the young. From the other perspective, the two genders within the couple remain separate. Within the perspective from which the couple appears as undivided, there is an association between 'big people' and rice-growing on the one hand, and between young people, the 'outside', and uncultivated land, including both primary forest (*polong kora*) and secondary forest cultivated in the past (*polong adi'*), on the other. Within the other perspective, from which there is a separation of the genders within the couple, there is an association between women and rice, and men and the forest.

I have pointed out that the married couple, the 'big people', are closely associated with rice, while young people, not yet parents, are associated with these wild and semi-cultivated foods. However, there is no doubt that there is a sense in which women are more closely associated with rice cultivation than men. As has been mentioned above, young women begin to involve themselves in the cultivation, processing and cooking of rice to some extent before they become parents, while there is often difficulty in persuading even young fathers to help in the rice fields; young men who are not yet fathers practically never enter the rice fields. Women also are more responsible for ritually important parts of rice cultivation, such as sowing of nursery beds and transplanting. It was certain women who, before the Kelabit began to convert to Christianity, used to have dealings with the deity associated with rice, Deraya.[7]

There is also no doubt that men are more closely associated with the forest than are women. Although women gather and also fish, they only do so in secondary forest while men hunt animals for meat, fish and gather forest produce in both primary and secondary forests. Men enter the primary forest without fear, they say, of spirits of which women are quite openly afraid. In the past, men, particularly when young, sometimes had personal relationships with a spirit of the forest called *Puntumid* which is associated with hunting success and some own powerful charms which they find in the primary forest. I know of no cases of women having such relationships or owning such charms.

At *irau* feasts, the rice meal is reduced to its clearest statement, consisting of rice and meat, with no vegetables. Here, the association of women with rice and of men with that which is eaten with rice[8] – here, meat – is also clear. While women usually cook meat for everyday rice meals, at feasts men cook it, boiling it in huge pots outside the longhouse[9] while women cook the rice at the hearth. The meat is distributed by the men; young men distribute the flesh, *uang*, while older men distribute the fat, *lemak*. Fat-eating contests are sometimes held in which the older men compete; in fact the ritual eating of fat is a major aspect of these feasts, with men pressing lumps of fat on each other and sometimes on women. Fat seems to be considered very appropriate, and even essential, to men, particularly older men who are *lun merar*, while it appears to be considered inappropriate and perhaps dangerous for women, particularly young girls; I witnessed a mother, in panic, telling her daughter not to eat fat because it would give her stomach ache, while she watched her son eat it. Fat may perhaps be seen as being the most 'meaty' part of the meat; an extreme statement of its derivation from the forest and thus appropriately associated with men rather than women.[10] The core event at the present-day *irau* is the rice meal, preceded by the distribution of sweet drinks and crackers which have replaced rice wine and *senape*, rice steamed in leaves and eaten without side dishes. The women distribute all foods made from rice or which have replaced foods previously made from rice. Young girls who are not yet parents, and new mothers, distribute the crackers and sweet drinks, while older women – established 'big people', mothers of teenagers and of young mothers – distribute the *nuba'*, rice to be eaten with meat.

101

Thus, at *irau*, there is a rice meal consisting of what may be construed symbolically as male and female food, meat plus rice, and a separation of the focal couple into its constituent parts, the husband and wife. The male role as rice-grower appears to be negated; this is underlined by the fact that it is those men who are most closely associated with rice as members of successful couples, *lun merar* men, who are here most closely associated with fat. Rice and the female are associated with 'inside', with the hearth, where the rice is prepared for *irau*, while meat and the male are associated with the 'outside', the non-hearth, where the meat is prepared.

Rice, then, is associated with women but also with the couple, male and female, while meat is associated with men but also with the young (*anak adi'*). The man is both part of the couple, which itself is the essence of what constructs the hearth – rice-growing success – and yet he is the epitome of what is opposed, though complementary, to rice.

It is the male role as one half of the married couple, itself the core of the hearth-group and of the house, which is emphasized on an everyday level. From this perspective, male and female are jointly associated with the cultivation and provision of rice. It is young people, those who do not grow rice and who do not have children, who are associated with the 'outside'. From this perspective, the 'outside' is not represented as positive. It is merely the absence of the 'inside', of rice-growing. But from the other perspective, which is made fully explicit only at *irau*, men are represented as being associated with the 'outside'. In this context, the 'outside', the forest, is represented as something positive and necessary to the successful celebration of the rice meal.

The very great importance of *irau*, in the generation of differential prestige between hearth-groups, and in the fact that they are held to confirm the position of their hosts as full *lun merar*, highlights the presentation of both rice *and* wild foods as essential to the rice meal.

GENDER SYMBOLISM IN THE KELABIT HOUSE

The internal division of the Kelabit house and hearth-group apartment reflects both the perspectives on gender which have been discussed. There is no explicit gender symbolism associated with different parts of the house. There is simply an 'inside' and an 'outside', respectively the hearth in the *dalim*, associated explicitly with the couple, and the *tawa'* or gallery. However, despite explicit Kelabit ideology, the hearth does appear, even on an everyday level, to be more closely associated with women than with men, just as rice is more closely associated with women. Women do most of the cooking, and are more assertively present in the hearth area than are men. Even men who are 'big people' do spend some time on the gallery, making baskets and doing other craft work, while women never do. Even in the past women would only spend time on the *tawa'* if visitors from outside the longhouse were present. In the past young men slept on the *tawa'*: young women slept in the loft above their parents. I have been told by women that they find that men get under their feet in the hearth area and that they send them to sit in the *tawa'* if this is the case (although I never saw this happen).[11]

The Kelabit house can be seen both as a statement of the focal nature of the couple, as contrasted to those who are not yet married, and at the same time, but from another perspective, as a statement concerning the differentiation between the two halves of the couple, which involves an association of the female half with the centre, the *dalim*, the hearth and rice, and of the male half with the *tawa'*, the periphery and the wild. The latter perspective, however, is less explicit and becomes apparent largely through observation.

CONCLUSION

Lévi-Strauss has argued that the house provides a way for antagonisms to be resolved. He suggests that, in Southeast Asia, this occurs through the conjugal couple. He, however, locates the antagonisms in the problems inherent in the necessity for groups to exchange wives. I have examined the conjugal couple among the Kelabit to see how far Lévi-Strauss's suggestion holds. I have argued that the main symbols associated with the house among the Kelabit are the hearth and the focal conjugal couple. Within the couple, and at the core of the house or hearth-group, is a statement about the significance of the difference between male and female; a difference which might be best described as a dynamic tension. It is not only what is achieved through the bringing together of the two genders that matters, but also what is made possible through the division of male and female; both of these achievements occur through the medium of the conjugal couple.

The Kelabit conjugal couple *is* the core of the 'house' (which is, I have argued, essentially reducible to what I have termed the 'hearth-group'), as Lévi-Strauss argues the couple to be for house-based societies of Southeast Asia (1987: 155). However, what is achieved through the couple as the core of the Kelabit hearth-group is possible not because they are the representatives of separate groups of people which include both men and women, but because of the difference in gender between the two people involved. Gender, then, is a very dynamic difference for the Kelabit. Onvlee argues that the expression *mini–kawini* ('male–female') in Sumba, Indonesia is used 'for a relationship between things that are distinguished in their relatedness and related through their distinction' (Onvlee 1980: 46, quoted in Jordaan and Niehof 1988: 173). This seems an apt description of the way in which gender difference is conceptualized among the Kelabit: male and female can only mean what they do divided from each other, at one moment, because they mean what they do when they are seamlessly joined, at another.

Although tensions over the residence of spouses would preclude this in practice, Lévi-Strauss's picture of the significance of the house as the site of the resolution of antagonisms might be seen as implying an ideally unidirectional process and that what would eventually be desirable, worked towards via the joining of man and woman in the conjugal couple, would be some kind of stasis. The impression is that the 'house', focused upon the couple, is utilized as a kind of weapon against disorder. This is not an appropriate way of looking at the role of gender within the Kelabit couple. Among the Kelabit, there is a constant realignment of focus between the achievement of the unity of the two genders and the importance of the difference between them. There is no reason to suppose that this process of constant realignment is in any way problematic; which is why it seems inappropriate to describe as a 'resolution' what is, at certain points, achieved through the presentation of the couple as a 'whole', a seamless united front. It appears rather to be central to the nature of gender among the Kelabit that such realignment should continually take place.

HOUSES IN LANGKAWI: STABLE STRUCTURES OR MOBILE
5   HOMES?

Janet Carsten

THIS CHAPTER EXAMINES the applicability of Lévi-Strauss's (1983a; 1983b; 1987) concept of 'sociétés à maison', house-based societies, to a Malay fishing village on the island of Langkawi, Malaysia. While it takes its inspiration from the ideas advanced by Lévi-Strauss, it is also the product of dissatisfaction with a preliminary discussion of these ideas (Carsten 1987a), and of the stimulation of other writings on this theme.[1]

Lévi-Strauss's argument relates principally to the Kwakiutl *numayma*, the medieval noble house in Europe, eleventh-century Japan and to certain Indonesian societies. A number of features of these societies are stressed by Lévi-Strauss. Firstly, continuity occurs through descent, that is, downwards in the inheritance of names and property (1983a: 174; 177–9). Second, he draws attention to the hierarchical ordering of the basic units of these societies. When both the houses themselves and members of these units are ordered according to birth order and proximity to a common ancestor, as he apparently considers to be the case in all his examples, marriage implies unequal status, and plays a central role in the ranking system (1983a: 181).[2]

Third, Lévi-Strauss emphasizes how the 'dialectic of filiation and residence' (1983a: 180) is a common feature of house-based societies. In other words, dual membership in a group with bilateral descent and in the residential unit creates conflicting obligations. He draws attention to a series of opposing principles, such as filiation/residence, patri-/matrilineal descent, hypergamy/hypogamy, close/distant marriage. In this context the house takes on a crucial significance: according to Lévi-Strauss it 'reunites' or 'transcends' (1983a: 184) these incompatible principles:

The whole function of noble houses, be they European or exotic, implies a fusion of categories which are elsewhere held to be in correlation with and opposition to each other, but are henceforth treated as interchangeable: descent can substitute for affinity, and affinity for descent.   (1983a: 187)

It is characteristic of such societies that filiation and alliance are equally important (Lévi-Strauss 1983b: 1224) as well as being mutually substitutable.

Discussing Indonesian societies specifically, Lévi-Strauss (1987) has emphasized the centrality of alliance: how it is a principle both of unity and of antagonism in house-based societies where neither filiation, property nor residence, taken alone, are criteria for the constitution of groups. The married couple is at once the centre of the family but also a source of tension between families – particularly over residence. The house then 'transfixes' an unstable union, and transcends the opposition between wife-givers and wife-takers and between filiation and alliance. It becomes

the objectification of a relation: the unstable relation of alliance which, as an institution, the house functions to solidify, if only in an illusory form.
(Lévi-Strauss 1983a: 155; italics in original)

In this respect Lévi-Strauss has applied the notion of fetishism to the house, using the elaborate constructions of Batak and Atoni architecture as examples.

As I will show, certain aspects of this argument seem to be highly applicable to Langkawi, others are more problematic. In part, these problems stem from a failure to distinguish clearly different types of social organization within Southeast Asia and to connect these to the analysis of the house. I return to a comparative discussion of the house in Southeast Asia in the concluding sections of this chapter, suggesting some of the reasons why Lévi-Strauss's ideas apply in different ways to different types of Southeast Asian social organization.

106

THE HOUSE IN LANGKAWI

Even the most preliminary attempt to describe the house in Langkawi is beset by a striking paradox. On the one hand houses are at the very heart of social organization; their material and symbolic significance is elaborated at many levels and in countless contexts; no account of social life can avoid reference to their structure or a description of relations within, and exchanges between, these units. On the other hand, in comparison to the well-known Indonesian examples of the Batak or Atoni, the symbolism seems curiously flat, the architecture unexceptional, the units themselves impermanent and mobile. Tension between a markedness and an unmarkedness runs through all that concerns the house and makes this unit's centrality to social organization always ambiguous. It is this tension which provides the focus of the analysis presented here and which renders Lévi-Strauss's discussion at once relevant and problematic.

House structure in Langkawi, as elsewhere in Malaysia, shows considerable variation in style and design. Hilton (1956) has noted the susceptibility of Malay house building to changes in fashion, and in Langkawi the marked variation in style and quality of housing is one of the clearest indicators of wealth. From the point of view of the developmental cycle of the domestic group, perhaps the most significant feature of the more traditional type of Malay house is that it can be easily enlarged and that it is moveable from place to place (Plate 3) (Hilton 1956: 144). These features of their design permit flexibility and mobility in the residence patterns of their occupants.

While the amount of building activity going on in Langkawi is striking, very little of it involves the construction of new houses, instead old ones may be repaired, extended and improved, creating the impression that the village is under continuous reconstruction. Major improvements or extensions to a house (for example, building a new room) are often undertaken by parents at the time of a child's marriage. Frequent changes in residence after marriage are normal: a couple may move house, *pindah rumah*, several times during the first years of their married life.

Rosemary Firth has commented that a Malay 'will think nothing of buying a house, taking it to pieces and re-erecting it elsewhere' (1966: 23). In Langkawi villagers may simply omit taking it to pieces. The practice of 'lifting the house', *usung rumah*, which may involve moving

Plate 3   The walking house: group of men lift a house on Pulau Langkawi, Malaysia.

to another site within the same compound or to an entirely different area of the village, is another aspect of the flexibility of residence. The *usung rumah* requires the co-operation of neighbours and kin and is a festive occasion. A house may be transported when land is bought or sold, after a death or the birth of a child, which leads to the reorganization of the household or the setting up of a new one.

The ongoing nature of house construction and the physical mobility of houses are thus related to stages in the developmental cycle of the domestic group, but they also underline the traditional impermanence of the house structure itself and its loose connection to a specific site. Rodman's observations on a Melanesian society in which both houses and residence are also strikingly mobile, are highly relevant here. She stresses how residence is in constant flux, and this process 'becomes part of the interweaving of place and people that creates Longana kinship' (1985: 69). A similar interweaving of locality and persons lies at the heart of kinship and community in Langkawi. Today, however, these features of the house are changing. Houses are becoming both significant items of property (with implications for inheritance practices) and more permanent structures.

The simplest houses are wood, palm and bamboo constructions raised on stilts and consisting of a kitchen, *dapur*, and one main room, *ibu rumah* (literally, 'mother of the house'), where woven mats and perhaps one cupboard form the main items of furniture. At the other extreme are large and more elaborate dwellings which may be partly built at ground level, with concrete floors, concrete and timber walls, metal roofs and glazed windows. These houses generally consist of a kitchen, *dapur*, and two main rooms: the *ibu rumah* which tends to be used for formal occasions, and the main living area of the house, also known as the *dapur*, which can be regarded as an extension of the cooking *dapur* (see Fig. 5.1). In such houses the *ibu rumah* tends to contain several items of furniture: a formica table, bamboo or formica chairs, a cupboard for clothes, a glass-fronted cabinet where unused kitchen items are displayed. The main living area appears almost bare by contrast: woven mats are laid out on the floor, bedding may be rolled up against one wall, but the central space is left clear.

The fact that houses are constantly improved and enlarged enables the different types of house structure to be considered partly as stages in a developmental sequence which parallels the developmental cycle of its occupants. Improvements also reflect the influence of changing

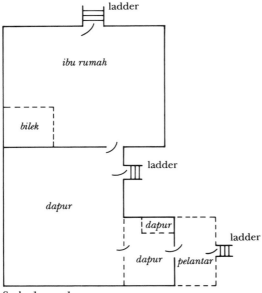

Scale: 1 cm = 1 m

Fig. 5.1   Langkawi house plan.

fashions: the simplest and smallest houses being generally also the more traditional in style, while the newest and grandest reflect current trends in house design and the increasing influence of urban values in rural life. Most houses in fact fall between the two extremes I have described. One part of the house, generally the *ibu rumah*, will show clear signs of having been constructed later than the rest and is built from wood and concrete with a metal roof and glazed windows.

Houses have certain essential characteristics – firstly, a *dapur*. Most significantly, a house never has more than one hearth. Villagers always emphasize that co-residence necessarily implies the sharing of one hearth. If the core meaning of *dapur* is cooking stove or hearth, both the room in which this is situated, and the living area adjoining this in the larger, three-roomed houses, can be seen as extensions of this core hearth (see Fig. 5.1).

The second essential feature of the house is the *ibu rumah*. In the more simple type of village houses this space corresponds to the 'living' *dapur* of more elaborate structures, and is the area where women spend most of their time. This room therefore, like the *dapur*, has an association with women which is revealed in the very meaning of the term, *ibu rumah*, 'mother of the house'. The same term is used to refer to the female household head.[3]

The strong association between the house and women is ritually expressed during house building. The mother of the house, *ibu rumah*, must hold the central pillar of the house, *tiang seri*, when it is erected. This central post is the abode of the house spirit, *semangat rumah*, or *manya rumah*, which is also believed to be female. Like other women, the house spirit must be suitably adorned. The top of the *tiang seri* is wrapped around with red, black and white cloths known as *bunga alang* and sometimes described as the clothes of the house spirit. The house spirit is vulnerable to attack from other spirits which are less benevolent. To protect her from this, iron is placed in the ground at the base of the *tiang seri*. While Stephen Headley (1987a) has suggested that bodies in Java are metaphorical houses, houses in Langkawi are conceived as female bodies and must be decorated appropriately.

THE SHARING OF SPACE AND FOOD

The association between the house and women has a more practical expression. On entering any house in the village, perhaps the most striking impression of the visitor is the contrast between the overwhelming presence of women and the near absence of men. Particularly during the day, men are almost entirely missing from the house, engaged in fishing, attending the mosque or coffeeshop, or undertaking errands in the local market town. Those that are present, often old or sick, seem confined to its furthest regions: they sit alone, huddled in a far corner of a room, or, appropriately, they occupy the very margins of the house space: perching on a door sill or verandah, half in and half out of the house, watching the comings and goings of the neighbourhood.

In contrast, women dominate the house space with their presence. They walk freely to and fro as they go about their tasks: cooking, looking after children, cleaning, weaving mats. They utilize the central areas of the room and sometimes the margins too; there is no sense of confinement or restraint in their movements or use of space. The sitting positions prescribed by Malay formal etiquette[4] are largely ignored: women may sit cross-legged, with legs stretched out in front of them, or even lie about on the floor.

This lack of restraint in the way they range themselves in space is also reflected in other aspects of women's behaviour within the house, particularly that of older women. Their conversation is neither dull nor subdued. In the absence of men it is likely to be particularly full of lively gossip and jokes spiced with sexual allusions. Laughter is frequent, conversation often bawdy. Nor does it necessarily change in character in the presence of men of the household. Subjects of local interest, feasts, rotating credit societies, marriages and disputes are all discussed in a lively and opinionated manner.

Even within the house it is rare to see physical contact between adult men and women but in other respects men and women of the same house behave towards each other in a relaxed manner. Women do not modify their movements, sitting positions or dress when male members of the household are present. Men and women of one house eat together and converse rather freely in each other's presence. Villagers minimize the association between specific areas of the house and men or women, saying *tak kira*; 'it is not calculated', strictly followed. It is difficult to ascertain whether such segregation is less strictly observed in Langkawi than elsewhere in Malaysia – partly because observers have tended to concentrate on formal contexts where such segregation is always marked (see Provencher 1971: 165).

Although relations between household members tend to be informal and relaxed, irrespective of gender, a strict age-based hierarchy operates between generations, and in weaker form, within generations when age differences are great. This hierarchy is particularly clear in the relation between mothers and daughters who between them share most household labour. Young women, who perform most of this labour, always comply with the constant stream of orders issued by their mothers.

Men of one house tend to be less close than women, and in adulthood relations between closely related male consanguines are often based on avoidance. Nevertheless, within the house affection may be displayed by fathers and grandfathers towards young children and between brothers of all ages. Particular ties may be less close than the corresponding ones between women, but the atmosphere is friendly, relaxed and informal, and this is reflected in conversation patterns and body posture.

When male strangers come to the house sex segregation becomes more marked. These guests are received by men in the *ibu rumah* (or on the *beranda*), while women of the household remain in the *dapur*. If female strangers come to the house they either enter the 'living' *dapur* directly or they graduate there rather rapidly from the *ibu rumah*. However, such formality is exceptional. Villagers say that the *ibu rumah* is for visitors, *orang datang*, but by this they do not refer to casual, everyday visits from neighbours, kin and friends who usually sit in the *dapur*, but to those of strangers.

Even when male strangers visit, it is mainly young women who are restricted to the *dapur*. Older women participate in the entertainment and, if no men are present, actually receive male guests in the *ibu rumah*. Sex segregation applies in varying degrees of strictness depending on the formality of the occasion and the degree of familarity between the visitor and the household. When they are at home men of the household spend most of their time, as do women, in the *dapur*, for it is here that the main activities of family life are performed. While different areas of the house are loosely associated with women and men, and this separation gains strength by the absence of men from the house for much of the day, villagers' own perception of such segregation is that it is rather weak.

This is one aspect of a more general lack of division of interior house space. Different areas of the house tend not to be strongly associated with particular people. Co-resident nuclear families never have a separate annex or room built onto the house for their use. Household members do, however, have their customary sleeping space either in the 'living' *dapur* or the *ibu rumah*, where it may be partitioned off by screens or wooden partitions to form a *bilek*, sleeping room. These are generally only constructed when more than one married couple co-reside in one house. Children may sleep near their parents, grand-parents or other resident adults while they are young; in general their space is less defined than that of adults. Individual household members do not have their own daytime space; at night means of separation usually consist of no more than mosquito netting or a flimsy screen. Household members usually prefer to sleep near to one another even when the size of the house would allow some distance.

The unity of the household is most clearly expressed in cooking and eating arrangements. I have already referred to the fact that houses only ever have one hearth, *dapur*, where most day-to-day activities are carried on, and this term refers to the cooking stove, the kitchen, and the main living area of the house. However many members, nuclear families, generations live within one house, they cook and eat together, and this is the most significant of household activities in terms of the attention it receives and the symbolism with which it is invested.

The preparation of meals by women and their consumption by members of one house take up much attention and time and these activities are highly enjoyed. The central constituent of such meals is steamed rice which is accompanied by fish and vegetables. Rice is produced through subsistence agricultural labour which is dominated by women, and in which kinship connections are frequently utilized. Fish are associated with commercial, individualistic exchanges and the labour of men (see Carsten 1989).

Even in informal contexts within the home, meals are rarely taken by one person on their own. When this does happen the person eating will always first invite others present to partake of the meal. If they refuse she will tuck herself away in a corner, out of sight of others and eat hurriedly and furtively and with considerable embarrassment. If visitors pass by during a meal they are always invited to eat and, equally consistently, they refuse. The invitation is a gesture of hospitality and inclusion; its refusal emphasizes the boundaries of the household.[5] Eating everyday meals in other people's houses is strongly disapproved of; even children are discouraged from doing so. It is significant that the taking of snacks or drinks in other houses is a normal part of visiting.[6]

Newly married couples avoid eating together on their own. When this occurs and is witnessed by others, the couple is teased and show acute embarrassment. As in many other cultures, Malays make an association between eating and sex; jokes often turn on this point. A newly married pair who have not yet had children, like the solitary person, cannot form a household; one expression of this is an avoidance of situations when they constitute a commensal group.

The site of cooking and eating, the *dapur*, can be regarded, then, as the very heart of the house. I will argue below that in the last analysis it is shared feeding that creates kinship. Cooking and eating are not only activities performed by household members together, they are also performed in an undivided way. This is what gives force to the prohibition on eating meals in other people's houses.[7]

HOUSES AND SIBLING SETS

Houses in Langkawi are not only associated with women and with undivided kinship in a general way; they also have a strong association with the sibling group. In order to grasp the implications of this association it is necessary to understand the centrality of siblingship to notions about kinship. Kinship in general and relations in the wider community are conceived in terms of siblingship. When villagers seek to emphasize that they are all related in an undefined way they say 'we are all kin here; there are no strangers'. The word they use for kin, *adikberadik*, is itself derived from that for younger sibling, *adik*. When asked to specify a kin connection, however distant, they always trace it back to the point where two ancestors are siblings. The emphasis on sibling unity is reflected in naming systems for siblings. Personal names are often selected by parents for their homophony; birth-order terms for sibling sets constitute some of the most commonly used terms of address and reference in the village. It is normal to refer to and address cousins by sibling terms and in almost all contexts it would be highly impolite not to do so.[8]

Affines too can be incorporated into this system. Husbands and wives should, at least in theory, refer to and address each other using sibling terms, although in fact they experience marked discomfort in doing so. Siblingship is at the very heart of kinship, and this relates to two of its unique properties. One is its capacity to express both hierarchy and equality. The other is its almost limitless capacity for lateral extension which I associate with a more general 'inclusive' tendency in this society. This occurs both in an endless connecting of co-villagers through ties of 'cousinship', where cousins elide with siblings, and in the way affinal connections can loosely be taken to imply consanguinity (siblingship) in previous generations. An assertion of distant kinship necessarily implies siblingship in the past; siblingship in the present often implies intermarriage in the future. I will refer again to this inclusiveness whereby distinctions between kin and non-kin or kin and affine tend to be blurred or ignored except in disputes when it is always possible to assert them.

It is in the context of a fundamental importance of siblingship that an association between the house and the sibling group takes on a wider significance. This is manifested at many different levels. It is made ritually at the time of birth which itself occurs in the symbolic

115

centre of the house, the *dapur*. Each child is believed to be part of a set of 'symbolic siblings' consisting of the child and its younger sibling placenta, *adik uri*. When a child is born, the afterbirth is washed and placed in a woven basket together with certain ritual objects. It is then buried by the father in the grounds of the house compound in a manner which echoes the burial of corpses outside the village in the graveyard. The *adik uri* is believed to exert an influence on the child after its birth. Similar beliefs and practices involving an expanded version of this symbolic sibling set have been recorded widely elsewhere in Southeast Asia and can be related to a complex cosmology which has been explored by Headley (n.d.; 1987a; 1987b). McKinley (1981: 371) has reported that the placenta sibling is the same for any group of natal siblings since it returns to the womb to supervise the birth of younger siblings. This further underlines the unity of the sibling group. What I would emphasize here is the way that the sibling set is in this birth ritual physically anchored to the house.

Parallel with a positive association between the house and sibling-ship is a negative association between the house and affinity. New houses are never established until a couple have at least one child. Although I have described how affinity can be converted into siblingship, and this is one aspect of a loosely conceived endogamy, it is also the case that siblingship and marriage are in many contexts opposed. In-marrying affines are conceived as threatening the unity of the sibling group. They are thought likely to cause quarrels between brothers and sisters, particularly over inheritance. It is explicitly in order to avoid such disputes which might threaten the harmony and unity of the household that married siblings never co-reside.

Above all other kin, adult siblings are required to render each other aid and support throughout life. Warm, affectionate relations should obtain between them; sisters are often especially close, and quarrels are highly upsetting for those concerned. If siblingship is paradigmatic of kinship morality in general, it also epitomizes the shared consumption that is at the heart of co-residence. The prime definition of incest is in terms of those who have 'drunk the same milk', *makan sama susu*, and this of course applies principally to siblings.[9] The indivision and sharing which unites those who live together is symbolically and practically lived out in the commensal act, in everyday terms this is the household meal. If houses can be materially and symbolically defined by their one hearth, *dapur*, their core relational configurement is the sibling set.

FROM THE HOUSE TO THE VILLAGE COMMUNITY

As different members of a sibling group marry and have children, they establish new houses which are most commonly built in the compound of either the husband's or the wife's parents. Different houses of one compound (a piece of undivided house land) thus come to be occupied by adult siblings and their spouses and children. In many respects the compound can be regarded as an extension of the house. Relations in both are characterized by a high degree of sharing and informality and are dominated by women. Visits between houses of one compound are frequent, especially between adult women. The relaxed manner in which these visits are conducted contrasts strongly with all other forms of visiting: 'guests' behave exactly as they would in their own house; 'hosts' do not modify their behaviour for their guests. There is a frequent exchange of goods, services, cooked food and raw produce between these houses, and it is notable that strict reciprocity is not observed.

To a very great extent, houses of one compound share resources: the land on which they are situated, water from one well, food to a more limited degree. Frequently such households own rice land in common. This is a consequence of a very great resistance to partitioning property by formal inheritance procedures. Such procedures, which in all senses import division into the sibling group, are associated with disputes as either cause or effect and tend to be deferred until long after the death of an original owner (see Carsten 1990).

Not only is it possible to see the compound as an enlarged house united by links between adult siblings, but this is in many respects also true for the village community. As the houses which make up a compound multiply, the land on which they are situated is eventually divided, and new compounds are founded on neighbouring tracts of land. The village grows through the process of house expansion. Lim (1987: 93) has commented on how 'house compounds flow into each other', boundaries between them are indistinct, and space is 'free-flowing'. This process of gradual enlargement is underlined by the fact that one term: *kampung*, is used for a compound consisting of one house, one of several houses, a neighbourhood of several adjacent compounds, and a village of several neighbourhoods.

The image of the community as an expanded house is lived out at communal feasts, *kenduri*, typically held to celebrate marriages. The most frequent participants in these feasts are male and female household heads who are often grandparents. However, men and women attend such occasions separately, not as married couples, and they often take one or more grandchild with them. Such feasts play on the central symbol of the house: they are particularly extravagant meals of which an important feature is the consumption of meat together with rice cooked in coconut oil. The prime constituents of everyday food are, by contrast, steamed rice and fish. In other repects too, the *kenduri* can be seen as both an elaboration and a reversal of the symbolic imagery of the domestic meal. Briefly, the food is cooked outside houses by men, and it is consumed separately by groups of men, women and children; the individual, sexual ties between these groups have been negated.

Although the community can be seen as modelled on the house, it is also true that in many respects relations between houses in the wider neighbourhood contrast with those within them. Instead of a sharing of consumption, resources and labour, based on principles of hierarchy, houses in the wider community are involved in directly reciprocal exchanges which are conceived as occurring on an equal basis. Visits are conducted with varying degrees of formality: the most informal take place in the space between houses without the offer of food or drink; more formal ones occur inside houses and involve the consumption of snacks, that is a hot or cold drink and cake or biscuits, but never a full rice meal. Before leaving their own compound, women always cover their heads and may also put on better clothes. Marked imbalances are not easily tolerated in these visiting relations.

The various systems of labour exchange which occur in the wider locality of the village, and which are particularly important at rice harvesting, all operate on a direct and short-term reciprocal basis in which like is exchanged for like. The same principle is even more evident during the fasting month when houses of one locality exchange different types of cakes each evening. Since only a limited range of cakes are made, exactly the same ones may be swopped between houses.

It is, however, marriage that provides the most striking example of the conception of the village community as made up of houses exchanging on an equal basis. Ideal marriage partners are those who resemble each other in as many respects as possible. Appearance, wealth, status, educational attainments and personal characteristics should all be closely matched. There is a high degree of endogamy in Langkawi, but this operates as much through locality as kinship – in fact, as I have stressed, the distinction between these tends to be blurred. The important criterion is to marry 'close', *dekat*, a word which conflates geographic and genealogical proximity. The betrothal and marriage rituals involve a series of exchanges in which equal reciprocation is a prominent theme. This is most vividly lived out when the newly married couple engage in a series of stays in the two parental homes. Following a ritually prescribed sequence, in terms of both order and duration, known as *sambut-menyambut* (exchange), they alternate between the two parental homes in a precisely balanced manner. Until the birth of children they continue to spend periods of varying duration in both homes; this period of to-ing and fro-ing is referred to as *berulang* (literally, a repeated action).

The two sets of parents of a young couple have a relationship that is continually stressed. Co-parents-in-law, *bisan*, are involved in a constant series of exchanges which show a striking concern for balance: visits, labour, services, raw produce and cooked food are exchanged on an equal basis. A failure to observe obligations leads to acrimony which can easily put the marriage of their children at risk. Since these two couples are the respective heads of two households, such exchanges in fact tend to operate between houses rather than between specific individuals.

It is highly significant that many of the rights and duties of *bisan* focus on their common grandchildren. This is especially clear when the grandchildren fall sick and during the rituals surrounding childbirth. It is through the birth of grandchildren that people in Langkawi perceive the *bisan*, who represent two distinct households, actually to become kin if they were not so before. The birth of grandchildren creates kinship between grandparents – kinship in the past, and it unites houses in the present.

HOUSES TRANSFORMED

I have shown how the community is in one sense modelled on the house, and we can see a continuity between the house, the compound and the wider community, and yet the community seems at the same time to be based on principles which are opposed to those on which houses are based. However, we can resolve this paradox by seeing the house as part of a dynamic process. In their internal aspects houses represent sibling groups, undivided consumption and shared substance; relations are founded on the hierarchy of close kin, and they are dominated by women. In their external relations houses are conceived as equal units exchanging according to rules of balanced reciprocity which are epitomized in marriage and relations between co-parents-in-law. Here both women and men as married couples may be said to represent the house.

The internal and the external aspects of the house seem in many ways contradictory. But rather than seeing these as static and irreconcilable oppositions, I would argue that it always remains possible to move between these two aspects of the house and to transform one into the other.

Symbolically, this process of transformation can be represented as one of cooking and eating whose locus is the *dapur*, the very heart of the house. An important part of the food that women cook there is acquired by men in individualistic, commercial exchanges of fishing. Relations between men who fish together are spoken of in Langkawi in terms which strikingly resemble those in which marriage is discussed. That is, they are seen as fragile, tense and competitive.

It is in the *dapur* that women transform raw food to cooked, and this transformation is completed when it is eaten there and incorporated by household members. Women's labour ensures the reproduction of the household, and co-eating creates the shared substance, the kinship, of those who belong to one house. The *dapur* is associated with another act of transformation performed by women, that of affinity. I have described how the relation between co-parents-in-law focuses on the production of grandchildren: *bisan* become kin once they have grandchildren in common. Immediately after a couple begin to have sexual relations, they are actually described as 'cooked'. And, conversely, their eating together implies sex. At childbirth, when women are thought to lose heat, the heat of the *dapur* is applied directly to them – in the past through their 'cooking' over a fire, and today by means of a stone heated in the *dapur* which is applied to their stomachs.[10]

Thus in childbirth, women almost literally cook themselves in the *dapur* where they lie after giving birth. Affinity is dissolved into the production of children, and once again the image of this act of transformation is cooking and the heat of the *dapur*. In the light of this it may be significant that the complex rites of childbirth tend to be closely observed only for the first child – the one who establishes the consanguineal principle.

So far, I have suggested how a community of similar houses which exchange and intermarry on a basis which is ideally equal can be transformed into a single household founded on hierarchical consanguinity, and how the image of this transformation is domestic cooking and eating. However, this transformation can occur in the reverse direction, and this is precisely what happens at communal feasts. Here exactly the same imagery is used to create a community out of the household. In this case it is not simply an ordinary meal that is consumed by household members but a highly elaborate one consumed by those whose individual sexual ties have been negated. And this of course is necessary in order for the community to appear as founded on the household but also as a more powerful reality. The cooking, consumption and incorporation of *kenduri* food create the commonality of the community. Further, it is highly appropriate that these feasts are characteristically marriage feasts. For it is through individual marriages that the notion of a community of shared affines equally exchanging is lived out.

It is now possible to build up a picture of the two-way process of transformation (see table at top of page 122). We can now see why the idea of shared grandchildren has particular force. For it is these grandchildren that represents the culmination of the process of transformation in both directions: at once the product of affinity as it is cooked in the house, and also the result of household consanguinity as it dissolves into shared affinity in the community at large. And it is not incidental that one of the images projected at the *kenduri* is that of a community of shared grandchildren. Further, we can see how it is possible to achieve a representation of the community which is at once modelled on the house and at the same time based on principles which are opposed to it, and how co-villagers may be both kin with whom marriage carries connotations of incest as well as potential affines.

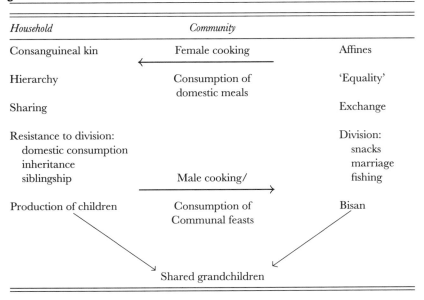

Household	*Community*	
Consanguineal kin	Female cooking ←	Affines
Hierarchy	Consumption of domestic meals	'Equality'
Sharing		Exchange
Resistance to division: domestic consumption inheritance siblingship	Male cooking/ →	Division: snacks marriage fishing
Production of children	Consumption of Communal feasts	Bisan
	Shared grandchildren	

UNITY AND DIFFERENCE IN THE SOUTHEAST ASIAN HOUSE

At this point it is worth placing Langkawi houses in a wider Southeast Asian context. Errington (1987; 1989) has provided a broad framework for the comparison of Southeast Asian societies in terms of their marriage systems, siblingship and houses. She draws a distinction between societies of 'Eastern Indonesia', which have assymetric alliance, and those of the 'Centrist Archipelago' which have cognatic kinship and endogamous marriage.[11] Following Lévi-Strauss (1963), she describes the former societies as underlain by a principle of 'concentric dualism' – that is, they cast a whole range of activities in dualistic forms. These societies have multiple houses with clear boundaries between them. In contrast, the societies of the Centrist Archipelago exhibit a strong centripetal tendency. Here

the 'Houses' or social groupings tend either to coincide with the whole society, and hence be wishfully complete and autonomous as in the Indic States, or to be centred on an Ego or set of full siblings and to stretch indefinitely from that center, with no clear boundaries.   (1987: 405)

What is illuminated by Errington is how these two forms, which seem very different, are in fact transformations of each other. Both principles – that of dualism and centrism – are present in Eastern Indonesia *and* in the Centrist Archipelago. In Eastern Indonesia the difference between brother and sister and their enforced separation at marriage ensures the whole system of exchange between houses. In the Centrist Archipelago cross-sex siblings epitomize unity and similarity. The hierarchical states conceive themselves in an image of encompassment and unity often envisaged in terms of siblingship. Unity, however, is threatened by the outside: the Centrist societies are shot through with dualism between 'us' and 'them'. As Errington puts it, 'Eastern Indonesia postulates unity but institutes fracture' (1987: 435), while the Centrist Archipelago 'institutionalises unity but is haunted by duality' (1987: 435). The fractured houses of Eastern Indonesia would disappear were marriage to be endogamous; while in the Centrist Archipelago, it is the incest taboo which prevents the whole system from collapsing in on itself.

At the beginning of this chapter I described how the house in Langkawi is not rigidly divided into different regions. Although the different parts of the house are on different levels, no great play is made of these. The association between above/below and superiority/inferiority is, however, clearly present in Malay culture. In Langkawi people are always careful not to seat themselves above those they are conversing with since this would constitute a breach of good manners. Similarly, some but by no means all houses are oriented on an east–west axis, however, ideas about orientation remain relatively unelaborated.

The Iban longhouse (Freeman 1970: 1–7), the traditional Minahasan house (Lundstrom-Burghoorn 1981: 28), or the Kelabit longhouse (Janowski this volume) seem at first rather different structures from the Malay house. They consist of rows of apartments leading off from a long gallery. Within these apartments the division of space seems to be rather minimal. Each apartment has its own hearth, *dapur*, and the Minahasa use this term to refer to the whole apartment. The Iban apartment consists of a single walled room, the *bilek*, with its own *dapur*, a section of the gallery and of the open platform which runs along the length of the longhouse. The centrality of the hearth is clear in all these cases. The rather simple division of space in the Langkawi, Iban, Kelabit and Minahasan cases can be contrasted with the assymetric alliance societies of Eastern Indonesia where differentiation of house space is highly elaborated.

The Purum house (Needham 1962: 87–96) is divided into two parts, *ningan* on the left and *phumlil* on the right (1962: 88). The *ningan* part is associated with affines, wife-takers, women, the inferior, the inauspicious, the west, and with death. The *phumlil* part is associated with kin, wife-givers, men, the superior, the auspicious, the east, and with life. These dualistic associations are clearly demonstrated in sleeping arrangements and in rituals associated with the house.

A similar series of divisions holds for Atoni houses (Cunningham 1964) in which orientation, right/left symbolism, as well as up/down and inside/outside, are all used to express difference. The areas which agnates, affines and guests may enter and sleep in are clearly defined. Cunningham notes that one of the striking features of the Atoni house is the continual division of space into halves, and the intersection of these divisions with units which are themselves halves of larger wholes. The house thus has inner and outer sections, and these are divided into right and left, back and front. Right and left are associated with male and female, and outer and inner areas. Wife-givers and wife-takers are also differentiated according to where they may sit in the house, and this seating pattern in turn expresses superiority and inferiority. Cunningham shows how

'order' (*atoran*) in the Atoni house expresses two simple, but pervasive, concerns – unity and difference – and their continual interpretation.
(1964: 64)[12]

House structure reflects in a complex way the social relations that are enacted within it. A comparison of the Langkawi, Minahasan, Kelabit and Iban houses with the Atoni, northern Thai and Purum, reveals significant if faint similarities which bear out Errington's insights. The themes of orientation, use of above/below symbolism, the centrality of women, play on the symbolism of the house in many life crisis rituals, all richly elaborated in the latter cases, are echoed in the former. In spite of these similarities, there is a more fundamental contrast between the two sets. If the house in all these cases is an expression and interpretation of unity/difference, the one set seems to be almost a reversal of the other. The Malay, Iban and Minahasan houses strongly emphasize unity. The Atoni and Purum cases, where spatial differentiation is greatly elaborated, stress difference.

If the conclusions of Needham (1962), Tambiah (1969) and others – that spatial classification shows homologies with sex and marriage rules – are put together with those of Errington, this contrast is not difficult to understand. Malay, Kelabit, Iban and Minahasan societies have cognatic kinship systems with a substantial degree of kin and/or local endogamy. They belong to what Errington calls the Centrist Archipelago. In these societies the distinctions between kin and affine, and kin and non-kin, tend to be blurred or ignored. They have a tendency to be 'inclusive' rather than 'exclusive' and to have an ideology of egalitarianism.[13] Exactly the reverse is true of the Atoni and Purum where descent groups and prescriptive marriage rules give a fundamental significance to distinctions between kin and non-kin, kin and affine, wife-givers and wife-takers.

Errington's observation that these two forms are in reality transformations of each other is born out when we look at the northern Thai houses described by Tambiah (1969) and Turton (1978). Turton (1978) shows the significance of the orientation of houses along an east–west axis, where west is associated with the setting sun, death and impurity, whilst the east is auspicious and pure. Sleeping arrangements reflect these ideas. Turton reports that a son-in-law must not enter the sleeping area of his parents-in-law, and the male household head sleeps to the north of his wife and other couples, and children further south. No married couple can sleep together in a house if they are of a different descent group to that of the householder.

Although both Turton and Tambiah describe societies which in many respects conform to the centrist model, both have hierarchical rather than egalitarian forms of social organization. Further, the Thai-Yuan described by Turton have endogamous matrilineal descent groups (see Turton 1972). In both cases the symbolism of spatial differentiation is more elaborated than in the Minahasan, Langkawi, Iban or Kelabit house. I would suggest that we might view these two cases as centrist societies in which dualistic principles are particularly evident.

CONCLUSION: THE HOUSE-BASED SOCIETY IN LANGKAWI

It is clear that there is a great divergence between the ethnography of Langkawi and the model proposed by Lévi-Strauss for the 'house-based society'. This divergence can in part be attributed to Lévi-Strauss's conflation of two types of social organisation in Southeast Asia. Lévi-Strauss (1987: 153) begins his discussion by referring to the cognatic societies of Indonesia, citing material from the Iban, the Rungus and the Bajau Laut of Borneo (1987: 154–5). As Howell and Gibson both note in this volume, he then turns to the Atoni of Timor and the Karo Batak of Sumatra (1987: 156–8) both of which may be characterized as Eastern Indonesian societies with assymetric alliance. In spite of his starting point – the nature of social organization in cognatic societies – many of the attributes of 'house-based societies' seem to apply rather better to the Eastern Indonesian examples than they do to the societies of the Centrist Archipelago of which Langkawi is one example.

Lévi-Strauss emphasizes the importance of the downward perpetuation of the house through descent and inheritance. In Langkawi, however, houses are often mobile and impermanent structures, and what is important is their *lateral* continuity. This process is materialized when new houses are established which ensure the expansion of the compound, neighbourhood and village. The material reproduction of the village is paralleled in the process of sibling group expansion: each process implies the other. Descent is less significant than lateral extensions through siblingship: it is in these terms that the reproduction of the community is envisaged.[14]

While it is true that relations *within* the house operate on a hierarchical basis in Langkawi, it is clear that, in contrast to the model proposed by Lévi-Strauss, in their external relations houses are not conceived in a hierarchical ordering but as equally exchanging units. This is evident in reciprocal visiting and labour arrangements and in marital exchanges. Marriage takes place between equals; the ideal union is one that is 'close'; the distinction between wife-givers and wife-takers, emphasized by Lévi-Strauss, is elided.

Perhaps the most suggestive part of Lévi-Strauss's argument for the material I have presented is his discussion of alliance. His points that in these societies alliance and descent are equally important and mutually substitutable, that alliance constitutes a principle both of unity *and* of conflict, and that this conflict is manifested over the question of residence of the newly married couple, are all highly pertinent (see also Bloch this volume). In Langkawi the tension over where a couple will live is vividly demonstrated in the marriage ritual itself when the couple oscillates between the two houses of their parents. Villagers always emphasize that the locality of residence of a betrothed couple is uncertain and unpredictable – neither the bride's nor the groom's family can be acknowledged to have prior rights. Even after their marriage a young couple remain mobile until they have had children.

Lévi-Strauss has argued that in 'house-based societies' the house resolves the conflict created by marriage by uniting a number of opposing principles: wife-givers/wife-takers, patrilineal/matrilineal descent, hypergamy/hypogamy, close/distant marriage, descent/alliance. In Langkawi while the tension of alliance is clearly evident in exactly the terms described by Lévi-Strauss, the house cannot be said to unite these opposing principles. Notions about kinship and community involve a complex elision of such oppositions: they become more or less irrelevant where marriage occurs *by definition* between those who are 'close', where the lateral extension of sibling-ship is more important than descent, and where continuity is ensured by including and incorporating people through their perceived similarity, rather than separating them out according to their differences.

I have shown how houses in Langkawi manifest these inclusive tendencies: space tends to be unified rather than differentiated; shared substance is created by co-eating. I have also described how the unity of the house is intimately connected to that of the sibling group. However, there is a tension between alliance and siblingship and a tendency to exclude affinal relations from the house. Rather than resolving an opposition between affinity and siblingship, the house in Langkawi seems only to succeed in subordinating one principle to the other depending on the context.

I have argued that houses in Langkawi do not fuse opposing categories so much as manifest them with all their contradictions. The internal and the external aspects of the house that I have described are based on opposing principles but it always remains possible to move from one to the other, to pass from the inside to the outside. Indeed this is necessarily the case where the community is both perceived in terms of the house and asserts itself as a reality of a different order. It is in this respect that the core of the house, the *dapur*, takes on a symbolic as well as a practical significance as the site of this transformative process. Both feeding and the production of children, in other words the creation of kinship, may be said to occur inside houses as well as between them.

The paradox of a stress on the house in some contexts and its negation in others can be explained if not resolved. An emphasis on the integrity of the house and a simultaneous possibility for breaking this down is central to notions of kinship and the construction of community in Langkawi, and also fits into the general Southeast Asian pattern elucidated by Errington. The house which is so central to social reality in Langkawi is part of a system of relations, a dynamic process. It actively participates in a process of transformation between different aspects of this social reality.[15] In this sense houses in Langkawi may be considered partly as stable structures, partly as mobile homes, without ever quite being either.

HAVING YOUR HOUSE AND EATING IT: HOUSES AND SIBLINGS IN ARA, SOUTH SULAWESI

6

Thomas Gibson

Lévi-strauss sees the 'house' as a solution to the problems of societies where 'political and economic interests' have not yet 'overstepped the old ties of blood', in other words where class divisions must still be represented in a pre-class ideology of shared descent and alliance. He sees the house concept as having special relevance in the context of Indonesia. However, in Indonesia, we find houses playing a key symbolic role in a whole range of social forms, from self-sufficient, egalitarian tribes, to maritime empires, to oriental despotisms. Societies at all these levels make use of the house as a symbolic device to represent social groups. I will argue here that Lévi-Strauss's concept of the 'house' cannot be applied in a straightforward way to the Indonesian societies characterized by Errington as 'centrist' (Errington 1989). This is because an idiom of siblingship, linked to an idiom of shared place, is far more important in organizing social life than are alliance and descent, the idioms to which Lévi-Strauss gives prominence.

In another sense, however, Lévi-Strauss's concept does have great relevance for some societies in Indonesia in which competition for wealth and power among the upper strata is intense but has not led to stable class divisions. These societies do make use of the house in a manner highly reminiscent of Lévi-Strauss's European, Japanese and Kwakiutl examples. It is this dual nature of the 'problems' to which the house is a 'solution' that makes the application of Lévi-Strauss's theory to feudal Indonesia so fascinating and so complex. Because of limitations of space, I will not be able to do justice to this second aspect of the problem. The rest of this chapter will be devoted to demonstrating the fact that the house is solving a different problem in 'centrist' Indonesia than in feudal Europe or Japan.

For Lévi-Strauss, the paradigmatic kinship system is one based on the idioms of filiation and alliance. In his early writings on kinship, he argued that classless, segmentary societies (Durkheim's 'mechanical solidarity') are integrated primarily through the exchange of women in marriage. Where 'positive marriage rules' are in operation (elementary structures), marriage alliance serves as part of the enduring structure of the society. In kin-based societies where 'negative marriage rules' alone are in operation, alliance may appear to generate only an 'individu-ating web of complementary filiation' within each descent group, and descent alone may structure the 'politico-jural domain'. In societies based on both 'alliance' and 'descent', filiation is the key idiom around which social structure is articulated.

A second important feature of classless, segmentary societies for Lévi-Strauss is that, while they suffer historical change, they reject it ideologically. They prefer to relate the present to a changeless originary past through myth. Modern societies, by contrast, valorize change, and relate the present to an ever-changing past through historical narrative. The difference between 'hot' and 'cold' societies is not so much one between a dynamic and a static *present*, but between a mutable and an immutable *past*. 'Hot' societies are based on an internal division into competing classes and interest groups which generate change internally. While a certain degree of social integration is still produced through the exchange of women ('complex structures'), an increasing degree is achieved through the exchange of material goods. Lévi-Strauss has at times explicitly linked this contrast to that made by Durkheim between 'mechanical' and 'organic' solidarity. Lévi-Strauss introduced the concept of the 'house' to help analyze societies he sees as making a transition from kin-based to class-based social orders. His definitions of 'house-based societies' have been discussed in the introduction to this volume and need not be repeated here.

It is highly significant that where Lévi-Strauss does refer to Indonesia, he devotes very little space to the 'bilateral' societies of the Philippines, Sulawesi, Borneo and Java. Unable to conceive of an alternative set of metaphors to those of filiation and alliance, Lévi-Strauss claims that:

in Borneo as in Java the conjugal couple constitutes the true kernel of the family, and, more generally, of the kindred. Moreover, this central role of alliance manifests itself in two ways: as a principle of unity, underpinning a type of social structure which, since last year, we have agreed to call the 'house', and as a principle of antagonism because, in the cases considered, each new alliance generates a tension between families on the subject of the residence – viri- or uxorilocal – of the new couple, and therefore of that of the two families which it is the couple's duty to perpetuate.

(Lévi-Strauss 1987: 155)

He then quickly passes on to a discussion of the Atoni of Timor and the Karo Batak of Sumatra, both of which are on the Indonesian periphery, and both of which operate more familiar unilineal systems with positive marriage rules. Errington has recently argued that they are structured by a principle of dualism, while the societies of the Philippines, Java, Bali and Sulawesi are structured by a metaphor of centre and periphery, or 'centrism' (Errington 1989: 208). Here I wish to argue that this spatial metaphor is everywhere rooted in the house as fundamental social unit, and articulated with the image of a set of coresident childhood siblings.

It has long been recognized that one of the consequences of 'bilateral descent' is that genealogical 'rules' do not unambiguously allocate individuals to discrete units which may then be linked by the exchange of women. All social relationships tend to be assimilated to kin relations, so that one is either a kinsman or a stranger, with no room left over for 'affines'. There is a tendency toward the endogamy of a localized group, and differences in origin between husband and wife are played down. The kin group tends to merge with the local group and with the in-marrying group. I would argue that Murdock's notion of the deme as a localized, endogamous, bilateral descent group constitutes only a limit case for most of these societies: in-marriage and localization are only tendencies within these systems and in practice there has always been a great deal of movement and even long-distance migration in these societies, as the distribution of the Malagasy and Easter Islanders attests.

This poses a set of symbolic problems quite foreign to societies organized in terms of exogamous unilineal descent groups, where concepts of place need not enter into the jural definition of corporate groupings (although residence may play a large role in practice). Shared place is of the essence to group identity of whatever scale in the 'centrist systems' of Austronesia, and it is the house as both residence and architectural construct that tends to take on the central role as symbol of social groups, ranging in scale from the nuclear family to the kingdom. A more problematic symbolic feature of these societies relates to incest. In a sense, a man always marries a kinswoman, and incest is always a matter of degree (cf. Conklin 1964; Bloch 1971). A recurrent ideological problem is how to open up a degree of difference between potential spouses sufficient to avoid the feeling of incest, without creating a permanent category of non-kinsmen. One solution is to stress sexual difference in the early years of courtship and marriage, but to see marriage itself as a process in which there is a progressive transformation of affines into kin, or more narrowly, of spouses into siblings. This transformation can be effected through a 'downward focus' on the offspring of a marriage through devices such as teknonymy (Geertz and Geertz 1975), the relation between co-parents-in-law as stabilized through shared grandchildren (Carsten this volume), or, as in the case in hand in the village of Ara, through a series of rituals designed to shift attention from the elder to the younger generation in a household, and to promote the image of the co-resident sibling set as the central image of sociality (cf. McKinley 1981; Boon 1977).

Instead of dealing with a dialectic of descent and alliance between discrete social units, then, one is dealing with a dialectic of unity and division within a nested set of encompassing socio-spatial units. The concept of 'bilateral descent' is highly misleading since it focuses attention on ties of filiation, when in fact the whole system is geared toward siblingship and shared place. It follows that the 'house' is 'solving' a different kind of problem in the symbolic systems of 'centrist Indonesia' than in the feudal systems discussed by Lévi-Strauss.

RITUAL IN ARA

In the remainder of this chapter, I propose to follow the course of the ritual cycle in Ara, a Makassarese village in South Sulawesi, Indonesia.[1] The people of Ara seem to be engaged in a never-ending round of ritual activities, an impression which is due in part to the fact that in recent times a good deal of practical economic activity has been carried out away from the village by men on temporary labour migration to build boats on distant islands. Even the ones who have taken their families with them tend to return to Ara to conduct the major life-cycle rituals of circumcision, marriage and burial. A key element in almost all such rituals is the preparation and momentary display of elaborate offerings of food, notable for the careful attention paid to colour and composition. The main ingredients are ordinary rice, and glutinous rice which comes in black, red, yellow and white varieties. Rice may be displayed in cooked or raw form, along with meat and eggs, palm sugar, coconuts, bananas, benzoin incense and the constituents of betel chews: tobacco, betel leaf, areca nut, gambir powder and lime. Such displays are called *a'patala*, the word used to describe the laying of a table for a meal. In this chapter, I will spare you the tedium of listing the ingredients for each and every ritual.

One magician explained to me that these offerings are intended as physical bodies in which the spirits can materialize, since they are composed of the same elements as human bodies. Thus the assembly of red, black and white rice and yellow curry represents the four elements of fire, earth, water and air, while the eggs placed on top of the mounds of rice represent the 'eggs' found within the human body that are the loci of human spirit. The trays of coconuts and bananas which are often placed beside the rice offerings are likewise tied to the human body, in that they represent ribs and the breasts. I never got direct confirmation of this interpretation from a female medium, although they listened to it with keen attention when I repeated it to them.

As a general rule, the female mediums emphasize material symbols, while male magicians emphasize linguistic incantations and exegesis. But as we shall see, even among the mediums, many ritual techniques are explicitly oriented to the embodiment and transfer of spiritual entities from one vessel to another. Ritual practice as a whole is a dialectic of container and contained, form and content, material symbol and linguistic incantation. This dialectic has been given a great deal of explicit theoretical discussion in the Sufi tradition, much of it going back to Greek neo-Platonic sources as filtered through Ibnul Arabi and others. In the local Indonesian version of this tradition, the visible world is seen as but the seventh in a series of emanations from the Godhead. But it is a more general dialectic that has been addressed in many other intellectual traditions. Many of the rituals and doctrines discussed in this chapter bear a remarkable similarity to those of more obviously Hindu-Buddhist derivation found in Java and Bali (cf. Headley 1987a).

In the next sections, I shall describe the rituals surrounding the creation of the human body and its associated soul, the creation of the house and its associated spirits and household members, and the creation of the village realm and its associated royal ancestors and deme members.

THE SELF

Marriage and the generation of vitality

I begin with the rituals surrounding marriage since they provide the most extreme statement of social difference in the cycle, a difference which is progressively covered over and denied by subsequent rituals. The differences are of three kinds: kinship, gender and social rank. Due to lack of space, I shall have to leave the issue of social rank aside except for a few brief remarks at the end.

As I mentioned in the introduction, the logic of much of the symbolic system points toward marriage with a close kinsman. In myth, the typical form of incest is that between opposite-sex twins who shared a womb and feel desire for one another because of the remembrance of a lost unity. In ritual, a brother–sister pair is systematically substituted for a husband–wife pair whenever images of solidarity or continuity are required. Since sibling marriage is prohibited by shariah law, the next best option is first-cousin marriage.

The point is that marriage is regarded as being a tie established within the group, not between groups. Nevertheless, a certain difference must be established between a prospective bride and groom in the prelude to their wedding. They must practise avoidance after the formal betrothal, and differences between the hard, erect qualities of male bodies and the soft, encompassing qualities of female bodies, as well as a certain antagonism between them, are symbolically played up.

Before consummation, a mock combat is staged between the bride and groom, in which the separation that has hitherto been enforced between them is violently overcome by the groom. The bride wraps her head and body like a mummy in a cloth and hides in the attic. The groom has to penetrate this most private section of the house, seize her, carry her downstairs, uncover her face and wash it with water. He then holds her tight while a rattan rope is passed around them. The final public ritual involves them mutually feeding one another. The groom first makes a ball of cooked rice and attempts to place it in the bride's mouth. Again she is supposed to struggle and refuse it out of shame. The bride then feeds the groom. The contest continues later in private, as the groom must correctly answer a series of riddles before being allowed to consummate the marriage. The sexual tension generated by these practices is great, and the end result of them is the overcoming of difference and the generation of new life.[2]

On the third day after the wedding, women from the bride's family distribute sarongs she has woven to the male siblings and cousins of the groom's parents. Later the bride goes to eat a meal in each of these houses, thus literally incorporating their food into her bodily substance. Subsequently, on the feast of Id and Maulid, the bride must take a complete meal of cooked food to all the siblings and cousins of her parents-in-law, particularly those of the men who received sarongs. They thus incorporate her food into their bodily substance. After a few years, their substance has so fused that she can be regarded more as a niece than as an affine. By this time one or more children will also have been born, linking the two sides by kinship in both the ascending generations, assuming the bride and groom were cousins, and the descending generations, through shared grandchildren, nieces and nephews.

Childbirth and the Seven Siblings

The Indonesian word for birth, *lahir*, is derived from the Arabic *zahir*, external form or manifestation. Birth is in fact considered to be the embodiment of a previously created soul. Birth magic to 'open' the mother's body during childbirth, and then to close it back up afterward, is one of the two forms of magic most sought by magicians when they go to meditate on top of graves. The other is invulnerability magic, which has the opposite objective of closing male bodies to hostile penetration. While male magicians are not actually present at births, they often sit in an adjoining room and give advice or make spells over medicines.

According to one of my most articulate informants, Hama, Seven (Spiritual) Siblings come into existence at a person's birth, each embodied in a different physical substance, as follows:

Ere inong, 'drinking water'. This is the amniotic fluid that bursts from a woman when she goes into labour. It is the first sibling to emerge, although it is not regarded as the eldest. It is the origin of the *nyaha*, spirit, breath or life force of the person. When it emerges it rises upwards, like water evaporating, and enters the attic of the house. It then descends again, like water precipitating, and enters the baby after its body emerges, causing it to begin breathing.

Muhammad. This was Hama's term for the body itself. The Prophet Muhammad is often taken as the paradigmatic human being, who represents the most perfect and complete human. In ritual contexts, all mankind can be included under his name. The body of the child already possesses an *alusu*, 'ethereal aspect', before it is born, but receives the *nyaha* mentioned above, only after birth.

Ari ari, 'placenta'. Although this emerges last at the time of birth, it is referred to as the baby's elder sibling. Traditionally, it was placed inside a coconut and stored in the attic of the house. Now, it is placed in a coconut and buried under a sprouted coconut near the house. The *ari ari* is a companion to the child in its early months. When a child who cannot yet focus its eyes is seen to smile to itself, it is said that it is looking at this elder sibling. Later on in life, certain illnesses can also be treated with the aid of this *ari ari*. According to Hama, the *nyaha* is continually moving back and forth between the *ari ari* and the body. When one goes to sleep, the *nyaha* ascends again to the *ari ari* stored in the attic, just as it ascended at birth, and descends again to enter the body when one wakes up.

There are four more birth siblings which appear to have less subsequent ritual importance: *lai*, the umbilical cord; *rara*, blood; *bohon*, the caul; and *daging*, flesh. As we shall see, each of these Seven Siblings is also brought into correspondence with some part of the house.

The bloodied banana leaf on which the child was born is folded up and placed in a bamboo pole with a basket at one end called a *tompong*. Not everyone was traditionally permitted to erect a *tompong*. In general, only the nobles were allowed to make use of bamboo constructions in life-cycle rituals, such as birth, marriage and death. The *tompong* is planted in the ground beneath the house with its 'mouth' open to the sky. It is thus able to catch the *dalle*, 'good fortune', that descends from heaven. Various other leaves are placed in it along with the birth leaf. Each leaf has a specific meaning and purpose. The mixture of the baby's blood with the medicinal leaves also serves to protect the baby from evil influences while it is in the extremely vulnerable condition of having an unhealed navel and soft fontanelle.

The *tompong* is left under the house for seven days, by which time the child's navel is healed and the next ritual can be performed. During this time, the child must remain in the house, and the mother is not supposed to leave it either, for fear her 'open' state may attract evil spirits to enter her which she would then bring back with her into the house. During these seven days, the midwife (also a kind of *sanro*) continually massages the mother's stomach with hot water to close her womb back up.

Between the third and seventh day after birth, after the infant's umbilicus has fallen off, a ritual is held to seal the infant's fontanelle and navel with herbal medicines rendering them more resistant to penetration by spirits. It also marks the release of the mother from a number of restrictions, including the prohibition on leaving the house. The first step is to invite a local Imam to come and recite Arabic prayers. Then the *sanro* who acted as midwife for the child's birth takes over. She applies the herbal medicine to the navel and fontanelle of the child, and to the stomach of the mother. When the *sanro* is finished, a number of other women invited for the purpose will also take turns applying medicine to mother and child. Then trays containing different substances are passed around the child seven times. Hama linked this to the ritual circumambulation of the Ka'bah in Mecca during the pilgrimage.

Death and the ancestors

During life, the *nyaha* enters and leaves the body during sleep, and especially during dreams. When a person dies, the *nyaha* leaves the body for the last time, rises into the air and disperses like mist, recalling its connection to water vapour at birth. Two aspects of the self do survive death, the *anja* and *alusu*. The first sign of the continuing existence of the dead is the possession of a near relative by the *anja*, or ghost, during the period when the individual identity of the dead person is still clearly remembered. This ghost makes demands through the possessed relative for offerings, such as its favourite cakes. It must be appeased and sent away again. The second step is the return of the *alusu*, 'subtle essence', of ancestors so long dead they have become anonymous, and their specific genealogical relationship to the living has been obscured. Unlike the dyadic relationship between a specific ghost and a living individual in possession, the relationship between an *alusu* and the members of a household is one of generalized, anonymous ancestor to an undifferentiated group of co-resident descendants. The co-residence of the descendants is crucial, for the ancestral spirit is installed in a shrine (*palangka*) located in the attic of a house. For the most part, in-married spouses are considered its descendants as well, given the preference for first- and second-cousin marriage. In some cases an in-marrying spouse may bring a *palangka* with them and install it side by side with the existing one. Thus the place of the ancestral/attic spirit must be located within the symbolic structure of the house as a whole.

The *alusu* announce their request for a *palangka* in which to stay by afflicting one of their descendants. Once installed, the spirit must be fed regularly with 'complete offerings' of rice, meat and betel ingredients. Because of the anonymity of the spirits, it is the shrine itself which begins to acquire a reputation, and the most powerful tend to accumulate many narratives about the miraculous events they have caused. Most *palangka* were destroyed by the village chief as un-Islamic in the 1930s. But he seems to have missed many of the most powerful *palangka* of the noble families. The *palangka* of the mediums also seem to have survived. Before this campaign, *palangka* spirits played quite an active role in community affairs, bothering some people and helping others. One could be afflicted by a *palangka* spirit in someone else's house, and be told by a *sanro* to go make an offering there. *Palangka* spirits were also of quite unequal power, some having a great reputation for working cures through their mediums. There was a fairly close correlation between their power and the rank of their owners, so that the *palangka* of the hereditary ruler of Ara was the most powerful of all (Plate 4).

Plate 4   'Having your house and eating it.' The house of Gallarrang Daeng Makkilo, the last hereditary ruler of Ara, who died in 1913. Note the four posts across the facade, the greatest number to which a noble with the rank of *gallarrang* was entitled. From front to back, the house is in four sections, with the last two sections built at higher levels. The highest section is the sleeping quarters of unmarried women.

THE HOUSE
The 'birth' of a house

Houses are constructed under the supervision of a ritual specialist called an *oragi*. The *oragi* must first of all be an expert in the properties of wood, both material and magical. He talks to the tree spirits before cutting the trees down to make sure they are willing to be made into a house. The *oragi* determines which posts should go in which part of the house by reading the whorls in the grain at the points where the branches were cut off. The most dangerous problem is the presence of bark that has been sealed up inside the wood in the form of an overgrown knot hole. This can cause illness in the future inhabitants of the house. All such holes must be located and chiselled out. The *oragi* must also make sure that all the posts and beams in the house are oriented in the right direction. That is, the end of the post or beam which was closest to the earth when it was growing in the tree must be closest to the earth, to the front, and to the 'foot' of the house.

When beginning a new house, the *oragi* must make the first cut in the post destined to be the male post. The first shaving is carefully saved and placed in a bottle of 'house oil', *minyak bola*, which is put away in the attic in the same manner as the afterbirth of a child (or the first shaving from the keel of a ship). When all the materials for raising the house have been assembled, and all the helpers have arrived, a ritual called simply *ja'ja'kang*, 'making an offering', is performed by an *oragi* or a *sanro* knowledgeable in such matters. The object is to fill the new house with *nyaha*, life force. It is said that every human construction like a house or a boat has a spirit of its own, called a *balapati*. Normally, this spirit cannot be seen, but occasionally it materializes (*a'talle*) as a small, shiny brown lizard with stripes down its back, about the size of a pen. One old man said that it is the job of the *oragi* to see that the *balapati* is introduced into a new house and remains contented within it thereafter. It has no parents, but is created by the *oragi* in the same way that the *nyaha* of humans is created and placed in our bodies by Allah, and does not derive from the parents of one's physical body. He said that the precise moment of the *balapati*'s entrance is when the beam that runs through the male and female posts from front to back goes through the central hole in the male post. The erection of a house is thus closely analogous to the birth of a child. (The same is true of the launching of a new boat.)

When a new house is to be erected, the *oragi* first lays out the usual range of coloured rice, bananas and other materials on a mat in the centre of where the house will stand. He recites a *mantera* over them, and they are packed up again for him to take home. Everything is now ready for the erection of the first house posts. I must digress a bit from the ritual to examine the significance of these posts. Two of the house posts are of the greatest symbolic significance. The *benteng polong* stands half way between the front and the back of the house, and is considered to be male. The *benteng bigasa* is the post immediately 'behind' it, and is female. One explanation of the meaning of *polong*, 'to cut', comes from the fact that traditionally the two posts would have been obtained from a single forked tree. The *bigasa* would be cut off above the fork, while the *polong* would include the other fork and the common trunk. Thus the *polong* typically had a strange curving shape, with a crotch in the middle where the two forks had come together. A hole would be drilled in this crotch to form the navel of the house, called the *talongko*, and various medicines called *bassiwaja* placed in it. Only some of the oldest houses still show evidence of this.

Marriage in Ara is uxorilocal and houses are always inherited by the eldest daughter. The owner of the house and her husband sleep in the area defined by the *bigasa, polong* and the two posts immediately to the west of them. The wife sleeps nearer the female *bigasa* and the husband nearer the male *polong*. Because of this, I originally thought the two posts were meant to be like a husband and wife. Indeed, I was told that this was the case by one *sanro*. But this turned out to be an unusual opinion: the *polong* is more often seen as an elder brother, and the *bigasa* as a younger sister. When I suggested the two poles were like husband and wife, another *sanro* commented sharply that they are *salimara*, too closely related to marry. The two posts traditionally came from the same 'body', or trunk, in much the same way that Eve was taken from the body of Adam.

Another explanation of the term *polong* is that it is derived from the Selayarese word for sibling, *polo*, associating it with siblingship in this way. Husband and wife often address one another as elder sibling/ younger sibling. Thus the husband/wife relationship tends to be assimilated to the elder/younger sibling relationship, rather than the other way around. We have already encountered this tendency to encompass difference and hierarchy within the elder/younger sibling relationship when I discussed the connection between the ancestral *palangka* and the placenta spirit. There will be further evidence of it below in the discussion of the *a'jaga a'kahajuang* ritual.

To return to the ritual creation of a new house, before the posts are actually put up, a bit of steel is buried under the pot where the male post will stand, along with red, white, black and yellow uncooked rice, a raw egg, a cooked egg and a bamboo shoot. The tier containing the male post is the first to be erected, following by the tier with the female post. The central posts should be erected on top of silver trays.

Before they are raised, a sarong appropriate to their gender is wrapped around each central post. Hama said that the two poles together formed the body of the house, an analogue to the human body, and the sarongs were like the *bohon*, caul, that is wrapped around the head of a newborn child. Various other ritual materials are hung on these posts at the same time, including coconuts, bananas

141

and palm sugar. After several weeks, these are taken down and cooked into cakes, to be eaten by the household members.

Once the posts have all been erected, a temporary platform is constructed around the central posts, and a rough shelter is built on it. The owner and his family must sleep here in exposed conditions for three nights, *a'dingindingin*, 'shivering', in order to *appasiama*, accustom themselves, to the new dwelling. The house will not be truly broken in, however, until the *a'jaga a'kahajuang* described below is performed. This may be years later.

Feeding the house spirits

While only male *oragi* have both the technical and ritual knowledge required to create a new house, many female *sanro* know how to look after the spirits of established houses. I got information about the *a'pakanre balapati*, 'feeding the house spirits', ritual from four separate specialists, and present a composite account here.

The ritual itself falls into two parts. In the first part, a set of offerings is prepared on a Thursday or Sunday night, and placed at various points within the house: where the male and female posts meet the floor, and in the attic. In the second part, often performed the following morning, a second set of offerings is prepared, and placed beneath the house at the base of the male, female and four corner posts, and in the earth in a hole dug in the centre of the house.

The first part of the ritual, conducted inside the house, involves the placing of offerings at the base of the male and female house posts inside the house, and in the attic. All these offerings consist of the same elements (rice, egg, banana, coconuts and betel leaves), which make up a complete ritual 'body' that can serve as a receptacle for spirit. They are opposed to one another only on a numerical axis, containing nine, eight and six mounds of rice, respectively. In the case of the male and female house posts, these numbers signify male (odd) and female (even). In the case of the attic offering, the rice is composed of an even set, but the bananas and coconuts of an odd set, indicating neutral or ambiguous gender.

The second part of the ritual is conducted underneath the house. It involves placing offerings at the base of the four corner posts, at the base of the male and female posts, and in a hole dug in the ground at the centre of the house. These seven offerings are all composed of the same materials, and are contrasted on a numerical axis and on a cooked/raw axis. In the centre are the three offerings for the two centre posts and for burial. Each has five sets of betel ingredients. On the periphery are the offerings for the four corner posts. Each has three sets of betel ingredients.

Next, the three central offerings beneath the house may be contrasted. As among the two central post offerings, there is an opposition between cooked (male) and raw (female). Otherwise, they and the buried offering are of identical composition, except that additional 'living' materials are placed in the earth: a coconut inflorescence, green bananas and, above all, a 'live' chick and sprouted coconut. One might say then that there is a three-way opposition between living (earth), raw (female) and cooked (male), representing different degrees of transformation of the materials from 'nature' to 'culture'.

Finally, one can contrast the offerings as central and peripheral on a vertical axis. The attic and base offerings are associated in that both contain three mounds of white and three mounds of black rice and betel leaves. They are opposed in that the betel leaves in the attic offering are folded 'standing', *kalomping*, while those at the base are folded 'sitting', *deppo*. The attic offering is further associated with the buried offering in that both are unitary and undifferentiated, while the two central offerings within and beneath the house are differentiated according to gender (odd/even, cooked/raw).

Going from top to bottom, then, there is a single offering in the attic which is unitary and undifferentiated, there are two offerings in the middle which are opposed on a gender axis, there are six offerings at the bottom which are opposed as centre and periphery, and there is a final, unitary offering beneath the earth.

This structure mirrors in some ways the view of the generations reflected in the kinship terminology. The kinship terminology recognizes gender difference only in the own and first ascending generations. It only distinguishes lineal from collateral kin in the immediately ascending and descending generations. Beyond this core, all ascendants and descendants within the bilateral descent group are merged into the undifferentiated categories of *bohe*, 'ancestor' and *ampu*, 'descendant'. The combined effect of the terminology and ritual systems is thus to transform gender difference from the point of greatest contrast and opposition at marriage to one of siblingship and, with the birth of grandchildren, unity. This transformation is brought about in part by mapping each individual and the household as a whole onto the house as a material symbol.

Completing the house/household

A'jaga a'kahajuang, 'performing a protective ritual'

This is a large-scale ritual with many components which represents a sort of culmination and synthesis of the human, house and household rituals discussed earlier in this paper. The term *a'jaga a'kahajuang* refers to a whole complex of rituals performed one after the other. Minimally, it involves the sacrifice of a buffalo, which can be used then for several different purposes. At one level, the *a'jaga* serves as a step in the initiation of children into religion, since it is always accompanied by a ritual cutting of the children's hair by three village Imam and, very often, the children are circumcised as well. Ritual expressions of devotion to the Prophet Muhammad through the reading of his *Life* by al-Barzanji, and to the local Saint by laying offerings on his grave are also usual.

At a second level, and more significantly for the purposes of this paper, the ritual marks a crucial stage in the transformation of affinity into kinship, since it contains several crucial conflations of spouses with siblings. In order to perform this ritual, the heads of a household must have at least one child of each sex and one additional child, i.e. a 'completed' sibling set containing all the relevant structural oppositions (male/female, elder/middle/younger) (see McKinley 1981). The children are often dressed in the costumes of a bride and groom. In this way a sibling set is ritually substituted for a married couple as the source of household fertility and completion. Further, this ritual repeats in part another ritual known as *a'jaga bunting*, 'wedding protection', which is held at the end of a wedding if there are still enough resources left to sacrifice another buffalo.

By recapitulating the linking of the married couple to the house, the *a'jaga a'kahajuang* celebrates the successful outcome of a marriage. The bodily union of a husband and wife constructs a material vessel into which Allah can place the soul he has created.

By producing a child, they become kin to one another and as members of the same house/household address one another with sibling terms. But the household is not complete until they really have produced a full sibling set, which ideally consists of the three relevant sibling positions: elder brother/elder sister/younger sibling. It is these three children who are the focus of the ritual which completes the construction of a house/household. In this ritual, the house is circled seven times, just as a newborn baby is circled seven times when its apertures are sealed. The successful raising of three children thus serves both to reproduce the household with an increment and definitively to transform marriage/affinity into siblingship/kinship.

At a third level, the ritual marks a stage in the 'initiation' of a new house, since it is the primary occasion for the ritual circumambulation (*a'ngale*) every house must undergo at least once to protect its resident spirit. An activity peculiar to this ritual (and to the one held at the end of a wedding) is the ritual circling of the house by the family, *a'ngale*. All the members of the family are supposed to hold onto a special heirloom sash while they circumambulate the house seven times in an anti-clockwise direction. According to Hama, this protects the spirits (*nyaha*) of both the children and the house. It need only be carried out once for each house, indicating that the house itself is the main focus of this phase of the ritual. This recalls the ritual circling of the newborn child in the *a'tompolo*, marking the 'closure' of a house which has obtained self-sufficiency through the internal generation of a complete sibling set/household, just as the child is 'closed' when its navel and fontanelle are medicated.

The ritual thus plays on the ambiguity of householders, houses and house spirits at many levels. Hama explicitly linked the three children in the ritual to the house posts, saying that the male child corresponded to the male post, the female child to the female post, and the third child to the peripheral posts, indicating the sort of male/female, centre/periphery oppositions we saw in the last section on house ritual.

Conclusions

The ultimate ideological effect of the ritual cycle I have been discussing in this chapter is to transform duality into unity, to take a young man and a young woman from separate houses/households and unite them. If there is a master symbol in all of this besides the house itself, it is that of siblingship. In the following schematic representation of this material, note that there is no room in this scheme for the sexually active married couple, and no room for the two most common forms of magic: invulnerability magic for young men which aims at closing their bodies to danger when they roam beyond the limits of the realm, and childbirth magic for young women which aims at opening their bodies to fertilization and the emergence of children while they are safely protected within the realm. Ideologically, the ritual system represents society as made up of self-contained, consanguinous households.

In summary, the mapping of alliance, descent and the human body onto the house and siblingship shows that the central concern in this ritual system is with the construction of a certain kind of social order. Society is seen as a series of nested, relatively self-contained units which reproduce themselves without needing to exchange with other units. The basic unit is the human self, which is differentiated from birth into a set of spiritual 'siblings'. This self is easily expandable into a household self conceived as a unit differentiated into sets of 'siblings' of successive generations. And while household members cannot, in fact, marry one another, deme members can. The deme itself can be thought of as a unit internally differentiated as a maximal sibling group of elders and juniors. Finally, spouses are ritually transformed into 'siblings' through a series of rituals that equate them with their children, on the one hand, and stress their descent from a common, anonymous household ancestor, on the other.

Lévi-Strauss interprets the metaphor of the house as 'solving' a symbolic problem caused by the corrosion of the 'blood ties' of alliance and descent by political and economic interests, without those interests having yet been able to dispense with the idiom of kinship. I interpret the metaphor of the house in Ara as solving quite a different symbolic problem, caused by the adoption of the idioms of siblingship and place as a means of conceiving the social order. At the symbolic level, my conclusion as to the direct applicability of Lévi-Strauss's argument to Ara and, by inference, to 'centrist' Indonesia, must be negative.

Body parts (at birth)	House parts (spirits)	Household (members)	Kin terms
Placenta/ Elder sibling	Attic/Anonymous female ancestor: even & odd offerings	grandparents (elder sibling)	Undifferentiated unity senior generaton
	Drinking water/Nyaha: Mediating element		
Muhammad/ Alusu	Male/female posts: : Elder brother/ younger sister: : odd/even offerings	B, Z, & younger sibling in a'jaga	Sexual duality medial generation
Caul	Sarongs on posts		
Blood	Base of peripheral posts/Descendants Offerings in fours	grandchildren (younger sibling)	Undifferentiated multiplicity junior generation

At a more pragmatic, or 'functional' level, however, Lévi-Strauss's concept may prove more fruitful. Following Bloch (1986), it would be possible to write a history of the political or 'functional' uses to which these rituals have been put over the past century. The rituals discussed in this chapter have been highly contested during this period in several different areas: there has been a political struggle over the use of 'feudal' symbols, a struggle of religion against superstition, and a struggle within religion over the true definition of Islam.

While one of the symbolic effects of the rituals discussed in this chapter was to represent each household as an undivided unity of ancestors and descendants, another was to legitimate the division of society into the ascribed ranks of nobles, commoners and slaves. Special bamboo structures, which were the prerogative of nobles, were used to claim high rank on the occasion of each ritual performance: at marriage, birth and funeral rituals. Thus while divisions internal to the house/household were played down in ritual, divisions between houses/households were played up. Honours and titles are accumulated by houses and passed down within them, just as in Europe or Japan. Moreover, there was a lot of scope for manipulation of the system to convert achieved status into ascribed rank. This characteristic has been stressed by virtually every writer on the Bugis-Makassarese peoples. One of the purposes of rituals was to push claims to higher status. If a house was allowed to get away with using certain symbols, its new rank would be secured. In this respect,

147

Ara in the nineteenth century would have looked very like one of Lévi-Strauss's ranked societies where the 'rules' seem made to be broken.

All of this came under sharp attack in the 1950s when an insurgency inspired by the values of the Modernist Islamic organization, the Muhammadiyah, extended its control over the countryside. When political 'feudalism' came under attack, so did the rituals, for two reasons. First, as I have said, they were attacked for reinforcing 'feudal' distinctions of hereditary rank. Second, traditional Sufi rituals honouring the Prophet and the Saints were an integral part of most life-cycle rituals. Modernist Muslims are as intolerant of these rituals as they are of the spirit cults practised by spirit mediums. Modernists have not rejected the life-cycle rituals as such, but have tried to detach them from 'religion' (*agama*) and practise them as 'culture' (*kebudayaan*).

In the course of this century, religious Modernism has often been adopted as a tactical means of advancement for those of middling status, and tends to be strongest among those who have progressed furthest by their own efforts, usually within the system of formal education. Modernists who have managed to land high-prestige salaried posts with the government have also tended to revive the most conspicuous forms of ritual display, which were suppressed in the 1950s, particularly at the marriages of their children. This is the classic route to social advancement. One thing that members of the 'revolutionary' generation of 1950–65 have learned is that you cannot reform religion and society at the same time. Their social revolution ultimately failed, and they have made their peace with a hierarchical social system. But they press on with their purification of religion.

It is perhaps at this more 'historical' level that we should look for the relevance of Lévi-Strauss's argument, for it is here that his concern with myth and history, kinship and class, is located. The 'house' and the rituals by which it is reproduced have shown a remarkable ability to survive in the face of enormous changes emanating from the political and religious domains. While my overall argument has been that the house is a symbolic device serving as a model for an enduring social order based on the idiom of siblingship, it is also a device whereby competition for wealth and power can be carried out under the cloak of innate differences in rank. Further refinement of this concept is clearly in order.

7 THE LIO HOUSE: BUILDING, CATEGORY, IDEA, VALUE

Signe Howell

'HOUSE-BASED SOCIETIES' – A GENERALLY APPLICABLE CATEGORY?

In his discussions about the social and symbolic role of the House, Lévi-Strauss was mainly concerned with finding a structuring principle common to cognatic (or 'undifferentiated') societies (Lévi-Strauss 1983a, 1987). As is well known, the idea that the House might constitute such a principle came through his re-examination of Kwakiutl social organization – a topic which had been puzzling anthropologists for some time because of the apparent lack of clear categories. Accordingly, he suggested that the House could be understood as a 'moral person' and be defined in terms similar to those used to define a noble house in the Middle Ages in Europe, that is, as 'a corporate body holding an estate made up of both material and immaterial wealth, which perpetuates itself through the transmission of its name, its goods, and its titles down a real or imaginary line, considered legitimate as long as this continuity can express itself in the language of kinship and affinity and, most often, of both' (1983a: 174). In addition, he pointed out that Houses in this sense frequently possess goods of supernatural origin (1983a). Initially, for Lévi-Strauss, the explanatory strength of Houses as encountered in cognatic societies was that they united a whole range of contradictory tendencies. Thus 'patrilineal descent, matrilineal descent, filiation and residence, hypergamy and hypogamy, close marriage and distant marriage, hereditary and election: all these notions, which usually allow the anthropologist to distinguish the various types of society, are reunited in the House' (1983a: 184). It gives an illusion of unity where one previously saw only contradictions and incompatibility, and provides a context in which 'Descent can substitute for affinity and affinity for descent' (1983a: 187).

In subsequent discussions of those cognatic societies which he suggests may be understood as 'house-based societies', Lévi-Strauss continues to develop these ideas. Casting his analytic net across all continents, he reiterates his primary concern with cognatic societies. He begins his introductory remarks to his final lecture series thus: 'This course, the last in a series covering six years *devoted to cognatic societies* ...' (1987: 185, emphasis added). In the chapter on Indonesian societies, he applies to advantage his concept of the House in a reinterpretation of Iban, Rungus and Bajau Laut social organization, all of which may be characterized as undifferentiated. But when he moves on to discuss the highly differentiated Indonesian societies of the Batak and the Atoni where the socio-symbolic significance of the House is also prominent, he appears to forget that central to his original argument is a separation between differentiated and non-differentiated societies. As a result, the analyses of both social types suffer.

Lévi-Strauss does himself a disservice, in my view, by including in his category of house-based societies a random selection of societies predicated upon very different ideological constructs just because the House is of prominent social and symbolic significance. Rather than debating whether the presence of Houses as moral persons in societies displaying diametrically different organizing principles might be understood according to different criteria he seems, rather surprisingly, to insist on the same kind of explanation. He claims to identify everywhere an inherent contradiction between different principles, principles predicated upon affinal relations. In certain circumstances when 'this relation of reproducers becomes strained, it will be perceived as a thing and objectified in the "house"; this is a specific institution which ... owes its existence neither to descent, property or residence as such, but as a projection of a relation capable of manifesting in one or more of these illusory forms' (1987: 155–6). Although this conclusion was reached from his examination of the highly structured societies of Atoni and Batak, he suggests that this particular conflict is also present in cognatic societies, but that it is more hidden; and that, 'what really happens in societies with "houses" is the hypostatization of the opposition between descent and alliance that has to be transcended' (1987: 158).

The purpose of this chapter is to make use of Lévi-Strauss's ideas and to see to what extent they help explain the situation as I found it in a highly differentiated Eastern Indonesian society, the Lio. While the House is significant in Lio society, my question is to what extent its significance is comparable to that of Houses is non-differentiated societies.[1] Having alerted us to the possibility that the House might constitute an organizing principle in cognatic societies, Lévi-Strauss has provided a new interpretative tool. But, as he himself says, the characteristic of such societies is that they do not have fixed categories that might otherwise constitute the said order. There are no units that may be defined either as families, clans or lineages and hence, 'in order to understand them it was necessary to introduce into anthropological terminology the notion of "house"' (1987: 151). But when houses are also significant in differentiated societies then it seems to me that some other, more fundamental questions have to be asked with regard to the interpretative use of units which may be defined as families, clans or lineages where these exist as ideological constructs. From an analytic point of view, and following Lévi-Strauss's formulation of the problem, there would appear to be two possibilities: there are non-differentiated societies in which social and moral unity is found through the House;[2] and there are differentiated societies where such a unity is found primarily in fixed kin and alliance categories and in the relations between these. If the latter societies can also be found to have 'Houses' then their meaning must be explained in different terms from those used in the case of non-differentiated societies. By generalizing from previous conclusions derived from the study of elementary structures, Lévi-Strauss reduces the usefulness of the concept when it is applied to non-differentiated societies, as the discussions by Carsten and Gibson (this volume) bear out.[3]

Moreover, it is unclear whether Lévi-Strauss is focusing upon relations *within* the House, or relations *between* Houses. While the two are not to be regarded as separable, they are clearly not of the same order and proper account should be taken of this fact.[4]

For comparative purposes within Indonesia, Errington has distinguished two major types of social organization. Firstly, the 'preferentially endogamous "cognatic" societies of insular Southeast Asia' which she calls the *Centrist Archipelago* and, secondly, *Eastern Indonesia* where asymmetric alliance is the norm (Errington 1987: 403–5). Focusing, as I do in this chapter (though for somewhat different purposes), upon the institutionalization of the 'incest taboo', she concludes that 'the political process and cosmo-political problem' of the two types of societies are, at different levels, both the same and different. Consequently, both semantically and sociologically the significance of Houses are not to be confused (1987: 437). What Errington's paper makes clear is that the significance of Houses emerges in each case through juxtaposing the two types of societies. This is what Lévi-Strauss should have done, but did not do.

In view of the above, and of my reading of Lévi-Strauss, I want to examine the House – as category, building, idea and value – as I interpret its significance among the Northern Lio of Flores, Eastern Indonesia. Remaining for present purposes within concepts and categorizations employed by Lévi-Strauss, my main problem is the following: Lio have all those fixed categories that Lévi-Strauss identified as constituting the organizing principles of differentiated (non-cognatic) societies, and yet Lio have named Houses – Houses that display many features similar to those of European noble Houses and which enable us to interpret them as moral persons – a point I myself made before having read Lévi-Strauss (Howell 1989: 424). For me the question then becomes: what do the named descent groupings *do* and what do Houses *do* and how do their functions and meanings differ? In earlier interpretations of Lio society I have treated Houses as synonymous with clans. Thus I wrote previously, 'Surrounding the dance-burial place are the clan houses, *sa'o*. This word is not used for any other kind of house and it could be translated as "clan". Here I will use the word House in the sense of the House of Plantagenet or the House of Fraser' (Howell 1989: 424). Rethinking this in more depth as a result of reading Lévi-Strauss, I have changed my perceptions, and my starting assumption is now that 'clan' and 'House' cannot automatically be collapsed into each other. While they overlap in many instances, the named patri-groups and the named Houses do not do the same thing, and semantically they express different aspects of Lio social life. My task will thus be to disentangle their respective significance. This leads to the suggestion

Plate 5   A Lio temple on top of the dance-burial space and three ceremonial houses along the side.

that it is misleading to think in terms of an analytic category of 'house-based societies' which can accommodate both differentiated and undifferentiated social organizations.

THE LIO HOUSE: A LIFE-PROMOTING COMMUNITY

Houses, in the Lio context, constitute separate semantic and moral universes that are informed by, and inform, other such universes in the society. Lio 'families, clans, and lineages' on the one hand and 'Houses' on the other are mutually constitutive in creating their separate semantic domains. However, both domains are encompassed by a third: the 'temple' (*kéda*) (Plate 5). While descent categories regulate inter-group relations of a strictly human kind such as marriages, births, deaths and property, Houses regulate intra-group relations and relations with House ancestors. The temple orchestrates the cosmogonic and cosmological anchoring. My argument will be

153

that none of these could achieve their particular significance in isolation from the others.

Lio Houses must be regarded as a cosmological reflection, as an objectivization of relationships expressed in and through them, and as actors in rituals. They have a mystical quality which is not reducible to any underpinning of a conflict between descent and alliance. Errington has called the Indonesian House a 'worship community' (1987: 406). I prefer 'life-promoting community', both to avoid the Christian overtones of worship and to emphasize, and expand, the often-stressed point that Eastern Indonesian societal organization can be judged as one that is preoccupied with the control of the flow of life (see Fox (ed.) 1980).

THE NORTHERN LIO[5]

The Lio live in the north-central part of Flores in Eastern Indonesia.[6] They live in ancient villages, clusters of which are centred upon a 'trunk' village and constitute independent socio/political/ritual entities. The only overall authority is ideological, namely a common conception of the cosmogonic past which is of major importance for the living today and which constitutes the parameters for everything significant in Lio social life – from the physical lay-out of villages, the construction and lay-out of houses, to marriage practices, cosmological understanding, ritual, and agricultural and economic practices. The existential reference point is a mountain, on the top of which the first human beings lived. The sea came almost to the top of this, and the sky was very close. Everybody lived together in one building called *kéda*. The *kéda* was a totality where no differentiations were made. There was no separation between mundane and ritual activities, there were no leaders, there was no death, there were no marriage rules, and there was no separation between kin and affines. Myths and descriptions of this time emphasize either individuals or brother–sister pairs – both categories explicitly presented as people with no parents, *ana kalo*. When the event occurred that led to sea and sky receding to their present-day levels, the people from the mountaintop started to move downwards. Different brother–sister pairs[7] settled in different places and started to cultivate the land. Their descendants still live and work in the same places, and memories of the original ancestors are kept very much alive and give shape to present-day activities and perceptions (Howell 1992).

Accompanying the descent from the mountain were numerous divisions and separations. The patrilineal principle came to the forefront. People were divided into marriageable and non-marriageable kinds and prescriptive marriage rules were imposed. Brother's daughter with sister's son (*ana weta/ana nara*) marriage[8] rather than brother and sister unions became the rule with accompanying asymmetric gift exchanges. This form of prescriptive marriage system results, of course, in agnatically composed descent groups that stand in a fixed and asymmetric alliance relationship with each other (see below for a discussion of the Lio categories of descent groupings). At the same time a distinction arose between older and younger same-sex siblings (*aji/kae*). These terms are applied to all meaningful hierarchical relations: the various types of patrilineally defined descent groupings, Houses, priest-leaders, villages and temples. Interestingly, relative age with its implied status differential is not reflected in the cross-sex sibling terms (*weta/nara*).

Once they had left the Mountain, the people never returned to live there, although pilgrimages are made irregularly. The *kéda* could no longer be built as a house for living in, but a building called *kéda* was, and continues to be, built which is best described as a 'temple'. The major objects kept inside it are two wooden sculptures of the ultimate brother–sister pair (Sun–Moon and Earth–Stone). Although I have very little information about them and their roles, it is clear that they are the most significant of Lio supernatural beings. A different kind of house (*sa'o*) had to be built for people to live in. Over time, some of these houses became more significant than others and are known today as ceremonial houses (*sa'o ng'gua*). It is these that I will call Houses in the sense delineated by Lévi-Strauss. Today ceremonial Houses are structurally different from ordinary houses. They are also different from the small houses built in the fields where most people spend a large part of the year.

Ceremonial houses and temples, however, are similar in their general layout and construction. They are both built off the ground on sturdy wooden pillars. The main difference is that the *kéda* is a platform with no walls – the tall straw roof hangs over the platform on all four sides – while *sa'o* have plank walls, a verandah, a front door and several sleeping compartments inside. The *kéda* thus has

155

nothing that separates sky (Sun–Moon) from earth (Earth–Stone), while the *sa'o* graphically enclose humans between the two. The *kéda* is always taller than any *sa'o* and, in some villages, the difference between them is further marked by the use of different roofing material. Furthermore, while the buildings cannot be interpreted as in any sense human (as has been suggested by Yamaguchi 1989), *kéda* has associations of maleness and *sa'o* of femaleness. Idioms for expresing the relationship between them are those of husband and wife/wives (the Lio are polygamous) or, in other contexts, of wife-givers/wife-takers. My argument is that an understanding of the *sa'o* can only be developed in relation to the *kéda*. The two other studies of the Lio house (Prior 1988, Yamaguchi 1989) fail to take any account of the *kéda*, thereby severely limiting the understanding of the semantic and moral complexity of the House.

Accompanying the descent from the mountaintop and the establishment of villages, *kéda*, *sa'o*, marriage groups, and the hierarchical older/younger distinction, was the establishment of differentially ranked social categories which persist in the present day. These were aristocrats, (*ata ria*) 'the big people', the commoners (*ana fai walu*) – literally 'children of women who stand alone', and slaves (*ata ko'o*) – nowadays abolished as a category, but the origins of those commoners who are descendants of former slaves are not forgotten. The aristocrats are most clearly identified with Houses – their persons are fused most intimately with the building, the valuables kept inside it, and its ancestors. Slaves are, morally and socially, least connected. Commoners are probably mostly poor relations of aristocrats, individuals or groups that have 'gone down in the world' for various reasons.

The big people are the priest-leaders (*mosa laki*) and their immediate patri-kin. They are the caretakers of Houses and of the House wealth. They are the orchestrators of rituals and they control the flow of life for all members of a House (Howell 1989). Each village is led by a council of priest-leaders – internally ranked according to their particular role. Each has a title that reflects the role, and these are attached to Houses.

Although there must be seven priest-leaders, there need not be seven Houses. In several cases, two or more priest-leaders belong to one House. Although there are individual differences between actual titles and the roles of the priest-leaders, the following three titles, normally distributed between different Houses, are always present. Firstly, there is the 'priest-leader of the land' (*mosa laki tana*); in important villages with temples he may also be called 'trunk priest-leader' (*mosa laki pu'u*). This man orchestrates the major village rituals and is head of the Big House (*sa'o ria*), one which comes first in all ceremonies and whose maintenance is the task of all villagers, not just of those who are House-members by virtue of descent or incorporation. Secondly, there is the 'priest-leader who stabs the pig' (*mosa laki wela wavi*). He orchestrates animal sacrifices and makes the first stab. Thirdly, there is the 'priest-leader of warfare' (*mosa laki ria bewa*).

Recruitment to these offices is by election, but constrained by agnatic descent. Ideally, it passes from brother to brother and then from father to son, reverting to the son of the eldest brother. In reality, the personal qualities of an individual are of paramount importance, particularly his knowledge of esoteric and historical matters, and his verbal skills. The person of the priest-leader is mystically associated with the ancestors and with the House and the well-being of the House members and their fields is to a large extent predicated upon his quality.

The Council of priest-leaders wields all public power in a Lio village. They act as arbitrators in conflicts, as mediators with the outside world, as mediators with the ancestors, and as orchestrators of ceremonial of all kinds.

THE LIO TRUNK VILLAGE AS MICROCOSM

The temple (*kéda*) stands at the edge of a circular, elevated flat space (*kanga*). The various Houses also stand along the same edge. Dead priest-leaders are buried inside this elevated space. At specific ritual events – mainly on the occasion of the annual planting ceremony, but also when the *kéda* is rebuilt – people dance on top of it. In the centre of the *kanga* is a standing stone (*tubu*) which ideally originates from the mountain, and also a flat stone (*lodondà*). The male and female symbolism of these stones is clear to the Lio. Other *tubu* may be erected without *lodondà* elsewhere on the *kanga*, but then their significance is particular. While all independent villages have a dance-burial place, surrounded by one or several Houses, only those that can maintain a claim of direct descent from one of the original people (brothers and sisters) who came from the mountaintop may build a *kéda*. The *kéda* enables its owners to maintain direct contact with the major deities and the original ancestors. Villages with no cosmogonic right to a *kéda*, but whose leaders have ambitions of autonomy and glory, may build a different kind of overarching building. This is the *kuwu*, similar to the *kéda* in terms of its construction and positioning, but it may not keep any sculptures and it does not constitute a means of communication with the major deities (Howell 1991).

Lio social organization derives its form and meaning from the central space and buildings of the trunk village. Together they constitute the significant locality: geographically, historically, politically, ritually and cosmologically for all members of a trunk village, even though – as is the case with many people – they may live in virtually independent satellite villages and have little actual contact with the trunk village except during the major ritual events. Satellite villages often have satellite Houses and satellite priest-leaders, but these are all subordinated to those of the core village. The occasion for prescribed attendance of all descendants of the original ancestors are: the rebuilding of the *kéda*, the rebuilding of the trunk House, and major agricultural ceremonies. However, everyone is a member of one of the Houses in a trunk-village and is responsible for matters connected with it, and they are subjugated to the authority of its priest-leader.

The building, or rebuilding, of both *kéda* and House are major events in the life of the village. The procedure in both cases is extremely complex and each sequence is prescribed. The various stages are accompanied by animal sacrifices. Before the Catholic Church forbade it, a live human being was placed in the hole dug for the main house post – the one to the right looking towards the entrance from inside – where the person was given some food before being crushed by the post.[9] The rebuilding of the *kéda* is the ultimate significant event in Lio life and involves the active participation of all those who claim descent from the original ancestors, i.e. all members of the Houses connected to the *kéda*, its 'wives' or 'wife-givers'. The rebuilding of a House requires the presence of all its members. Both events are marked by highly ritualized behaviour and numerous animal sacrifices and offerings.

The layout of both buildings can be broken down into a series of hierarchical opposites. In the Houses, there are connotations of right–left; up–down; front–back; male–female; priest-leader–commoner;

wife-givers–wife-takers and, most importantly, of ancestors–the living. In the *kéda* the main emphasis is on the distinction between the Mountain and the village. In both buildings, each beam and marked space has a name and meaning.

In order to highlight a conceptual fusion between the House and human well-being, I wish to mention some significant attributes of ceremonial Houses. Suspended from the ceiling in the centre is a bundle containing last year's unhusked rice from the priest leader's special ritual field. Some of this is mixed with rice from the House members' own fields and cooked and eaten communally at the start of the planting ceremony. The rest is planted in the ritual field before the commoners may plant. A branch of areca nuts wrapped in the leaves of the wine-palm is also kept in the right-hand back corner tied to the top beam of the wall. This is replaced with great ceremony each year as part of the planting ceremonies. Together with the House gold and other House valuables – also kept in the upper space of the House and denoting the patri-group – these substances: rice, betel, and palm-wine denoting wife-givers, are those that I have argued elsewhere (1989: 430–1) are imbued with life potential.

Suspended from the ridgepole into the centre is the 'heart of the House' (*ate sa'o*). This is a basket in which various ritual paraphernalia are stored attached to deer antlers. Thus, contained, and maintained, within the building are all Lio valuables: non-perishable wealth – both the inalienable and that temporally stored before it resumes its wandering in future alliance exchanges – as well as perishable, but ritually renewable, wealth of rice, areca and palm-wine. Their obligatory presence in ceremonial Houses expresses the intimate and vital connection between the House and its members.

In each House, towards the back, there is a sacred area consisting of a horizontal beam along the floor. At both ends are sacred stones over which sacrifices are performed and offerings to the House ancestors placed. A tall upright panel is placed at the centre of the beam on which are relief carvings. These may represent the ancestral couple of the House, or more commonly just a female figure or a pair of breasts, thus graphically denoting the female quality of Houses.

When the priest-leader of a House dies, he must be placed on a mat in the centre of the House, wrapped in cloth provided by the wife-givers. His head faces the panel, his middle is below the rice bundle and the 'heart of the House', his feet towards the door. House gold is put on the body. Today he is buried after a couple of days. In the past his decaying flesh fell onto the ground below until only the bones were left. These were buried. His widow had to sit next to the body and eat all her meals there. In other words, the person of the priest-leader – a future communal ancestor – literally merges into the building – and vice versa.

The *kéda* by contrast is not a building for humans. It is dominated by the two wooden sculptures which are positioned on a shelf halfway up the roof above the main house post. In front of them are offering places. It is their house. There is also a fireplace in the centre, and there are numerous carvings and paintings of animals and plants on the beams. These all refer to the period on the mountaintop and the descent from it. In addition, the horns of sacrificed buffaloes are kept there. The temple is hardly ever used. It dominates the village landscape, however.

Priest-leaders and their families frequently told me that they are too frightened to live inside their ceremonial House because the building itself has become too sacred (*bhisa*) through being actively involved in numerous sacred events. It may therefore stand empty the whole year except for times of ceremonials when the *mosa laki* has to sleep in it. The *kéda* is sacred by definition, and several adults have never been inside the one that belongs to their own trunk village.

While I would certainly argue that the Lio ceremonial House should be understood as a moral person, and that its very structure expresses significant existential ideas and values, it is not possible to argue that it is a microcosm of the universe in quite the same way that Cunningham argued for the Atoni house (1964). It must be interpreted in relation to the *kéda*, to the other Houses, and to central ceremonial space with its graves and standing stones. Thus it is not the House on its own, but the central space and significant buildings of a Lio trunk village that can be said to constitute such a microcosm. The significance is derived from all the components in interaction, not from any one in isolation. This makes for a more dynamic overall conception. Different localities, buildings, objects, and aspects of the trunk village are brought into play at different times and for different purposes, carrying over the meanings from other contexts.

160

HOUSE, *KÉDA*, DESCENT AND MARRIAGE

It is possible that in the past each House, constituted as an agnatic descent group (*embu*), stood in a fixed wife-giver/wife-taker relationship with other Houses inside a village; possible, but undemonstrable – either actually or ideologically. This is not the way the Lio talk. They certainly talk about Houses and they talk about the need to marry BD/ZS. They talk endlessly about wife-givers and wife-takers. Kin relations and obligations are also significant elements of daily life, but of a less public concern than affinal ones. Further, they talk about the various rituals that have to be performed, about the *kéda*, about Sun–Moon/Earth–Stones, their House and, last but not least, about the ancestors. These are the significant elements of their lives.

There are several categories of agnatically composed descent groupings. The largest of these is the *kunu* which in older anthropological writings would have been translated as tribe. Strictly speaking, among the Northern Lio there are only three *kunu* and each one of these claims direct descent from the ancestors on the mountaintop. Consequently, there should be only three temples, one for each. In reality, although I was never given the name of any other *kunu*, I came across villages which had temples but whose priest-leaders denied that they were members of any of the three *kunu*. Legitimate new temples may be built which become designated younger siblings to existing ones upon agreement of the Council of priest-leaders and upon the receipt of large gifts together with a continuing acknowledgement of the inferior status. Not surprisingly, many villages try to get out of this relationship by manipulating mythic history (Howell 1991).

The next descent category is the *embu* which displays many of the characteristics usually attributed to a patri-clan. The word also means great-grandparent and older ancestors. Wife-takers may also be referred to as 'children of the clan' (*ana embu*). All *embu* have names which usually do not correspond to the names of the Houses. Men volunteer their *embu* affiliation more frequently than women. Upon marriage and the accompanying exchanges, a woman is incorporated into her husband's *embu* and ultimately, although this is more complex, his House. In my experience, when discussing her premarital status a woman tends to emphasize her House rather than clan affiliation. Depending on whether she is fully transferred to her

161

husband's House (see below) she continues to participate as a House member in the most important ceremonies of her natal House. Her formal relationship with her natal descent group, on the other hand, is marked by them being wife-givers to her husband's group. However, both she and her brothers are members of another named descent group (*tebu*) reckoned through their mother. There is an offering place for the ultimate ancestress inside every House so that both male and female descent are acknowledged as part of a House. Unlike *embu* affiliation, the *tebu* affiliation can never be changed.

Finally, the smallest descent-based category is the *ngewa'u* (literally descent) which, unlike the *embu*, is not named and consists of brothers, fathers and father's brothers. The actual cut-off point of this group is not absolute, either vertically or horizontally. The *ngewa'u* has no special ritual functions. It is operative on a day-to-day basis of co-operation and obligation.

While BD/ZS marriage is the idiom used to express Lio marriages, not all marriages are of this kind. It is imperative, however, that the priest-leaders contract such marriages, and that they contract them with women from the same wife-giving group over several generations. Such wife-giving groups are called 'trunk' wife-givers (*ine ame pu'u*). In brief, I argue that the significance of regularly contracting marriages across generations between the trunk wife-givers and the patrilineal descent group of the House-based priest-leader is that, in effect, such marriages symbolically transform wives into sisters (Howell 1990) and that such a transformation is necessary because it emulates the conditions on the Mountaintop and makes the House the replica of the *kéda* there. While classificatory sibling marriages are strictly forbidden, marriage between actual or classificatory BD and ZS is prescribed. This means that at the same generation level, classificatory brothers and sisters are like siblings and may not marry, while at the second and subsequent descending generations their cross-sex (ZS and BD) children must marry while all children of all other sibling relations remain forbidden. By applying different definitional criteria of forbidden marriages (*piré*) at same and subsequent generational levels, new generations of Lio male and female priest-leaders are created by 'brothers' and 'sisters', albeit at one generational remove.

There are several myths that exemplify the importance of the brother–sister pair among the Lio which I cannot go into here. For present purposes the point to stress is that when a classificatory trunk-brother's daughter is properly married to a priest-leader, she is *ipso facto* priest-leader. It is only she who may 'enter' the House and perform all the ritual female tasks that are a necessary part of House, temple and village ceremonies. She alone may wear the female House gold. Wives who do not fulfil these criteria may not perform the rituals. In such cases, an unmarried sister of the priest-leader, or if he has none, a younger brother referred to as 'the sister' stands in.

Alliance relationships are primarily expressed with reference to descent and descent groups rather than to House affiliation; although occasionally a priest-leader might specify the House of origin of his wife. I have argued that, in the case of the priest-leaders, the protracted asymmetric alliance exchanges are the catalyst for the transformation of wives into sisters. The rule of brother's daughter with sister's son marriage combined with the fact that the House constitutes a moral person enables the Lio to satisfy both the rules of incest avoidance and the demand for the re-creation of the cosmic brother–sister relation that forms the basis for the meaning of the House.

In the *kéda* where there are no differences between kin and affines, the brother–sister relationship is directly represented (see p. 155); in the House it is implied and brought about by marriages between unequal agnatic groups which allow wives to be transformed into sisters at second or subsequent generational levels. Here then, it would appear that clan and House do not do identical things.

The House objectifies the social link with the House ancestors. For the individual Lio the House is a concrete proof of origin and continuity. Upon entering a House for the first time a stranger must 'greet' it ceremoniously, just as she must 'greet' the *kéda*, by walking in silence to the sacred wooden partition towards the back and placing the right foot on it. A House brings people together in an idiom of common agnatic descent that transcends the present and continuously creates the future in conformity with the past. It does this by virtue of the fixed relationship that it occupies with the communal concrete symbols of *kéda*, dance-burial place, central standing stones, graves, and other significant parts of the landscape. Moreover, the House is a physical structure that has mundane purposes as well as ritual ones. Each House does this for all its members, but not for the village as a whole. By contrast, the *kéda* is concrete evidence of totality; of absolute origins, of timelessness and perpetuity, and of ultimate cosmological order. It also represents the pre-social life of non-differentiation, while the House denotes the claims of social life for differentiation.

Every member of each House also participates in the *kéda*. Their identities are fused with it. Yet it is the House that constitutes a moral person for the Lio and it becomes that not only because it orchestrates social life and social relations with the living and the ancestors specific to the House, but also because it encloses valuables that are life-promoting. People participate in their Houses in profound ways which are made manifest on ritual occasions but which are ever present and always shape their perceptions. But the *kéda* overshadows them all. It makes the cosmogonic past part of the present, while Houses make the social past part of the present.

If we return to the clan/House relationship, how can we further demonstrate that they do different things? Houses have names, and clans also have names. In some cases these are identical, but this is the exception, not the rule. Clan names often employ the name of the founder, for example Embu M'bele. House names reflect their ritual role, for example *Sa'o Susu Nama* or *Sa'o Ng'gua Ka Uwi* (where the agricultural ceremony is performed), *Sa'o Ria Bewa* (war), *Sao Keti Uta* (harvesting first vegetables), *Sa'o Ine Ame* (wife-giver to *kéda*). The major House is universally called *Sa'o Ria* (the Big House) or, in trunk villages *Sa'o Pu'u* (the Trunk House). Each House may have other, subsidiary titles also, but these are operative in connection with specific rituals only. In theory, the actual occupier of the office of priest-leader should be an agnatic descendant of the original officeholder. However, there is evidence to suggest that this is not always the case. My guess is that the actual clans in occupation vary depending on the contingent circumstances of which kin group has become powerful. The group in power may also die out and another take over. Several clans may be members of the same House. This may be the result of migrations (probably recent) from one village cluster to another. Conversely, the same clan may provide priest-leaders for more than one House.

Land is ultimately owned by Houses, with the *mosa laki* as its guardian and controller. *Mosa laki* dispense the right to cultivate certain parcels of land, but it is not possible to alienate land from the House. People may cultivate land belonging to more than one House. Then they have to pay tribute to each although, because of descent, their affiliation to one is of primary significance. Similarly, people from one trunk village may have moved and settled within the jurisdiction of another, cultivating their land. For the annual agricultural ceremonies they will be subjugated to the main House there. However, they usually retain their natal clan affiliation, and are also tied to their House and *kéda* of origin for more important ritual purposes there. So while descent groups of priest-leaders may change, the House and its name and role remain unchanged. This does not mean that descent and descent idiom are unimportant. Priest-leaders constantly recite the names of their ancestors, placing a high value on the number of generations they can identify.

LÉVI-STRAUSS AND THE HOUSE IN DIFFERENTIATED AND NON-DIFFERENTIATED SOCIETIES

Where does all this take us with regard to Lévi-Strauss and his specific considerations of 'house-based' societies? In particular how useful are his findings in relation to societies whose ideology is unilineal? And is his use of the term House compatible with mine? I believe I have avoided doing what he warned against – that is, starting with genealogical group or territorial organization which he maintains are not primary data – and have instead concentrated upon relations. His conclusion, however, that the House constitutes a spatial projection of a relation between groups – those related in a descent idiom and in an alliance idiom – which establishes a fictitious unity (1987: 157), seems unsatisfactory in the Lio case. I have sought instead to isolate those elements in the Lio social and semantic universe which seem to me to be significant, and have focused on their internal relations. And here some synthesis may be found, for *kéda*, ceremonial House, agnatic descent groups, wife-givers and wife-takers all constitute each other. None has privileged ontological or epistemological status, but each derives its particular meaning in relation to the rest.

I will end by returning to my original problem: given that, on the one hand, the House is of major social and symbolic significance in Lio society, but that, on the other hand, one may discern in it all those features ('families, lineages, clans') whose absence in some societies made Lévi-Strauss search for alternative organizing principles, is there any useful sense in which Lio society can be described as 'house based'? I wish to emphasize, however, that the problem is to some extent artificial, arising as it does out of postulations made by Lévi-Strauss. It is unlikely that I would have focused a discussion on the significance of the Lio House in such a way had I not been asked specifically to relate my discussion to his writings.

The Lio House is no reification of a conflict-ridden relationship. The Lio House is laden with significance; it is a moral entity that brings together the past, the present and the future for its members. As such it creates a participatory unity, and the boundaries between a House and its members – both dead and alive – are not clear. The relationship between House members and House ancestors is expressed through offerings and sacrifices by the living (Howell in press) and the benevolent provision of food and health by the ancestors. Houses remain unchanged, their names and functions continue through generations – but only so long as their living members honour them.

The 'tribe', *kunu*, also remains unchanged. Clans, *embu*, on the other hand, may be interpreted as more contingent groupings, directly resulting from powerful individuals and the injunction on men to marry matrilaterally. Clans orchestrate group relations outside the House idiom. Wife-givers and wife-takers are the operative groups upon which actual human life is predicated; 'they walk together forever' is a common expression and they thus ensure human occupancy of the House. The endless alliance exchanges between the priest-leaders of different *embu* enable the trunk BD to enter a House as a 'sister'. This relationship emphasizes differences, not unity. Furthermore, as necessary partners in the creation of ancestors, and new humans, marriage is just one social instance of the relationship. In the final pages I will seek to elaborate further on the above suggestions.

Conceivably, Houses might have been proposed as the medium and focus for all necessary social and ceremonial tasks in Lio life. But this would leave one with unanswered questions about the role of descent and marriage groups, as well as the meaning of the *kéda*. In an article discussing Lio exchange practices and the role of valuables (Howell 1989), I argued that one may distinguish three significant levels of exchange: that pertaining to the House, to alliance relations, and to the trunk village. Exchange relations at the first and last levels,

I suggested, are to be understood as concerned with creating unity, whereas those between alliance partners are better understood as effecting a necessary separation between them. However, it is only by maintaining such a separation between wife-givers and wife-takers that Lio society can continue (cf. Wagner 1975). Alliance relations are 'between' relations (cf. Sahlins 1974). House and trunk village/*kéda* relations are not.

Alliance relationships ensure a continuous reproduction of actual human beings – and actual ancestors. While alliance relations are embedded in the past, they are nevertheless more directly associated with the present, with contingencies, with actual social relations and with the future; Houses and their ritual, moral and political roles are less so. However, actual human beings live in the Houses and they change through the generations. The humans are made through the alliances. By contrast, the *kéda* is empty of humans. It is full of the ultimate deities, the ultimate brother–sister pair. It is the static, concrete proof of cosmogonic past; the reminder of absolute, undifferentiated and static power. Without the *kéda*, Lio Houses would mean very different things to the people who inhabit Lio land. Ultimately, I wish to suggest that the clue to the significance of Lio Houses is to be found in the semantics of this relationship.

I wish to end with a deliberation on this last point, the nature of the differences between Lio Houses and Lio *kéda*. A premise has been that the aristocrats are the main actors. They control, orchestrate and ensure the correct flow of life and they do this, primarily, through the two kinds of significant buildings and through the various rituals that are performed with and via these buildings. My argument is that the ceremonial Houses, not, perhaps surprisingly, the *kéda*, are earthly transformations of the original *kéda*. Their guardians (the priest-leaders) are the earthly transformations of the original inhabitants of the *kéda*. As the living representatives of the original ancestors, the guardians of the flow of life, the priest-leaders must emulate the social conditions of life in the *kéda*. As already stated, these were characterized by a thorough lack of differentiation. All were kin, none was superior to another. Single individuals or brother–sister pairs were the operative human categories. Descent from the mountain resulted in hierarchical differentiations. Among the most important were those between cognates and agnates, wife-givers and wife-takers, elder and younger, aristocrats and commoners, living and ancestors, between ritual and ordinary activities, and between temple and houses. The guardians of the Houses and the ceremonies became the senior males, those held to be closest in direct descent from the original occupants of the land. So, descent and House were from the very beginning intertwined. The senior men, the priest-leaders who originally were agnates and today constitute the council of seven priest-leaders, are distanced from the commoners. They are the embodiments of original values and also, at times, the human personifications of the ancestors from the Mountain.[10]

Through marrying trunk MBDs across generations, the male priest-leaders have been observing the incest taboo on sibling marriage, at the same time as the original brother–sister marriages semantically were recreated through the ideologically prescribed marriages between BD and ZS. According to Lio perceptions, the ritual duties – the overall control of the flow of life – can be properly effected only inside the House and through acts of its true male and true female guardians: the priest-leaders. Their marriage is a marriage of equals; the terms *weta/nara* carry with them no hierarchical ordering. So while the idiom for all Lio marriages is that of *ana nara/ana weta* (child of sister's brother/child of brother's sister) it is imperative only that this is continually contracted at the level of the priest-leaders of the ceremonial House.

The continuation of the House as a category and as a value is predicated upon the reproduction of a relationship between asymmetrically ranked agnatic descent groups of wife-givers and wife-takers. But the paradox in Lio society is that those with political and ceremonial power maintain this through a fictive egalitarianism and agnation. The priest-leader is a 'brother', who is married to his 'sister' – a woman who, by virtue of her category (BD) and of the alliance exchanges performed, may 'enter'[11] her husband's House whereby she is transformed into a 'sister' who performs all the ritual duties of a sister and the mundane duties of a wife. In their roles as the embodied custodians of life as lived on the Mountaintop, no separation is operational between affine and kin; between ritual and mundane within the Houses. This ideal runs parallel, but in direct contradiction, to a social organization which is highly stratified, both ideologically and institutionally. However, such a necessary paradox could not be achieved without the *kéda*. So the significance of the House is predicated upon the idea of the *kéda*, and upon the *kéda* as a building. Being the house for the ultimate, and *actual*, brother–sister couple and deities only it marks the irrevocable end of an era. Humans can no longer live in it since actual brother–sister couples are no longer allowed. The House manifests in the mortal persons of the priest-leader and his wife the conditions of that era in earthly representations.

Kéda and House together maintain the memory of life on the Mountaintop. Perhaps, embedded within this relationship can be discerned that between the two ideal types of Indonesian society discussed by Errington and referred to above.

Lévi-Strauss's starting premise was an attempt to find some organizing principle in cognatic societies. His identification of the House as a unifying principle in many such societies is of real value. My argument, however, has been that, from an analytic point of view, Lévi-Strauss rendered his original insight impotent because he deviated from his original aim. A new understanding of cognatic societies remains unachieved; both because he was unable to abandon his analytical heritage from the study of elementary structures, and because he tried to incorporate highly structured societies into the same model. As a result, the category of house-based society finally included virtually every kind of society and thereby lost its usefulness as a concept. Nevertheless, by identifying the central role of Houses as 'moral persons' and a constituting *one* structuring principle in many societies, Lévi-Strauss has alerted us to take proper interpretative account of them. But his attempts at identifying a universal significance, or indeed purpose, of Houses are rendered void.

HOUSES AND HIERARCHY: THE VIEW FROM A SOUTH MOLUCCAN SOCIETY[1]

8

Susan McKinnon

PARADOXES OF SINGULARITY AND MULTIPLICITY

Evans-Pritchard may have been the first to formulate the problem as a paradox – for the Nuer, the paradox of a patrilineal principle so unchallenged as to allow for the realization of practically everything *except* patrilineality (1951: 28; cf. Sahlins 1965). Yet, in part because of the force of his own rhetoric, he has hardly been the last. Moyer, for instance, has recently rephrased the Nuer paradox to fit an Indonesian context. Speaking of south Sumatra, he has asserted that the 'paradox of unilineality' implies that 'the more unilineal a system is or becomes the less likely it is to remain unilineal' (1983: 257). The situation, however, is not unique to the Nuer or to south Sumatra. Across the ethnographic spectrum – from Africa to Indonesia – the multiplicity of the forms of affiliation and residence found within societies has confounded ethnographers and defied the simple exclusivity of their analytic categories.

In Indonesia, the problem has been further compounded by the multiplicity of the forms of marriage that are found both within and between societies. Describing the aim of his book *Types of Social Structure in Eastern Indonesia* (1968 (1935)), van Wouden noted, some years later, that he had

... attempted to deal with the erratic distribution and intermingling of patrilineal and matrilineal forms of social organization and of unilateral circulating marriage systems with mother's brother's daughter marriage, father's sister's daughter's marriage and symmetric alliance with brother–sister exchange.   (1977: 184)

In the end, van Wouden's analysis was severely limited by the historical reconstructions – including circulating connubium, double descent, moiety and phratry dualism – that he devised to account for the complexity of the phenomena at hand.[2] Nevertheless, he clearly understood that the articulation of different possibilities of marriage and affiliation was integral to the particular shape of these societies.

Notwithstanding the promising beginnings forged by van Wouden, many subsequent scholars directed their efforts in the opposite direction and focused upon the classification of various societies in terms of a single mode of descent and a single terminological marriage prescription (Needham 1956, 1957, 1966, 1967, 1968, 1970, 1980; Fischer 1957; Barnes 1973, 1974, 1977, 1978, 1980b; Forth 1981). There resulted, predictably, a parallel paradox – that of societies in which actual marriage practices rarely coincided with the structural ideal as expressed in the terminological prescription. Although the problem of the relation between multiple forms of marriage is every bit as evident in other parts of the world (again Evans-Pritchard's description of the variety of Nuer forms of marriage comes to mind), it was only in places like Indonesia, where societies came to be characterized in terms of exclusive 'elementary structures', that the problem began to take on the form of a paradox.

Rather than assuming that the relation between contrastive forms of affiliation, residence and marriage might be central to the dynamics of the society concerned, their simultaneous presence has been explained away by recourse to various theoretical tropes that require the classification of societies in terms of a single form of affiliation, residence and marriage. Hence the paradoxes of patri-lineal descent systems in which few people actually affiliate in the 'ideal' manner and of prescriptive marriage systems in which few people actually marry in accordance with the 'ideal' type. In place of an analysis of the dynamics of contrastive social forms, the formulation of such paradoxes has substituted a meta-discourse concerning the relation between the ideal and the real, structure and practice, which is, in the end, the product of their own theoretical limitations – in particular, their insistence upon singular, substantive categorizations.[3]

It would seem far preferable to assume that different forms of affiliation, residence and marriage have value, and that their value is, in part, derived from their explicit opposition to one another within a common system of relations (Boon 1977; Valeri 1975–76; 1980). From such a perspective, it makes little sense to describe a society in terms of either one or another form of affiliation, since it is the tension between a number of contrasting forms that is significant. Indeed, in Indonesia as elsewhere, it is the negotiation of this set of differential values that forms the central focus of social life.

BETWEEN KINSHIP AND FETISHISM

It is precisely his attention to the simultaneous presence of contrastive social forms that is important in Lévi-Strauss's formulation of the concept of 'house societies'. As he notes:

Patrilineal descent and matrilineal descent, filiation and residence, hypergamy and hypogamy, close marriage and distant marriage, hereditary and election: all these notions, which usually allow anthropologists to distinguish the various known types of society, are reunited in the house, as if, in the last analysis, the spirit (in the eighteenth-century sense) of this institution expressed an effort to transcend, in all spheres of collective life, theoretically incompatible principles. (1983a: 184)

By creating this new category of house societies, Lévi-Strauss has, in one stroke, reassembled the complexity of societies that had been suppressed by the incompatibility of previous typological distinctions.

Following upon Lévi-Strauss's formulation of the concept of house societies, various authors have attempted to define, refine and apply the idea in their own work (see Barraud 1979; Fox (ed.) 1980, 1987; Waterson 1986; Errington 1987, 1989; Macdonald (ed.) 1987; McKinnon 1991). But one senses an unresolved tension between the dead weight of old kinship categories and the effort to transcend these in the face of the integrity of resistant social forms. Despite the fact that the term house does not, in itself, suggest a descent ideology, many authors continue to equate the idea of the house with that of a unilineal descent group (see, for instance, Fox 1980 (ed.): 11). Throughout the literature, houses are glossed as patrilineages or matrilineages, notwithstanding the fact that almost everywhere they contain alternately affiliated members who have been recruited by virtue of the workings of the system of marriage and exchange. The idea of the house has thus been subverted by a commitment to the concept of descent: it has, as a result, become a hybrid descent group with a lot of awkward appendages.

Part of the reason for the ambivalence may derive from the nature of Lévi-Strauss's original formulation of the concept. The value of the term house society is, in large part, determined by the more or less explicit evolutionary framework in which he situates it: 'it was necessary', Lévi-Strauss writes, 'to introduce into anthropological terminology the notion of "house" ... and therefore that a type of social structure hitherto associated with complex societies is also to be found in non-literate societies' (1987: 151). House societies, then, are located midway between elementary and complex structures of kinship.[4] He suggests that

... they originated in a structural state where political and economic interests tending to invade the social field did not yet have distinct languages at their disposal and, being obliged to express themselves in the only language available, which is that of kinship, inevitably subverted it.

(1987: 152)

In one sense house societies depend upon the language of kinship; in another, they go beyond and transform this language. Rooted in elementary structures of kinship, house societies provide the missing link between kin-based societies and those governed, presumably, by the political and economic forces of the market.

As if he was trying to transcend the language of kinship himself, Lévi-Strauss declares that

Anthropologists have therefore been mistaken in seeking, in this type of institution, a substratum which they have variously thought to find in descent, property and residence. We believe, to the contrary, that it is necessary to move on from the idea of *objective substratum* to that of *objectification of a relation*: the unstable relation of alliance which, as an institution, the role of the house is to solidify, if only in an illusory form.

(1987: 155)

173

Extending the rhetoric of a transitional form between elementary and complex structures, Lévi-Strauss sees the house as a proto-capitalist image of the commodity fetishism found in capitalist societies – only here the relations of reproduction substitute for those of production (1987: 155).

To the extent, then, that Lévi-Strauss situates the house in an evolutionary position betwixt and between elementary and complex structures, it remains in a liminal position theoretically – tied down, at one end, by the old 'objective substratum' of ill-fitting kinship categories, and suppressed, at the other end, by a vocabulary that turns the house into a 'fetish'. At the one end, the house reverts back to a jerry-built unilineal descent group; at the other end, the house becomes a proto-capitalist transformation of elementary structures on the brink of becoming complex.

Nevertheless, in the opposition between kinship and its transcendence or objectification, Lévi-Strauss has captured something central to our understanding of house societies. I would suggest, however, that this opposition does not define two distinct types of society so much as a tension within a single society that is central to the delineation of hierarchy. The contrast I am concerned with here does, in part, implicate something that we could call personification and objectification.[5] Yet it can also be characterized, on the one hand, by the opposition between the particularization and the generalization of relations and, on the other hand, by the contrast between the dispersal and the concentration of value. Whereas, in each set, the first is realized through persons, the second is realized through houses and valued objects. It is this double, contrastive movement that I would like to resituate, removing it from an external, evolutionary framework that makes the house a liminal entity caught between two worlds and instead framing it in terms of internal, indigenous understandings that give to a house society its own integral dynamics.

In the Tanimbar Islands of eastern Indonesia, such a framework is immediately found in indigenous representations of the generation of life. For it is the differential value accorded to the source of life and its issue[6] that distinguishes houses (in accordance with their relative ability to generalize relations and concentrate value) and gives shape to the hierarchical order. In the remainder of this chapter, I draw from my work on the Tanimbar Islands in order to show how a focus upon such processes – read through an indigenous ideology concerning the anchorage and flow of life – provides a framework for understanding the creative role of contrastive forms of affiliation, residence and marriage, and thereby also for the processes productive of the hierarchical order of society.

HOUSES AND THE ESTATES OF HOUSES

The double movement outlined above is immediately evident in the manner in which Tanimbarese conceptualize and differentiate the basic social units of their society.[7] Here I wish to outline the shape and structure of that differentiation.

Tanimbarese distinguish between houses (*rahan*) that bear a 'name' (*naran*) and those that have 'no name' (*wol naran*). Both are characterized by the relative permanence of their 'forest estates' (*abat nangan*) and 'village estates' (*abat ahu*). The 'forest estates' of named houses comprise both tracts of land as well as plantations of trees, while those of unnamed houses consist of trees only. Similarly, the 'village estates' of named houses comprise 'rows' (*lolat*) of allied wife-taking houses as well as pathways of 'sisters and aunts' (*ura-ava*), while those of unnamed houses consist of 'sisters and aunts' pathways only.

Within the category of 'forest estates', the relative permanence of named houses is marked by their enduring relation to land, which connects the house back to the past and to the ancestors. By contrast, the relative impermanence of unnamed houses is marked by the fact that their 'forest estates' of trees are but temporary growths that will, at best, endure only a few generations. The same can be said of the difference between the rows of allied houses and the pathways of sisters and aunts that differentiate named and unnamed houses. In order to understand these constructs, however, it is necessary to say something about the structures of exchange.

Exchange follows along extended pathways that link houses through affinal relations and along matrilateral lines (McKinnon 1991). There are two general levels of these exchange pathways (see Fig. 8.1). The lower level consists of sisters and aunts pathways. These are composed of the descendants (connected by affinal links along the female lines) of women who have married out of a house in the last three or so generations. The descendants (along the male line) of the men who have given these women are called both 'brothers and

Fig. 8.1   The relation between 'sisters and aunts' pathways and 'rows'.

uncles' (*ura-memi*) and the 'masters' (*dua*) of their 'sisters and aunts'. These relations are based upon recent marriages of women whose names are still remembered, and the pathways are thought to trace the lines of life-giving 'blood' (*lara*) that has flowed through specific women. They are considered to be highly impermanent, tenuous projections into the future.

The higher level of exchange pathways consists of the 'rows' (*lolat*) (see Fig. 8.1). These comprise named houses that are linked by affinal relations that have been established four or more generations ago and have endured either through repeated marriages or, more generally, through the continued exchanges of valuables that take place along the rows. Both an established wife-taking house and an extended series of such houses are called a row, while an established wife-giving house is called 'house master' (*rahan dua*). It is presumed that rows are based on the marriages of women and that they trace the female bloodlines that have extended from them. But the specific women will have long been forgotten and the relationship will no longer be conceptualized in terms of blood. Rather, *lolat* are simply rows of named houses that stand in a relation of enduring alliance.[8]

Sisters and aunts pathways are differentiated from rows, then, along a number of dimensions. Sisters and aunts pathways involve relatively impermanent affinal relations that are seen in more individualizing or particularizing terms: that is, in terms of 'persons' (*tomata*), of 'bodies' (*tena*), and of 'blood' (*lara*). Rows, on the other hand, involve relatively permanent affinal relations that are seen in more collectivized or generalized terms: that of houses and rows of (named) houses. If, for sisters and aunts pathways, it is persons and the personification of bloodlines that are stressed, then, for the rows, it is houses and, in Lévi-Strauss's (1987: 155) term, the 'objectification of relations' – or of alliances traced along female bloodlines – that are stressed.

Not surprisingly, the terms that distinguish sisters and aunts pathways from rows of allied houses parallel those that distinguish unnamed houses from named houses. Named houses, like their estates of land and *lolat*, are considered inherently permanent and, through their relation to the ancestors, they bear a relation to the founding of the fixed order of the world. Unnamed houses, like their estates of trees and their sisters and aunts pathways, are impermanent and bear no relation to the founding of the fixed order of the world.

The permanence of named houses is not only manifest in the particular nature of their estates, but also in the fact that they possess heirloom valuables (gold earrings and breast pendants) and, formerly, an exquisitely carved altar panel (*tavu*) in the form of a highly abstracted human figure, which stood – almost as a structural support – opposite the doorway of the house and constituted its ritual centre. As much as the estates of the house, these heirlooms and the ancestor altar made a named house 'weighty' (*aleman*) in contrast to the 'light' (*maraan*) quality of unnamed houses, which possessed neither heirloom nor an altar to the founding ancestor.

Altogether, the land, *lolat*, heirlooms and altars of named houses speak of an enduring ritual relation to the founding ancestors through

177

which the potential for life may be realized in the fertility of their estates. The relation of unnamed houses to these ancestors exists only to the extent that they remain attached to named houses as younger brothers. Indeed, the relation between named and unnamed houses – those who occupy an enduring ritual centre and those who move about on the periphery – is further conceptualized in terms of the relation between 'elder and younger brothers' (*ya'an-iwarin*) and should also correspond (although it does not always) to the relation between nobles and commoners.

The character of named houses, then, is expressed in their concentration of value and weight in an immobile centre, their generalization and objectification of relations in land, houses and valuables, and their immediate relation with the founding ancestor as represented in an abstracted image that was aesthetically merged with the very structure of the house (McKinnon 1987). By contrast, the character of unnamed houses is manifest in their dispersal of value, their lightness and mobility at the periphery, their particularization of relations in terms of blood, bodies, people and trees, and their mediated relation with the founding ancestor.

Yet, this is to give a static frame to what is otherwise a dynamic process; it is to freeze, as if given in the nature of things, a set of relations that in fact must be continually created and constantly negotiated. It remains, then, to show the manner in which these differential relations are engendered. Here, we must return to the logic of contrastive forms of affiliation, residence and marriage.

CONTRASTIVE FORMS OF AFFILIATION AND RESIDENCE

I begin with the contrastive forms of affiliation and residence. To speak of these, however, is immediately to speak of the relations of exchange, since the membership of houses is not ensured by a rule of patrilineal descent or patrilocal residence. Rather, the shape of houses is created through the differentiating effects of exchange (Wagner 1967, 1977; Strathern 1988).

The dynamics of social relations are founded in a conception of the house as constituted by the initial androgynous unity of a male and a female aspect – a brother and a sister (Strathern 1988; McKinnon

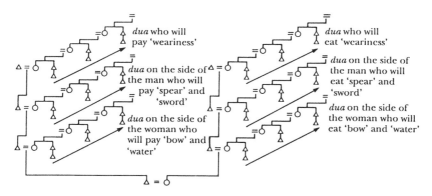

Fig. 8.2   The exchange pathways implicated in a man's marriage with an 'other' woman.

1991). When a relationship between a previously unrelated man and woman has been initiated with the intention that it should result in marriage, the immediate effect is not, as we might assume, the separation of the woman from her natal house, but rather the incorporation of the man as a part of the 'female' aspect of that house.

This is most explicitly evident in the initial uxorilocal residence of the man (a position described as being analogous to that of a slave) and the potential matrilateral affiliation of the couple's children. Indebted on account of the woman and the life-giving potential she bears, the man is thus completely encompassed by his wife-givers. It is only through the preliminary marriage prestations and the later bridewealth prestations – called 'bow', 'water', 'spear', 'sword' and 'weariness' (see Fig. 8.2) – that a man's own 'brothers and uncles' and 'masters' are able to 'redeem' (*rtevut*) him from his subservient, slave-like incorporation within his wife's house.[9] These prestations extract the man, his wife and their children from her natal house: they establish not only the patri-virilocal residence of the couple, but ultimately also the patrilateral affiliation of their children. They thereby establish the separate identity of the 'female' wife-taking house as distinct from the 'male' wife-giving house and, as a consequence, they lay the foundation for their continued relation (Valeri 1980). If, however, the exchanges are only partially completed, this may mean uxorilocal residence for the man and/or the matrilateral affiliation of children. There results the subordination of the wife-taker as an inferior female aspect of the wife-giving house and the consequent dissolution of the affinal relation between the two sides. Moreover, if there is a complete failure of exchange and a man is unable to mobilize his masters or his own family to pay either the separation fine or the initial bridewealth prestations, a man could (formerly) be seized and sold into slavery or, alternatively, he could flee and seek asylum as the younger brother client (and virtual slave) of a man of a named house.

The bridewealth and, more generally, all the male goods and valuables that move from wife-taker to wife-giver are meant to sever the more immediate effects of the slave-like incorporation and subordination of the female wife-takers. It is also true, however, that the female goods and valuables that move from wife-giver to wife-taker are meant to counter this severance and stress the continuity of relation and the inevitability of the encompassment of the female wife-takers by those who represent the source of life, the male wife-givers.[10]

Indigenous ideas about health, growth and life focus upon the negotiation of this tension between the forces of separation and those of encompassment. Although one's wife-takers will remain the female aspect of the male wife-givers, it is important that their separate – that is, externalized – identity be established and maintained. For to remain completely encompassed – that is, absorbed and incorporated – within the house of their wife-givers is a kind of social death, a relinquishment of the potential for growth and expansion.

The contrastive modes of affiliation and residence outlined above take on differential value, therefore, in accordance with the value given to the processes that ensure the growth and extension of life out from a source. Patrilateral affiliation and patrilocal residence effect the separation and externalization of the female issue from the male source at the same time that they ensure the continued relation between male wife-givers and female wife-takers, source and issue. This, in turn, makes it possible for the wife-takers to maintain a fixed centre of male continuity within their own house, from which point of anchorage they are able to foster the growth and extension of life through the female aspects of their house. Matrilateral affiliation and uxorilocal residence, by contrast, fail to effect the externalization of the female issue from the male source at the same time that they negate the relation between wife-giver and wife-taker. Unable to maintain a separate centre of male continuity within their own house, the wife-takers are subordinated and incorporated as a female aspect of their wife-giving house.

The forms of affiliation and residence therefore articulate with the larger hierarchical order of Tanimbarese society because the permanence of named houses requires the achievement of an intergenerational continuity and concentration of males who main- tain a fixed relation to the estates and patrimony of the house. The impermanence of unnamed houses and their estates is paralleled by the indeterminacy of the affiliation of their members. Not only is it the men of unnamed houses who are most likely to be dispersed through matrilateral affiliation, it can also be said that those who do affiliate matrilaterally may eventually come to constitute unnamed houses.

THE ANCHORAGE AND EXTENSION OF LIFE

The creation of the hierarchical superiority of named houses can be understood when one traces the changes, over time, in the affinal relations centred upon a brother–sister pair and their descendants. For it is here that the relative hierarchy of affinal relations (seen in terms of persons and blood) is transformed into a permanent hierarchy (seen in terms of the relation between named and unnamed houses).

The representatives of the male line of a brother retain rights to act as the life- and wife-giver to the sister's children and their descendants. This means that they must either provide women, life- blood, and female valuables for their sister's sons or, should they marry 'other women', redeem them of their debts for another source of women, life-blood, and female valuables. In the latter case (following Fig. 8.3), this means that the representatives of the house of the brother (A), together with his 'masters' (X, Y and so on), are obligated to pay the 'bow' (and 'water') portions of B1's bridewealth, the 'spear' (and 'sword') portions of B2's bridewealth, and the 'weariness' portions of B3's bridewealth. At the same time, they maintain the right to receive the equivalent portions of the bride- wealth paid for these men's sisters. These rights and responsibilities therefore continue for three generations, since the representatives of

181

Susan McKinnon

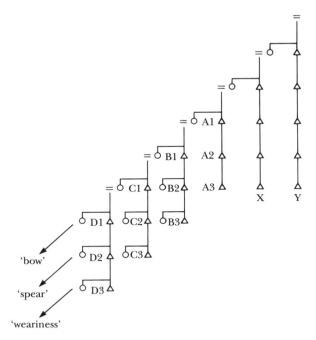

Fig. 8.3   The continuity and limitations of bridewealth obligations.

the house of the brother remain implicated in the bridewealth exchanges of the descendants of the sister and her husband for this period of time.

Over three generations, then, the descendants of a brother and a sister are related by the female bloodline that links them and by the bridewealth exchanges implicated by the marriages of the sister's children. By paying the bridewealth of the male descendants of the sister (or providing them with a daughter in marriage), the descendants of the brother ensure the continued redemption (patri-lateral affiliation and patrilocal residence) and separate identity of these men, just as their own redemption and separate identity are ensured by the descendants of *their* mother's brothers.

Beyond three generations, however, the two sides will no longer be implicated in the bridewealth exchanges engendered by the sister's marriage. The perpetuation of the asymmetric relation between the two sides beyond this point depends upon the fulfilment of one of two conditions: the renewal of the affinal relation through matrilateral cross-cousin marriage (which, in fact, is only intermittently practised); or the further extension of the female line that emanates from the sister. In the latter case, because the female line has 'multiplied its sprouts a thousandfold', the two sides will both continue to be recognized as the source of life of those who stand along the lower reaches of this female line. Their relationship will continue to be implicated in the exchange of valuables that centres upon the marriages of these people. Following Fig. 8.3 again, the men of A may be called upon to pay and receive the relevant portions of the bridewealth of the men and women of C and D, and so on indefinitely.

Once perpetuated beyond three generations, the relation between the side of the brother and that of the sister will be transformed from one conceptualized in terms of female bloodlines and the marriages of particular people that are characteristic of sisters and aunts pathways to one conceptualized in terms of permanent relations of alliance between houses that are characteristic of the rows. Only intermittently reconstituted through the marriage of their own men and women, the relation between allied houses along the rows is continually reconstituted by the exchange of valuables resulting from the marriages of other men and women further down the row and along the sisters and aunts pathways. Their relation is therefore renewed not so much by reengaging the movement of their own 'persons' and 'blood', but rather by negotiating the movement of valuables that express the condensed value of the movement of other 'persons' and 'blood' – and by the continued extension of life out from the source.

It is the ability to transform the impermanent pathways of sisters and aunts into permanent rows of allied houses, to transform the movement of blood into the movement of valuables, to maintain a separate identity, and to become a fixed and enduring source of life for others that effects the generalization and objectification of relations that is the hallmark of named houses. And it is this ability that transforms the transitory relations of hierarchy, which constitute wife-givers as superior to wife-takers, into the permanent forms of hierarchy, which establish rows of named houses as a superordinate form over pathways of sisters and aunts and which thereby distinguish the nobles of named houses from the commoners of unnamed houses.

The generalization and objectification of relations anchors the source of life in named houses. Yet the extension of life depends upon the particularization of relations in unnamed houses. These latter relations are continually dissolved in a flux of shifting (but always personalized and individualized) identities that are formed and reformed as life extends out from the source. As much as the source of life must be anchored by the immobilized weight of concentrated value, the extension of life must be realized through its fluidity, mobility, and lightness of being. The generalization and particularization of relations are therefore the two sides of the double movement that links source and issue in an organic figure of growth.

CONTRASTIVE FORMS OF MARRIAGE

Having come thus far, it will be easy to see how the contrastive forms of marriage that exist in Tanimbar articulate with the processes described above. An explicit injunction that two brothers (of the same 'house') may not marry two sisters (of the same 'house') ensures that, in what nevertheless remains a thoroughly asymmetric system, matrilateral cross-cousin marriage cannot be the only type of marriage accorded value. Indeed, in Tanimbar, there is a range of women a man might marry, including: the 'women of one's master' (*vat dua*), who belong to established wife-giving houses along the rows; 'same-sex siblings' (*ya'an-iwarin*), who include both a man's matrilateral cross-cousins (*fatnima*), and his brother's wives and wife's sisters (if they have been widowed) and 'other women' (*vat liak*), who belong to previously unallied houses.

Marriage with an 'other woman' is most often initiated by the young couple as a result of a secret love affair. Such an affair blossoms from the recognition of the uniqueness and particularity of individuals and individual desires. It is here that a man must be specifically redeemed of his bridewealth debts and that the payment of bridewealth becomes the prerequisite to the establishment of patri-virilocal residence of the man and patrilateral affiliation of his children. As a result of the marriage, the relation between the two sides is subsequently seen in terms of an asymmetric and hierarchical relation between wife-giver and wife-taker, male and female, 'brothers and uncles' and 'sisters and aunts', who come to be related in terms of the flow of blood along the female line that joins them.

Both matrilateral cross-cousin marriage and marriage with a 'woman of one's master' preserve the asymmetric and hierarchical relation between wife-giver and wife-taker. Yet the two forms of marriage differ in significant ways. Matrilateral cross-cousin marriage has reference to a man's own female bloodline, and it entails a reciprocity of exchange that has previously been established between the 'brothers and uncles' and the 'sisters and aunts' who are linked along his own female bloodline. By contrast, a marriage with a 'woman of one's master' has exclusive reference to the row that connects specific named houses, and it entails a series of reciprocal exchanges between these houses. In marrying her father's sister's son, a woman follows the bloodline of a particular person: 'she follows her father's sister' (*norang avan*). In marrying a man from a house that is the traditional wife-taker of her own house, a woman does not follow a particular person, but rather 'follows the row' (*norang lolat*) of named houses that are wife-takers relative to her own. In both forms of marriage, it is the continuity of exchange – rather than the payment of specific portions of bridewealth – that ensures the patri-virilocal residence of the man and the patrilateral affiliation of his children.

These contrasting forms of marriage take on their differential value by relation to the contrary processes of particularization and generalization, dispersal and concentration, that trace the trajectory between source and issue. In marriage with an 'other woman', we see the extraction of life from new sources, its externalization, dispersal and extension. Here new pathways are forged as asymmetric extensions of old pathways; new relations are formed as impermanent projections of life into the future, following the onward flow of blood.

In marriage with a matrilateral cross-cousin, we see a return to an old source of life. In the process, the fertility of a pathway of blood and life is reconfirmed and its generative forces reactivated. By replicating a marriage along such a pathway, what had been only a tenuous projection into the future anchors itself in the past. In the process, the pathway and the affinal relation are strengthened and become 'weighty' with the multiplication of people and valuables that travel upon it. Although still seen in terms of people and particular bloodlines, matrilateral cross-cousin marriage moves toward the generalization and objectification of affinal relations as the concentrated movement of people and valuables etches the figure of an enduring pathway.

In marriage with a 'woman of one's master', a woman from a long-allied house related along the rows, we see a return to a founding source of life. Such a marriage, which (unlike other forms of marriage) is the privilege of members of named houses only, replicates an ancestral marriage, that which established the original identity of the house. It celebrates not a relation between particular persons, but rather the continuity of the alliance itself. Marriage with a 'woman of one's master' occurs only exceedingly rarely because of the vast number of important, named valuables that it requires. But it is precisely the concentrated weight and number of valuables that move on such occasions that completes the generalization and objectification of the relation between source and issue, as it creates a row that is permanent and fully anchored in the past of the ancestors.

Seen as a whole, the system of marriage and exchange comprehends a double movement: one of generalization, objectification and concentration, which connects back to the past and anchors the source of life; and one of particularization, personification and dispersal, which expands ever outward into the future and fulfills the potential for life. The two are integrated through the asymmetric movement of women and life-blood, and mediated by the reciprocal exchange of valuables. In light of this double movement, different forms of marriage mutually imply one another. The continuity of the old, permanent alliances that connect back to the past and the source of life is dependent upon the movement of valuables engendered by the initiation of new affinal relations that issue forth from out-married women. Conversely, these latter are supported by the reciprocity of exchange that operates along the pathways and rows that trace old, established alliances.

CONCLUSION

By reference to this double movement, it is possible to understand the manner in which contrastive forms of marriage, affiliation and residence are mutually implicated in the articulation of the hierarchical order of Tanimbarese society. In terms of marriage, it is the marriages (with a 'woman of one's master' and, to a lesser extent, with a matrilateral cross-cousin) contracted by elder brothers and nobles of named houses that effect the continuity of relations back to enduring sources of life. Yet these alliances would not be possible except for the fact that the marriages (primarily with 'other women') that remain the province of younger brothers and commoners of unnamed houses extend female bloodlines and are productive of a wealth of valuables that gives new content to old pathways of alliance.

In terms of affiliation, the membership of houses is determined by the process of exchange, through which the forces of separation and encompassment are negotiated. Thus, exchange articulates the double movement that achieves not only the fixity of the (male) source, but also the fertility and growth of the (female) issue – both of which are necessary to the continuity and identity of a house. It is in the context of this relation between source and issue that the contrastive forms of residence and affiliation are given value and contribute to the creation of the hierarchical order of society. For elder brothers and members of named houses are those who have been able to realize the continuity and permanence of the male line that stands as a source and the growth and extension of the female lines that reach out into the future. Discontinuity and impermanence, along both lines, define the fragile position of commoners and members of unnamed houses – and, even more so, of slaves.

Finally, considered within the framework of these processes, it is the objectification and generalization of relations, and the condensation of value, in particular forms of marriage and affiliation that make it possible for elder brothers and nobles of named houses to convert the relative hierarchy of affinal relations into an enduring hierarchy of named and unnamed houses, nobles and commoners.

In order to understand the hierarchical dynamics of Tanimbarese social relations, it has been necessary to move away from a theoretical framework that conceptualizes social units in terms of *a priori*, essentialist and exclusive criteria. Within such a framework, not only have societies been characterized by reference to external categories, but these categories have also been seen as exclusive of one another. It has been necessary to substitute a more dynamic conception of social relations that reveals (rather than conceals) the contrastive logic of relatively valued social forms and the processes by which they are brought into being. This move has been possible because a consideration of indigenous ideology has compelled a reevaluation of inherited analytic categories.

A house society, at least in Tanimbarese terms, does not simply permit a random 'compounding of forces which, everywhere else, seem only destined to mutual exclusion because of their contradictory bends' (Lévi-Strauss 1983a:184). It is, rather, the explicit and differential articulation of mutually implicating contrastive social forms. Nor is the house society a kind of monstrous child, born in the world of kinship, transfigured by the world of the market, and governed by the forces of an evolutionary logic external to it. It is, rather, an integral form governed by processes that have their own, internal logic. If I have called these processes the generalization and particularization of relations, and the concentration and dispersal of value, that are productive of a hierarchical order of society, Tanimbarese would call them the forces that anchor the source of life and those that foster its growth and extension.

HOUSES, PLACES AND PEOPLE: COMMUNITY AND
9 **CONTINUITY IN GUIANA**[1]

Peter Rivière

THIS CHAPTER CONSIDERS the concept of the 'house' among the Carib-speaking peoples who live in the interior of the northeast corner of South America, a region often referred to as Guiana but politically divided between Brazil, French Guiana, Guyana, Surinam and Venezuela. This is a large area populated by numerous small native groups which, however, have enough in common for it to be possible to generalize about them with some degree of confidence.[2]

In the absence of any clearly defined social structure among these peoples, ethnographers have often found settlements an invaluable hook on which to hang their descriptions. Thus, to a large extent, the house, which is often physically identical with the settlement, has been a crucial element in the theoretical and comparative literature of the region. The issues which this raises both in the wider South American context and in relation to Lévi-Strauss's ideas on house societies are taken up in the second half of the chapter.

There are within the region three main types of settlement pattern. These are the single communal house settlement; the nucleated village; and the ceremonial centre settlement. This chapter will concentrate mainly on the first two forms, but it is necessary to say something about the last since all the settlement patterns of the region have some common characteristics. The ceremonial centre settlement, of which the best reported example is that of the Akawaio, is characterized by dual residence with family groups owning dwellings both at a nucleated village with a ceremonial centre and at outlying garden sites and moving seasonally from one to the other (Butt Colson 1970: 36–42).[3] Included in this category are the savannah-dwelling Indians such as the Macusi and Pemon. Some of these Indians live in scattered nuclear and extended family dwellings but the ceremonial centre pattern also survives, as Thomas (1982: 94), for example, indicates with reference to the Pemon. Furthermore there is evidence that the Pemon at the beginning of the century had single communal house settlements as well as villages of the ceremonial centre type (Koch-Grünberg 1923: 16). So that while it is possible to distinguish between different types of settlement, it is likely that there is no fundamental difference between them and that they are all variations of one another.

When we turn to consider what constitutes a 'house' in Guiana, in some cases it is very obvious for the house, the settlement and the community are one and the same thing. In these cases the settlement is formed by a single large roundhouse in which all members of the community live. The main alternative to this is the nucleated village composed of a number of smaller constructions. Although there are visible differences between these two types of settlement, there are good reasons, which will become apparent in the course of this chapter, for treating them as similar organizations. I will use the terms 'house' and 'village' interchangeably, reserve 'settlement' for the geographical location, and refer to the residents of such a unit as a 'community'. This is in keeping with native usage because most groups, whether they have single- or multi-house settlements, make terminological distinctions between 'house' as a dwelling-place and the 'settlement' as a geographical location. For example,[4] among the Trio of Surinam, who have multi-house settlements, the term for settlement is *pata* and the generic term for a house is *pakoro*, whereas among the Ye'cuana of Venezuela, who have single-house settlements, the terms are *juata* and *atta*, respectively. Most of the groups also have a term for a social group, defined by the criteria of kinship and co-residence, which could roughly be translated as 'community' (Rivière 1984: 31–9). In one case at least the identification between settlement and community is taken further for Dumont claims that 'the Panare call their buildings and themselves as a group by the same name' (1976: 88–9).[5]

Houses are built from similar materials throughout the region.

They are wood framed and thatched with a range of different palm leaves. However, a great variety of house types is to be found, and most groups build more than one type of house. The Trio distinguish and name eight main types of dwelling house and there are, in addition, variants and subtypes of these.[6] On the other hand, the Ye'cuana have only two types of house, one round, the other rectangular. In fact, several other groups (the Panare and the Waiwai, for example) that have single-house settlements have only two types of dwelling, one round and the other rectangular, oval or oblong.[7] In general, it would not appear to be the supply of construction material that dictates the type of house built although there is among some people the expectation that specific types of material be used. For example, the northwestern Panare use one type of palm to thatch the roundhouse, and another for the rectangular (Mattéi-Muller and Henley 1990: caption to Plate 9). Among the southern Panare, where roundhouses are more common, four different types of palm thatch may be used, each having its correct place on the conical roof (Henley: pers. commun.). A similar thing is found among the Ye'cuana who thatch the upper part of the roundhouse roof with one type of the palm leaf and the lower part with another. This constructional feature is, as will be seen below, a reflection of the symbolic and cosmological significance of the house.

However, what seems generally true is that whether there are several types of house or only two, only one of them will be regarded as a 'proper' house in the sense of fulfilling certain spatial, social, ritual and symbolic specifications. Such houses are in almost every case roundhouses although there is considerable variation in their actual shape. Thus the main Trio house is beehive shaped with thatch reaching to the floor (Plate 6) whereas that of the Ye'cuana is conical with the thatch stopping at a vertical wall of wattle or wattle and daub a metre or more from the ground. On condition that the construction and layout fulfil local expectations, the size of any particular example is symbolically unimportant. Thus, Henley (1982: 15) reports that the largest Panare conical house he saw was 25m in diameter and 12m high, and the smallest was 7m in diameter and 5m high. In another sense, as we will see, the size of a house or settlement is important for it is indicative of the status and standing of its leader.

The discussion so far has been confined to dwelling houses, but most settlements contain various other constructions. Such buildings,

Plate 6   The beehive-shaped Trio house known as *mïnë* in the village of Alalaparu in 1963.

often of different types, are used for a whole range of purposes including workhouses in which women process food, temporary shelters for visitors, kennels, and menstruation or birth huts. These will not be taken into further account here although their existence and position are not insignificant for understanding social relations and the symbolic ordering of space.

A difference between single- and multi-house settlements is that the social and symbolic significance of the former's layout appears to be far more explicit and elaborated. This may reflect the quality of the ethnography but I think not because, although the layout of multi-house settlements exhibits similar basic features to that of single-house settlements, no single house provides the same degree of community focus. The basic layout of a Trio village is quite simple. There is a cleared area which is more or less surrounded by houses depending on the size of the village, although in the smallest villages consisting perhaps of only one or two dwellings it will appear to be just in front of the houses. This space is used for collective activities such as communal meals, rituals and, on moonlit nights, as the place where men congregate to chat. The Trio word for this area is *anna* and it is

largely a male space, for although women are not excluded from it
men tend to occupy the middle of it whereas women keep more to its
edge and closer to their houses. Between the village and the gardens
or forest is an area of half-cleared land onto which the houses back
and where rubbish is deposited.[8] The gardens may or may not form a
further encircling band of cleared land and beyond them lies the
forest. The most important spatial distinction that the Trio make is
that between village (*pata*) and forest (*itu*).[9] In small villages it is a truly
striking contrast with the wall of the forest hemming in the village
clearing so that it is like living in a well. In all cases the dusty glare
and heat of the village is opposed to the damp darkness of the forest
and the passage from one to the other is seen as important and
marked by ritual attention.

This basically concentric pattern is very much more clearly
displayed in the layout of the large communal houses that form the
single-house settlements. Thus at the centre of the Ye'cuana roundhouse (*atta*) is the *annaka* (cf. Trio *anna*), basically a male arena where
bachelors sleep, rituals and dances are performed, communal meals
are taken, visitors are welcomed and community decisions are made.
Round the periphery lie the family compartments and hearths, the
domestic space or *asa*. The main door, facing east, gives straight on to
the *annaka*, whereas the other doors lead into family compartments.
Not all communal roundhouses have more than one door, but where
they do the main door at the front is usually associated with men and
male guests, and the other door or doors with women. The contrast
between back and front is also found in a layout where the communal
and ceremonial part of the house is offset towards the front and the
rear of the house is associated with privacy and domesticity.

That the layouts of the single-house and multi-house settlements
are not fundamentally different is evinced by that of a Ye'cuana
village in which the traditional form has been abandoned. This village
is composed of a number of separate dwellings, grouped round a
central plaza with a building called the *annaka* located to one side of it.
This house 'serves the same function as the inner circle in the round
houses' (Arvelo-Jimenez 1971: 147).

It should be noted at this point that ceremonial centre settlements
exhibit a similar pattern, although spread over a much wider area. At
the centre lies the nucleated village associated with collective and
ceremonial life, and round it at varying distances are the nuclear or

extended family dwellings where the main economic pursuits of farming and hunting are carried out. In the case of the Akawaio it seems clear that this settlement pattern is an adaptive response to the growth of large population centres and a similar development is recognizable among the Trio under external influence and the appearance of settlements with medical, religious, commercial and scholastic functions (Rivière 1981). This pattern, although dictated by practical needs, at the same time remains consistent with the symbolic ordering of space noted.

In clearer or less clear form the spatial organization of the Guiana settlement or house reflects what seems to be an almost Pan-amazonic pattern of concentric dualism whereby the centre is opposed to the periphery, front to the back and the inside to the outside. However, the evaluative connotations these basically spatial terms carry in English are very misleading in the Guiana context especially since these oppositions are often associated with a range of non-spatial terms including men:women, public:private, sacred:secular and essence:process.[10] However it is important to regard the relationship between these aspects of concentric dualism as both complementary and encompassing. Whereas the centre cannot exist without its periphery and vice versa, both centre and periphery together stand as centre to some further periphery. In a Trio village the *anna* is opposed to the encircling houses, but both houses and *anna* together form a settlement (*pata*) in opposition to the forest (*itu*). This situation is even more obvious in the case of the Ye'cuana as we will see when we now turn to the symbolic meaning of the house.

The house is not just a shelter for the spatial organization reflects certain fundamental social and cosmic distinctions. More or less explicitly the house is a microcosm. Nowhere is this more fully evident than in the case of the Ye'cuana house. The first Ye'cuana house was built by the culture-hero Wanadi, in the form of Attawanadi (House Wanadi), during his third and final visitation to this world. On that occasion he created the Ye'cuana (as well as other people) and their particular cultural identity. The house he built is still visible today in the form of a conical mountain located at Kushamakari in the centre of the Ye'cuana homeland. At the same time he created an invisible counterpart to it and the present-day *atta* still has an unseen double. Wanadi also initiated the ritual *waijama*, still used to inaugurate a new roundhouse.

The house is an exact replica of the universe. At ground level the *annaka* is equated with the 'sea' (*dama*) at the centre of the world while the *asa* is the inhabited earth (*nono*). The conical roof is the sky, also divided into an upper and lower part, physically represented by two different types of thatch of which the more valuable and durable covers the upper section and the part occupied by the *annaka* at ground level. The outer circle of the house, the *asa*, is covered by a more perishable thatch. The main transverse roof beams run north/south and represent the Milky Way, and the other main roof beams are referred to as 'sky trees'. All these beams are fixed at their lower ends to a ring of twelve outer posts called 'star supports'. The central housepost connects earth to sky and the visible to the invisible world.

An unusual feature of the Ye'cuana house is the skylight in the roof which most authors have explained in practical terms as a means of introducing light to the dark interior and of letting out smoke. Wilbert (1981), however, has gone further than this and sees the skylight together with the layout and orientation of the house as suggesting that the Ye'cuana used their houses as astronomic calendars, rather on the lines of the explanations proposed for Stonehenge and other European megalithic monuments. Whether or not we agree with Wilbert's interpretation there is no doubt about the powerful meaning associated with the Ye'cuana *atta*. Guss (1989: 32) writes:

In addition to presenting a faithful visualization of the structure of the universe, the Yekuana *atta* also provides a template upon which all other symbolic systems may be measured. The duality so central to Yekuana thought is reproduced in the spatio-temporal relations that determine their lives. As with all other forms, the *atta* is the result of two interlocking realities – an illusionary and material outer one encasing a more powerful and invisible inner one. It is in this latter or 'inner one', the *annaka*, that all ritual events take place, as communication with the unseen spirit-world is facilitated by the direct link provided through the centrepost. But the *annaka* and its surrounding *asa* also reflect the interdependence of these two realities and as such are as indivisible (and interpenetrating) as any daily economic activity is from its spiritual counterpart.

However, even if Ye'cuana house symbolism is exceptionally elaborate (or well reported) by the standards of the region, it is not different in kind from that found among other people. It is clear that the Waiwai house carries a heavy load of meaning (see Fock 1963; Yde 1965) as does that of the Panare as described by Dumont (1976: Chap. 5).

The situation in the case of groups with multi-house settlements is rather different for none of the ethnographies relating to such villages spells out the cosmic and symbolic significance of the house with the explicitness that is reported for the Ye'cuana. Even so there are clues to suggest that the house amongst these groups does have, if in an unelaborated form, similar meanings. The Trio are a case in point. They are certainly not explicit about the microcosmic nature of the house, and the origin of the house as recorded in the myth of the culture-hero Përërërëwa simply involves his being taught how to build one (type unspecified) by the daughter of Ariweimë, the giant alligator (Koelewijn and Rivière 1987: 16–17). Whereas they do not have an idea of the house, like that of the Ye'cuana, modelled on a house constructed by a culture-hero which is still visible in the form of a mountain, they do see rock outcrops, hills and mountains as the houses of spirits and the masters of game animals. Thus the Trio also subscribe to an association between hardness, durability and invisibility. One also finds this in other areas of their culture. For example, in the manufacture of stools the hard wood used is a substitution made by men for the rock out of which a culture-hero carved the prototype (Rivière 1969: 236).[11]

If there is a single type of Trio house that has meaning it is the round beehive-shaped dwelling, which is regarded by some Indians as the most traditional form. The word for it is *miñë* and the term applies also to the small construction in which a shaman conducts a seance, and to the hide used for shooting birds. What all three structures have in common is that they conceal those inside them, that is they become invisible. In cosmic terms this is most significant in the case of the shaman's hide for whilst in it and in a trance he travels to the different layers of the cosmos. He is not simply invisible but becomes part of the invisible world. In the case of the dwelling house, there is a direct parallel with the Ye'cuana *atta* as expressed by Guss in the passage already cited where he contrasts the outer visible reality with the inner invisible reality of the house. Thus while I have no evidence that the Trio conceive of an invisible counterpart to the visible house, the interior of the *miñë* is invisible compared with the visible exterior and, like the inside of the shaman's hide, closer to the powerful invisible reality.

Despite the wealth of meaning attached to houses, everywhere in Guiana the settlement is shortlived. Rarely does a settlement last more than ten years and the average duration is closer to six years. There are a good many reasons given to account for this; some of them of a practical nature, others less obviously so. Among the former one may note the exhaustion of economic resources in the vicinity, whether these be the availability of suitable cultivable land, the decline in hunting returns or the absence of other raw materials. Another reason that is frequently given is that after a certain number of wet seasons, a house no longer provides adequate shelter from the rain and the thatch is likely to be infested. Now it would be possible to pull the thatch off, burn it and rethatch the wood frame which is usually perfectly sound. In fact it is quite common for the main hardwood posts to be salvaged for use in another building. The preference, however, is to relocate the settlement by building a new house elsewhere.[12] Another common reason for the abandonment of a settlement is the association of misfortune with the place. This may be serious illness or the death of a number of infants, but the archetypal situation is the death of the village leader. Although whether the corpse is buried in the floor of the house or disposed of elsewhere varies from group to group, this has no bearing on whether the house is abandoned, which inevitably occurs. This opens up a question of fundamental importance: the relationship between a settlement and its leader.

A settlement, in a certain sense, belongs to its leader. Throughout the region there are various ways in which settlements are referred to. They are commonly known by a particular geographical or other feature in their vicinity; the name of a rapids, an oddly shaped rock, or the occurrence of a certain botanical species, for example. But they are equally known by the name of the person who founded the settlement, and who, in turn, is automatically its leader. Thus, in Trio, a settlement might be known as Eoyari *pata*. Eoyari is the name of the village founder/leader, so it is his 'village' or 'place'. In keeping with this the village leader is also known as the *pata entu*. The term *entu* can be glossed as 'owner' but its semantic range is wider than that. It also has the sense of 'origin' or 'root', something from which a thing has sprung.[13]

With some variation, the Trio case is widely true throughout the region. Thus, among the Ye'cuana, a small, incipient village is referred to as a headman's place or people, and as it grows older and larger it comes to be known by some local geographical feature. Arvelo-Jimenez (1971: 59) states that these different name-forms distinguish between a developing community and a fully autonomous settlement. Henley (1982: 14) also notes that although the Panare often fail to name their settlements, when they do so it is by reference to those that live at a particular site or by association with someone (usually a senior man) living there. In the case of the Akawaio the relationship between the house and the leader is made completely explicit, since one of the terms for the latter is derived from that for a housepost. The housepost is *ebu* and the village leader *ebulu* (Butt Colson 1971: 82–3).[14]

The association between house or settlement and its leader is most dramatically portrayed on the death of the latter. As already mentioned, when this occurs, almost invariably throughout the region, the village is abandoned, and the house is often destroyed. Barandiarán (1966: 63), who refers to the Ye'cuana leader as the 'soul' of the house, states that when the leader dies the house also dies. In a sense this is true for whereas a settlement is a geographical location, just as the house or houses contained within it are physical constructions, it is also a community of people. As a community the settlement is composed of a network of social relationships that has the leader as its centre. A leader's death results not simply in the abandonment and often the destruction of the house but often also in the demise or the dispersion of the community. At this point it is important to turn to a consideration of the settlement as a sociological phenomenon.

The settlement, as a community, is the basic social unit in the region. It is politically autonomous, and, ideally, is socially and economically self-sufficient. Guss claims that a ceremony associated with the final building stage of the Ye'cuana roundhouse seals it 'both physically and symbolically, reinforcing the autonomy and self-reliance that is the ideal of every Yekuana community' (1989: 26). This native view faithfully reflects the inside:outside conceptual organization of the world, but in practice it is quite false. The average size of settlements throughout the region is around 30 people and rarely exceeds 50 people for long. A population of such a size is not self-sufficient, simply on demographic grounds. There is, for example, a preference for settlement endogamy, but the chance of finding a marriageable person within the community is very low. Accordingly the search for a spouse forces people to look elsewhere. There is also extensive intersettlement trading and a considerable degree of ritual interdependence exists. Indeed, whereas there is the ideal of the settlement as a closed community, in practice there is high population mobility with people constantly moving from one settlement to another for an assortment of reasons. This, together with the fact that settlements are relatively ephemeral, means that the distribution of settlements and their constituent populations are forever changing although the basic underlying pattern remains the same.

On turning to consider the social composition of Guiana communities it is important to note that coresidence is often as important as kinship in the ordering of relationships and it is often difficult to distinguish between them. Most languages in the region have a term which applies to a group of which the criteria of membership are indistinguishably kinship and co-residence (see Rivière 1984: 31–9). Indeed these terms are often the only words in the various languages that refer to any form of social grouping, a term for the family often being absent. Furthermore there is no social grouping outside that created by kinship and co-residence in a single settlement. The Guiana region is characterized by the absence of such social formations as moieties, local descent groups and age-sets reported from elsewhere in Lowland South America, a fact which puts particular emphasis on the house as a stable community, if only for a given moment, in what is otherwise a world of fluid social arrangements.

A community normally has at its core a shallow bilateral kindred, often matrilaterally skewed as a result of the statistical tendency towards uxorilocal postmarital residence. Because the relationship terminologies are of the two-line prescriptive type, a bilateral kindred will contain both kin and affines, and this fits with the native view of the settlement as endogamous. However, a feature of the region is that this distinction tends to be played down, and co-residents are represented as consanguines. This apparently paradoxical position has to be explained by the disruptive nature of affinity in the region. Several authors have drawn attention, with reference both to Guiana and to elsewhere in Lowland South America, to what they refer to as the suppression of affinity. I have argued (1984: 67–71) that it is more in keeping with native ideas to express this as the emphasis on consanguinity.

199

A close marriage, and close in this context may mean kinship or co-residence since they are interchangeable and conflated, does not involve the difficulties that marriage between strangers creates. It is important to distinguish between related affines, that is, those who are kin, and unrelated affines, although it should be understood that there is a gradation rather than a contrast between these statuses. The behaviour and attitudes between these two types of affines, depending on degree of relatedness, are quite distinct. Kin who become affines remain kin whereas it takes a long time for unrelated affines to become accepted as kin. This distinction between kin and unrelated affines reflects the concentric ordering of the world that has already been noted. This is most clearly expressed in the opposition of inside to outside and gives the spurious impression that the community is a self-sufficient and enduring entity. However unrealistic this conceptualization of the community – as we have seen, in practice the settlement itself has an ephemeral life and its population is transitory – it does have an important influence on social behaviour and attitudes.

It has been pointed out that among the Ye'cuana 'village history is political history' (Arvelo-Jimenez 1973: 4), and this is widely true in Guiana. The decision where to live is often made on political grounds in the sense that there is often advantage to be gained from living in the village of a competent leader. Accordingly the number of a settlement's inhabitants is a good indicator of the quality of its leader. In the case of single-house settlements, the size of the communal house gives a similar indication since this depends on the workforce, in other words the number of followers, a leader can attract. Goldman (1963: 155), writing of the Cubeo of the Northwest Amazon, has remarked that 'the building of a maloca constitutes an election', and this remark is equally applicable to Guiana. People elect a leader by choosing to live with him, and in the case of single-house settlements they vote by helping to construct the house. The more successful a leader the more populous his village will be, but paradoxically in this success lies the seeds of failure. As a community grows in size, the more likely are there to be disputes and the more difficult are they to settle. The larger the village grows the more unstable it becomes. The situation becomes acute when the population is large enough for two bilateral kindreds to develop. When this happens, it is almost certain that two factions will emerge and the result of this is that the village will inevitably fission. The reason for this, a phenomenon which I have earlier referred to as 'single-cell' political units (see Rivière 1970),[15] is that, in Guiana, there is no political mechanism for coping with internal factionalism, and villages which develop in this way inevitably divide.

Let me try to summarize some of this. The house is the crucial social institution throughout the Guiana region. It is the focus of social and cultural life. At the same time in its claims to self-sufficiency and to consanguinity it is a fiction. Its ephemerality equally denies it any role in the transmission of qualities from one generation to the next. It is a moral entity but only for as long as it survives; otherwise it has none of the qualities of a corporate group. The only evidence against this is a comment by Arvelo-Jimenez (1971: 366–7) with reference to the Ye'cuana when she writes that it is important in the context of disputes and confrontations for a person to know the history of his ancestral village. 'There is prestige attached to belonging to a kin group which has a history, and shame in being publicly uncovered as belonging to a kin group with none.' Such knowledge indicates that a person is descended from an independent residential group that formed the core of a village and provided its leader for several generations. This would presuppose rather more stable kin and residential groups than exist today, but I certainly would not dismiss that possibility given the social, cultural and demographic upheavals that have occurred since the conquest.

There is one further and speculative point to be taken up. It was noted with reference to the Ye'cuana that the first house, built by the culture-hero Wanadi, exists in the form of a mountain located in the centre of the Ye'cuana's homeland. As already mentioned, there is throughout the region a commonly made association between rocks or mountains (often regarded as the houses of spirits or game masters), permanence and durability, and the invisible world. However, there is more to it than this because when Wanadi made the first house he also constructed an invisible counterpart to it, and Guss (1989: 32) claims that every *atta* still has its invisible double. If this is so it suggests that the visible house with its transient existence is less important in terms of societal continuity than the invisible counterpart. To express this in other terms but in keeping with the transformational ideas common to the region, just as the inner circle of the *annaka* is opposed to the outer circle of the *asa* in terms of permanence to impermanence, and essence to process, so the invisible *atta* is related to the visible. The mountain/house at Kushamakari is the visible and durable representation of invisible continuity and perpetuity. If this is right, and it is certainly in keeping with widespread ideas about the nature of the invisible reality, then the visible 'house' as category, group or building is no more than a fleeting phenomenon in a noumenal world. Indeed the observable nature of the settlement, with its ephemeral existence and fluid population, lends support to this interpretation. Further support may also be derived from Dumont's claim that for the Panare the shaman, who deals with the invisible world, is conceptually related to permanence and the headman, who deals with the visible world, to impermanence (1977: 73), and from Morton's (1979) reworking of the Waiwai material .where he adopts the terms 'continuous' and 'discontinuous' to refer respectively to the spirit and the human worlds. I have also argued that:

Continuous time is not in any sense linear time, but rather it is just and always there, indistinguishable from the cosmos of which it forms part. Continuous time is like space, but like space is not undifferentiated; it is broken up by discontinuities. Settlements are both geographical locations and historical episodes. Discontinuities are located in continuous time in the same way as settlements are dispersed throughout the forest. (1984: 99–100)

Settlements are spatial and temporal discontinuities in a visible world that is, in a sense, contingent on an invisible reality.[16] Settlements are the visible but ephemeral evidence of an invisible continuity.

If this is correct, and its speculative nature must be stressed, can it be said that the 'house' in the sense of a corporate group or a moral person exists at one level of reality and not at another? Logically this is possible, but in this case I think it does not occur, because while these ideas provide the conceptual basis for societal continuity, they do not give rise to discrete social units. Elsewhere in Lowland South America the division of essences and their physical representations between groups of people give rise to enduring social units. This is not so in Guiana, where settlements are merely transitory evidence of a continuous and real although invisible world.

At the empirical level, however, the Guiana groups belong within Lévi-Strauss's class of 'house societies' solely in his formalist sense where 'only the type of grouping, but not their variable content or their always brief duration, remains constant' (1987: 154). In other words, the Guiana case belongs to the very weakest end of the spectrum that house societies constitute, and I wonder what value there might be in a classification so flexible that it seems possible to incorporate within it such a wide range of disparate societies. I cannot say that I have learnt anything new about the peoples of Guiana by reordering the material in the way in which I have presented it here, but then the very nature of these societies has always pushed ethnographers to look at them in terms of residential units. It is possible, of course, that unbeknownst we have been using the concept of 'house society' all the time, although concealing it under the notion of 'co-residence'. Indeed I am unconvinced that it is useful to distinguish between the two concepts when the notion of house society is being applied in its formalist or weakest sense.

Whereas I can see little advantage in applying the concept of house society in Guiana, this may not be more generally true of Lowland South America. Although I do not wish to digress too far in making comparisons, it seems to me that the notion may have more applicability in the Northwest Amazon where the transmission of non-material wealth is important, and even more so among the Jê and Bororo. For example, not only do we find among the Bororo the transmission of non-material wealth, what Crocker (1985: 33–6) refers to as 'totems', but there has been some difficulty in defining just what the social groups are which transmit these valuables. It would be quite reasonable to regard them as 'houses' for they are certainly associated with such physical structures. The location of these houses in the layout of the village is carefully defined and pan-Bororo in its application, to the point that a Bororo visiting a strange village will know where on the periphery he can expect to find his 'house'.

The chapters in this volume by Hugh-Jones and Lea support the contention that the notion of house society may be helpful in elucidating features of some Lowland South American societies. Lea's discussion of the Kayapó is particularly useful in this regard since she makes it clear that their house is both a visible and an invisible (what she calls 'non-material') entity. The striking difference from the Guiana case is that the Kayapó house has a membership, individuals who inherit certain names and prerogatives and the possession of which, in turn, defines them as members of the house. In Guiana there are no possessions, material or non-material, that define membership in a house or other social formations, because no such groupings exist. As a building, group or category the visible Guiana house is a contingent entity dependent on its invisible counterpart.

To end I would like to look further afield, to Southeast Asia, given the predominance of that region in this volume. Carsten's 1987 paper 'Analogues or opposites: household and community in Pulau Langkawi' (1987a) offers some remarkable similarities between the situation as she describes it for Malaysia and that in Guiana, but with some interesting differences. These are mainly due to the fact that in Guiana the house and the community are a single unit, whereas in Pulau Langkawi the community is composed of many houses. For example, Carsten points out that descent is of little importance and that siblingship is used to extend the house outwards into the community rather than downwards. Likewise in Guiana, descent is unimportant and the method of incorporating people into the community is by extending siblingship to them through the fiction that co-residents are consanguines. This act of incorporation at the same time redefines the distinction between inside and out. The Guiana house, like that in Pulau Langkawi, stands for 'undivided consanguinity' and is opposed to affinal relations (in the sense referred to above) which are excluded from it. Carsten (1987a: 167) writes that 'while it is true that consanguinity and affinity are on one level opposed, and at the same time, on another merged, this fusion cannot occur within the house'. It occurs in what Carsten calls the 'shadow house' of the community which is notionally endogamous. In Guiana, it is just within the house, which is also the community that, through endogamous marriage, the possibility for merging consanguinity and affinity, in the former's favour, lies.

However, this potential for merging does nothing to resolve the basic opposition between consanguinity and affinity because they are part and parcel of a general and more fundamental series of concentric oppositions. The outside, the other, is crucial to the reproduction of the inside, for while they are opposites they are equally complementary, one cannot exist without the other (see Overing 1981). However, it is not in everyday life that the opposition between them can be overcome or mediated. In both localities it is only under certain ritual conditions that it is possible to transcend the difference, although in contrasting ways. Thus in Guiana, through ritual the outside is brought inside, and for the period of the ritual a unitary world is created (see Rivière 1969: chap. XI). In Malaysia, it would appear that this is achieved by taking the household in the opposite direction – out into the community. In both cases, it might be argued, it is through the house that similar categorical oppositions are transcended, although in each case, responding to different values systems, this is achieved in opposite ways. Interesting though this is, it is doubtful whether it is insight enough to give the 'house' the status of a cross-cultural analytic category.

THE HOUSES OF THE MẼBENGOKRE (KAYAPÓ) OF CENTRAL BRAZIL – A NEW DOOR TO THEIR SOCIAL ORGANIZATION

10

Vanessa Lea

LÉVI-STRAUSS defines the house as 'a moral person which possesses a domain that is perpetuated by the transmission of its name, its fortune and titles, along a real or fictive line, held as legitimate on the sole condition that this continuity can be expressed in the language of kinship or of alliance, and more frequently of the two together' (1984: 190).[1] The Mẽbengokre, a Jê-speaking society of Central Brazil[2] recognize Houses (as opposed to houses, dwellings or abodes) as moral persons in the sense alluded to above. I shall show here how Lévi-Strauss's conception of house-based societies offers the possibility of a new perspective for understanding Mẽbengokre social organization but first it is necessary to distinguish between those of its characteristics which are compatible with the Mẽbengokre case and those which are not, discussing the incompatibilities that exist.[3]

The distinction between Houses and dwellings is invisible to the eye of a casual observer. The dwellings are very similar to one another and are regularly spaced around the village circle (Plate 7). Their only distinctive external architectural feature is their size. A dwelling may house only one nuclear family, though ideally it is occupied by an uxorilocal extended family. Nowadays, matrilateral parallel-cousins (and sometimes even uterine sisters) tend to inhabit separate dwellings, but in such cases they consider themselves to belong to the same House. In the Mẽbengokre case, 'House' is a synthetic gloss for*kikre dzam dzà*

Plate 7   Mẽbengokre houses in Kapòto Village, 1987.

(House/on foot/place). Each House occupies a fixed position within the village circle in relation to East and West and each is considered to have a place of origin in a specific portion of the circle where its members have built their dwellings since time immemorial.

In recent years the men have taken over house-building from the women and have adopted the regional style: oblong constructions with windowless vertical-pole walls and thatched roofs. Dwellings generally lack any internal divisions but have one or two doors (depending on size) which open onto the village circle. The doors serve as windows and light also filters through the spaces between the poles. The floors are of beaten earth. The women construct pole beds where they sleep with their husbands and small children, separated from the next couple by no more than a few feet. Pots and pans are strewn about the floor or stored on pole racks; other possessions are hung from the walls or from the rafters. The senior woman of the dwelling tends to occupy the centre of the house with her daughters (along with their husbands and children) distributed to either side. The daughter of a dead sister of the senior woman tends to occupy one extremity of the dwelling or to construct a separate dwelling, but next door to her maternal aunt. The number of inhabitants per dwelling ranges from two to thirteen. The size of a dwelling depends upon the number of its inhabitants and is independent of its symbolic wealth; its upkeep reflects the number of resident able-bodied men available for rebuilding and restoration. There is generally one stone oven per House, out in the patio, though each dwelling also has one or more cooking hearths inside too.

Mention is made of the absence of any House, in a particular village, by saying *dzam dzà kaprù*, which can be glossed as 'vacant position'. When new villages are built, spaces may be left between the occupied dwellings in the hope of filling them, in due course, with the arrival of representatives of the empty positions. If a House is definitively subdivided (*aben ngrà*), its patrimony is also subdivided and the members of the two Houses that result from such a fission start to intermarry.

The Mẽtùktire (also known as Txukarramãe) are a Mẽbengokre sub-group, who consider themselves to be members of a community linked by kinship relations and sharing a cultural heritage distributed amongst nine villages in the states of Mato Grosso and Pará, Central Brazil.[4] In conceptual terms, each actual village has as its reference an ideal village which is constituted by the totality of Houses distributed amongst these villages, each one with its own distinctive patrimony[5] of personal names and prerogatives. No contemporary village has dwellings representing all the Houses. In Kapòto, for example, in 1987, there were 31 dwellings representing 14 Houses. All Houses have their members unevenly distributed amongst the above-mentioned villages. I therefore disagree with Turner when he claims that for the Jê and Bororo,[6] the individual village community constitutes the highest level of the social structure (1979a: 174).

Each House is an exogamous unit whose distinctive identity is substantialized, metaphorically, by the symbolic goods which compose its patrimony and that are considered inalienable. It could be argued that all goods are symbolic, nevertheless, this term is particularly appropriate in the sense that heritable goods in Mẽbengokre society are non-material – personal names and prerogatives (*nekrets*). The latter include:

(a) for both sexes, the right to make and use particular adornments, play specific ceremonial roles, and collect or store certain goods in one's House;

(b) for men, the right to specific cuts of meat from large game animals;

(c) for women, the right to raise certain animals as pets.[7]

Traditionally, and nowadays sporadically, a House may be visually distinguished from the outside by its pets which wander in and out like live emblems. Inside each House hang its members' masks and ornaments which are stored in order to be publicly displayed during ceremonies.

The patrimony of the Houses is not static. It can be enriched through new acquisitions or impoverished through robbery. For instance, people are accused of stealing names and *nekrets* from enemies who died at their hands. Nevertheless, each House has a nucleus of goods which is conceived (rightly or wrongly) as attesting to its immemorial origins. Rather than possessing a name as such, the Houses are referred to by the name of one of their most prominent items of wealth, such as 'the House of the yellow feather headdress', which is also 'the Eastern House'.[8]

The most highly valued names and *nekrets* are the 'purest' in the sense that they belong indisputably to one House. Names and *nekrets* which have started to circulate in another House can be renounced (*kanga*) by those who consider themselves to be their legitimate owners since they have lost their differentiating role. The Mẽbengokre claim that in the past women used to engage in physical combat due to the illegitimate appropriation of names and I witnessed various verbal disputes over names and *nekrets*.

From the Mẽbengokre perspective, mythical time converges with historical time with no significant rupture between the two. Along the mythical–historical trajectory of each House, the exploits of its uterine ancestors account for the origins of its patrimony of names and prerogatives; this is why they form a seemingly arbitrary collection. The use of the names and *nekrets* of the ancestors erases the temporal vacuum between them and the living. What the ancestors had that is non-perishable can be found amongst the living. It is as if the essence of each House were transmitted along a vast genetic-like thread.

Of the 29 myths that I collected, 22 were associated with one or more Houses; 9 myths mentioned an individual in one House and his or her spouse in another. Mythological figures tend to have various names; these belong to specific Houses and are passed on in the same way as any other names. Some of the ornaments and roles which are *nekrets* of certain Houses have their origin explained in myths which legitimize their possession of them. Other acquisitions mentioned in the myths benefit or prejudice society as a whole. The myths demonstrate that, from the Mẽbengokre point of view, not only did some aspects of the cosmos emerge from society – the sun, the moon, the night – but also certain physiological processes – old age and death, and even the pupils of the eyes.[9]

In the literature on the Jê, the women's domain (the ring of dwellings at the edge of the village circle) is usually depicted as 'peripheral', with connotations not just of space but also of value. Bamberger, for example, describes the female area as weakly social (1967: 128), claiming that women have an almost nonexistent role in communal affairs (1967: 162). According to Bamberger: 'The localization of women on the periphery of the village is symbolic of their apolitical and marginal social role in Kayapó society' (1967: 173).

In synthesizing the research carried out by members of the Harvard–Central Brazil project and focused on the Jê and the Bororo, Maybury-Lewis expresses the opinion that these societies share a sharp distinction between the public and private spheres, between the ceremonial domain and the households to which everyday matters are relegated (1979: 305). But when the Houses are recognized as moral persons it becomes clear that they control all scarce goods in Mẽbengokre society. These goods include beautiful names which give rise to the great naming ceremonies, adornments, a large quantity of ceremonial roles, songs, and even the maracas which are used to mark the dance and song rhythm in all ceremonies.

Ceremonies are supremely aesthetic events because they achieve the most complete composition of the social corpus, articulating together the members of each House through their respective roles. Even the dead come to attend the ceremonies which is why the Houses are abandoned to them by the living who camp out in the plaza. J. C. Crocker stated that '... the Bororo have created an organic solidarity which is no less real for being symbolic' (1985: 35). This is perfectly applicable to the Mẽbengokre.

The Houses are private, not only because access to them is limited to certain individuals, but also because they constitute the domain of particularities – symbolic goods, political interests and the male duty to avenge homicides which victimize its members. The cultural heritage of Mẽbengokre society is segmented by the Houses which, added together, form a totality. The village is decribed metaphorically by the Mẽbengokre as a body, with its legs to the East, its head to the West, and with the plaza representing its belly.

The Houses converge toward the centre because it is in the men's house that matters of collective interest are discussed and communicated to the entire village.[10] In other words, the men's house, which brings together members from all the Houses, represents a neutral space where an effort is made to harmonize the particularistic and factional interests that constantly threaten to disrupt the integrity of the village.

A Mẽbengokre belongs automatically to his or her mother's House. Half siblings who share the same father are distinguished from uterine siblings; only the latter are designated by the term *atsikot apoy* which could be glossed as 'brought out in a series'. When a man marries and is installed in his wife's dwelling, she should regularly send part of the fish and meat that she obtains from her husband to his mother and sisters. When a man inherits the right to eat a specific cut of 'beautiful' meat – that is, one that constitutes *nekrets* – this is taken to his mother's House, where it is cooked, consumed and ideally shared with his sisters' sons, his legitimate heirs within his House. The Mẽbengokre claim that hereditary meat cuts are not shared with the wife or children of their owner.

Consequently, I cannot accept Turner's interpretation that the Mẽbengokre have developed to the maximum the principle of separating a man from his natal family and integrating him into his family of procreation (1979b: 181 and 189). Turner also argues that as a man's children grow older, he comes to be considered less as an affinal member of his wife's household and more as a consanguineal one (1979b: 184). In my opinion, Nimuendajú's view of the Timbira reflects Mẽbengokre reality with greater clarity. According to him, a man has much stronger links with his mother's house because these are indestructible, than with his wife's house, for these links can be dissolved at any time (1971: 126). Dreyfus expresses the same point of view when she states that Mẽbengokre men are merely habitual guests in their wives' houses and never the heads of the family, and that the strongest ties are those that link men to their sisters, ties which are detrimental to the conjugal relationship (1963: 61).

PERSONAL NAMES

The transmission of names and of *nekrets* is identical. For reasons of space I will concentrate on the former. Ideally a man transmits the names he bears, if they originated in his own House, to one or more of his sisters' sons or else to the sons of his female matrilateral parallel-cousins (i.e. 'ZSs'). The Mẽbengokre of both sexes have between a minimum of five and a maximum of thirty names. On the occasion of their transmission, the names borne by one person are divided out amongst various name-receivers. This phenomenon could be attributed to a dialectical logic. Each person is identified with an eponym[11] or 'name source' with whom he or she shares one or more names in common but, at the same time, they should also be distinguished from him or her by receiving a name(s) from one or more other sources as well.

The actual name-giver, who merely proclaims the names being transmitted, is much less important that the eponym, a person in the ascending generation who is the bearer and source of the names transmitted to a baby or child. Thus, when a mother transmits her dead brother's name to her son, she acts as the name-giver but it is her brother who is the eponym. The splitting up of names on the occasion of their transmission, and the fact that people normally receive names from various eponyms – even when all of them are transmitted by the same name-giver – results in the fact that nobody is the exact replica of another person. The simultaneous process of identification and contrast is possibly due to the fact that the dead are held to be a threat to their close living relatives; they want to carry them off in order to be together. When names are split up amongst various receivers, this dilutes the eponym's identification with any one of them.

Another reason why each Mẽbengokre has so many names is that although individuals can choose the people to whom they transmit their names they only have the right to transmit names which originate from their own House. Names may be lent out in one generation but they must be returned to the House that owns them in the following generation. Thus a woman who receives names from her FZ has lifelong usufruct of such names but she cannot transmit them to her BD or other person of her own choice (see Fig. 10.1). The borrower may return the names to her FZDD or may simply

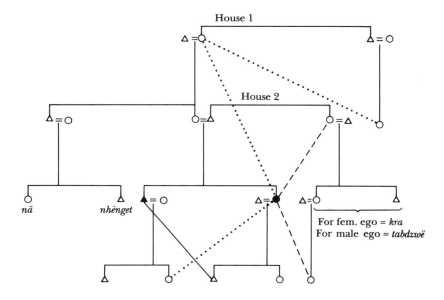

Male and female ego use the same terms *nã* (M) and *nhènget* (MB) for their matrilateral cross-cousins.

Female ego's patrilateral cross-cousins are her classificatory children *(kra)*; for male ego, these same cousins are classificatory sister's children *(tabdzwë)*.

Example 1:————— male ego transmits names to ZS.

Example 2: – – – –female ego receives usufruct of names from her FZ which she later returns to her FZDD. Since ego is not the rightful owner of these names, she must return them to their House of origin.

Example 3: ·········· female ego's MM gave usufruct of her names to her BD and later retransmitted them to her DD, thereby enabling female ego to transmit these names to her BD, since they are the property of ego's House.

Fig. 10.1 Cross-cousin terms and examples of name transmission.

relinquish the right to transmit them to the owners of the names, i.e. to the closest uterine relatives of the person who loaned them to a member of another House.

Ideally opposite-sex siblings name each other's children, men giving their names to their sisters' sons and women reciprocating by giving lifelong usufruct of their names to their brothers' daughters. Since parents can under no circumstances give their own names to their children, mothers have to await the birth of a granddaughter *(tabdzwë)* in order to transmit their names (names that they received from their MM for example) to a uterine heiress. For men, it is their sisters who produce their uterine heirs. Names and *nekrets* pass solely from the categories *nhènget* (MB, MF, FF ...) and *kwatëÿ* (FZ, MM, FM ...) to *tabdzwë* (for male ego, the ZC; for female ego, the BC; and for both sexes, the CC). These terms indicate a bilateral or cognatic kindred. A uterine ideology is expressed through the claim that names and *nekrets* must always return to their House of origin, from whence they sprang (*katòro dzà*; spring out/place) and where they have their roots (*dzà kray*; place (of) origin/base/beginning).

The combination of this ideology and the uxorilocal residence rule, together with the existence of a cognatic kindred, generates certain tensions. Grandparents have a relationship of strong affection with their grandchildren, independently of whether they are their uterine heirs,[12] whether they merely reside together,[13] or whether they live in another House.[14] The fact that the grandparents who are not in the uterine line (MF, FM, FF) can transmit lifelong usufruct of the names and *nekrets* they own to their grandchildren helps to diminish the conflict between affection and duty, or between the rules and their manipulability inherent in the Mẽbengokre social system. In other words, individual agents have various strategies available and choose the one best suited to their interests at any particular time.

This is reinforced by the fact that if their sisters neglect their duties in the reciprocal exchange of food and names, the men claim that they can reprimand them by handing over lifelong usufruct of their own names to their grandchildren. This obliges their sisters to await the birth of a great-grandson (DDS) to recuperate these names – since names should be held by only one person in each generation.

The bilateral aspect of the naming system, frequently noted in the literature, is deceptive. The term *kàymêtã* designates the usufruct of names and prerogatives. This term was explained to me by the Mẽbengokre through the following examples: when people go off to the city they ask someone to keep an eye on their house for them; the owners get back the house upon their return. If somebody lends out a name to a child in a different House, when another child is born to the owner's own House, the name must be returned.

The terms for cross-cousins (people with whom marriage is prohibited) are compatible with the naming system (see Fig. 10.1).[15] For both female and male ego, the female matrilateral cross-cousin is the potential name-receiver of their own mother's names and is thus a 'M' (*nã*). The brother of this 'M' is a 'MB' (*nhènget*). For women, their patrilateral cross-cousins are their classificatory children (*kra*); for men they are classificatory sister's children (*tabdzwë*). This is intelligible when we remember that, for a woman, the daughter of her female patrilateral cross-cousin is the legitimate heiress of the names that she herself received from her FZ and which she should later renounce in favour of this heiress, who is a *tabdzwë* for both her MM and her MMBD. Thus, in the Mẽbengokre case, these Omaha-like features of the terminology make sense in terms of female name transmission. As I have noted elsewhere (1986: 234), Héritier's claim that Omaha terminologies entail the dominance of the male principle (1981: 48–50) is not valid in the case of the Mẽbengokre.

Melatti's observation about the Timbira that the transmission of names seems to negate the incest prohibition (1979: 78) is in fact relevant to all the Jê. This is because although a man's semen creates the bodies of his children, it is his Zs and his WBs who create his children's social personae by transmitting their names and prerogatives to them. The women give up their brothers who leave to procreate children in another House; in return they recuperate their brothers' names and *nekrets* (prerogatives) for their own children.

SUBSTANCE VERSUS ESSENCE

The so-called 'relations of substance' have received much emphasis in the Jê literature. They refer to the sharing of food restrictions by members of the nuclear family when one of these is ill.[16] Seeger calls groups with such relationships 'corporeal descent groups' (1980: 131). I do not consider them to be descent groups for they denote substance in a very specific and limited way. Nimuendajú described such relations of substance as a mystical tie which links the (organic or corporeal) well-being of parents and children (1983: 80). For the Mẽbengokre, people's individuality perishes with their flesh and with the memory of them as individuals. Their essence or metaphysical substance, contained in personal names and heritable prerogatives, is non-perishable because it is recovered by society.

Names have a mystical aspect which is expressed by the fact that, before its skin or wrapping hardens (*kà tëÿts*; wrapping hard), a baby can neither receive many names nor have them ceremonially confirmed without placing its life at risk. A series of food prohibitions is applicable to people with determined categories of names. To infringe such taboos results in a skin disease (kà noy noy). Turner describes the Mēbengokre notion of skin as the boundary of the individual as a social and physical being (1966: 476). The same word is used to designate clothes. This suggests that names and *nekrets* are considered as a wrapping for the organism, a second skin that society recuperates from individuals at their death in order to reproduce itself.

Turner implies that names and *nekrets* can circulate *ad lib* from house to house. Consequently, although he recognizes that ceremonial activity is the focal point of Jê and Bororo life, he makes the enigmatic claim that, for the Mēbengokre, 'Most ceremonial activity is devoted to name-giving and other forms of celebration of marginal relations' (1979b: 206). Both he and da Matta define as marginal the relationships between those who transmit and receive each other's names – between the *nhènget* (MB, MF, FF) and his *tabdzwë* (ZS, SS, DS) and between the *kwatëy* (FZ, MM, FM) and her *tabdzwë* (BD, DD, SD) because these relatives do not form part of the nuclear family whose members are responsible for each other's physical well-being through the mutual observance of dietary and other restrictions.

Da Matta associates the domestic area with the realm of nature and biological ties (which include the 'relations of substance'), whilst he associates the ceremonial area, an area he describes as juridical (or moral) and/or public, with the realm of culture (1976b: 154–5). In my own view, the Mēbengokre Houses constitute the jural domain of society as much as the domestic one.

In sum, if genitors make and nourish the human being's organism it is the *nhènget* and the *kwatëy*, the sources of names, who transform it into a person, transmitting to their *tabdzwë* the metaphysical substance of the ancestors.

FORMAL FRIENDSHIP

In Mēbengokre society one acquires formal friends (*krab dzwë*) through one's father. Men, but not women, transmit their formal friends to their children. This gives rise to patrilines rather than patrilineages because there is no founder of the line. I use the term patriline to emphasize its unconscious aspect. Unfortunately, lines and lineages have tended to be used as synonyms in writings on the Jê.[17] The Mẽbengokre focus on the patrilateral aspect of formal friendship, that is, as a dyadic relationship between a man (or a woman) and his (or her) father – who share the same formal friends. Since transmission follows this pattern for *n* generations, it generates *de facto* patrilines. A notion of descent is not necessarily involved, for if someone lacks formal friends, his or her parents may appoint someone to this role.

There is not space here to enter into details of the roles played in ceremonies by formal friends. Of greater interest is the avoidance of cross-sex formal friends and the joking relations maintained with the close kin or affines of one's formal friends. The Mẽbengokre state that one must not marry one's formal friends, yet it is good for a man to marry his female formal friend's daughter, reciprocally envisaged as marriage between a woman and her mother's formal friend. I lack data on the extent to which this ideal is complied with in practice.[18] The relationship of formal friendship is inherited patrilaterally but such friends are not considered to be relatives. Inheritance of formal friendship could suggest the presence of a system of double descent, where one inherits, for example, movable property matrilineally and immovable property patrilineally, as in the case of the Yakö of Nigeria (cf. Forde 1950). In the Mẽbengokre case, however, one has full rights (i.e. the right to transmit to any person of one's choice) only wealth received through one's uterine line. All that a Mẽbengokre inherits from his or her patriline are formal friends, and the basic duty which this entails (besides ceremonial obligations) is that a man should transmit them to his children.

If a man marries his female formal friend's daughter, his behaviour to this friend, now his mother-in-law, is unaltered. He avoided her as a cross-sex formal friend and he will continue to avoid her as his mother-in-law. While Houses exchange men in order to procure genitors to give continuity to the uterine descent group, patrilines exchange women. In the case of Houses exchange is conscious; in the case of patrilines it appears to be unconscious for it is never verbalized as such.

J. C. Crocker's depiction of the Bororo rings true for the Mẽbengokre when he says that the men are caught between the demands of their uterine and of their affinal bonds. They are intruders in the female-dominated households in which they reside with their wives, and the ritual and normative emphasis on patrifiliation may represent an effort to escape the almost total domination by women (1977b: 189–91). The patrilines of the Mẽbengokre could be seen as an attempt to redress the imbalance posed by the all-pervading uterine logic of the Houses in favour of a male-dominated logic. This, in turn, could help to explain how divergent interpretations of the Mẽbengokre have arisen.

In the Jê literature, the formal friend has been characterized as a metaphor of otherness.[19] As far as the Mẽbengokre are concerned, what seems to be in question is inherited affinity. In sum, there is seemingly a Dravidian-like aspect to Mẽbengokre social structure – the inheritance, albeit indirect, of affinity.[20] I intend to elaborate on this question in a forthcoming paper. For the moment it must suffice to emphasize that since formal friends are not considered to be relatives it seems inappropriate to talk of double descent in the Mẽbengokre case.

Clues to Houses

As I have shown above, reference to the House, as an indigenous category, provides an explanation for some hitherto ignored or puzzling aspects of Mẽbengokre social organization. In this section I shall consider to what extent an explanation in terms of the House might be applied to other groups in the same cultural area.

The names and *nekrets* of the Mẽbengokre Houses are similar to the clan property of the Bororo, property which is bound up with the Bororo concept of *aroe*. J. C. Crocker comments that for the Bororo, *aroe*, which might be termed 'totem' (1977a: 247), denotes the soul or sometimes a name (1985: 33). Amongst other ideas it '... designates some immaterial essence which is the metaphysical dimension of a human being ...' (1985: 15). Thus Bororo *aroe* and Mẽbengokre names and *nekrets* would seem to be equivalent.

On the other hand, Crocker is confusing when he argues that the Bororo are functionally but not ideologically matrilineal (1985: 32). He argues this because, when the Bororo infer that the members of a clan are linked by common descent:

> ... the reference is to this matrilineal relationship with the clan's mystic self, its totems, rather than to an ideology of hypothesised genealogical connexions. (1969: 47)

218

Lévi-Strauss has argued that when an exogamous group grows so large that its members can no longer define its membership directly in terms of known genealogical links, then membership is defined instead through a clear rule of filiation or descent and through a name or other distinguishing mark transmitted in accordance with this rule (1962a: 20). Lévi-Strauss characterizes the Bororo as having clans and his description of these (1973a or 1989: 103–13) is sufficient for one to recognize striking analogies between Bororo clans and Mẽbengokre Houses. Rivière (in this volume) considers that both the Bororo and the Jê might profitably be analyzed as house-based societies. This, in turn, might help to approximate them to the Barasana and other Tukano speakers of the Northwest Amazon, a point taken up by Hugh-Jones (this volume).

As I have already shown, Mẽbengokre Houses occupy fixed positions around the perimeter of the villages; this same layout is maintained in camps during the trekking season. A similar pattern occurs amongst the Bororo whose eight clans have an invariable spatial distribution which determines a fixed sequence of clan-dwellings in their villages and temporary camps. This same constancy has also been noted for the Timbira (Nimuendajú 1971: 44; Melatti 1979: 51) and for the Mẽbengokre and Xicrin[21] (Turner 1966: 32; Bamberger 1967: 131; Verswijver 1983: 302; Vidal 1977: 63), but there is no agreed explanation as to why this should be so.

If one reads the anthropological literature on the Northern Jê, looking for the existence of Houses, whilst no other author makes explicit reference to them, some interesting if fragmentary analogies can be found in reference to 'longhouses', 'residential segments', 'domestic clusters', 'matrilines', 'matrilineages' and 'clans'. Both da Matta and Melatti adopt the term 'residential segments' to designate uxorilocal extended families, occupying two or more dwellings which are usually contiguous. Melatti points out that among the Eastern Timbira these segments are exogamous and exist at the supra-village level (1979: 51). This clashes with Turner's claim that exogamous groups are nonexistent among all the Northern Jê (1979b: 180). For da Matta, these segments are part of the Apinayé political scenario and only function as corporate groups when they take on the role of factions (1976a: chap. V). Named, exogamous residential clusters were also discovered by Seeger among the Suya. He considers (1981: 74) that these Northern Jê residential segments or clusters are relatively transient and that they are important socially and politically but not ceremonially. My data suggest otherwise.

W. H. Crocker, who studied the Ramkokamekra, notes (1979: 239) that longhouses (or matrilines within them) are the owners of particular, named rites. He mentions the temporary transmission of rites by women to their brothers' daughters, with the assumption that they will be returned to the lineage which is their rightful owner, where they should remain forever (1977: 260). This is directly analogous to what happens with names and ritual prerogatives amongst the Mẽbengokre. In her study of the Krĩkatí, Lave uses the term 'domestic cluster' rather than 'residential segment'. She mentions but cannot explain why sets of names are held to remain in one place, i.e. in the same domestic cluster (1967: 315). From accusations of name thefts Lave deduces that names are conceived of as property (1967: 148).

Heelas (1979) and Schwartzman (1987) have identified the Panara or Kreen-Akore as Southern Kayapó.[22] Heelas characterized them as having spatial descent groups, units which Schwartzman later designated as clans. There are four such clans, situated in a specific portion of the village circle, and a person belongs automatically to his or her mother's clan. The clans are exogamous but, in this case, the clans do not appear to possess any specific property or prerogatives. Schwartzman considers the existence of Panara clans to be self-evident (pers. commun), consequently, he does not enter into a theoretical discussion concerning them.

Turner claims that the Mẽbengokre '... do not think in genealogical terms and are generally indifferent to the genealogical nature or degree of relationships' (1966: 302). This surprises me because I collected genealogies covering five to seven generations, totalling approximately 1,260 people, directly related to the 184 members of the village Kretire in 1981. Turner (1979b: 180) and Bamberger (1974: 377) consider that the Mẽbengokre lack any form of descent. Turner's model of Mẽbengokre society does not take account of Houses, for their existence was something that he overlooked.

Vidal (1977: 55; 115) associates exogamy and heritable riches with the female-dominated and uxorilocal residential segments of the Xicrin, yet she considers that heritable wealth is more important for males than for females (1977: 116). She fails to use her findings to question Turner's interpretation of the male-oriented nature of Mẽbengokre social institutions.

Verswijver's view of the Mẽbengokre is much the same as my own, but he uses the term residential segments as synonymous with matrilineages (or matrilines) to which personal names, ceremonial prerogatives and other rights belong (1983: 313; 1984: 113). In my view, the term 'segment' tends to generate confusion; two or more dwellings which form a segment of a House in a particular village, constitute simultaneously a segment of that same House divided up amongst various villages. In other words, it is important to distinguish between two levels of segmentation – intra-village and inter-village. Although Verswijver and I are discussing the same phenomenon, I chose to interpret my data with recourse to the notion of house-based societies for it permits an analysis which accords with the Mẽbengokre's own conception of their society.

What have been variably described as longhouses, residential segments, domestic clusters, matrilines, matrilineages and clans are obviously related to one another and to the Mẽbengokre Houses, though to what degree is difficult to deduce from the existing literature. Within the continuum formed by the Jê and the Bororo, the focus adopted in this paper approximates the Mẽbengokre to the Xavante (Central Jê), whose clans and patrilineages dispute amongst each other the prerogatives to which they are entitled.[23] It also approximates them to the Bororo, who jealously watch over their clan property, and to the Canela, despite the fact that the latter's incipient matrilineality is now on the wane (W. H. Crocker 1977; 1979; 1990).

HOUSES, CLANS OR LINEAGES – CONCLUSION

In Lévi-Strauss's view, house-based societies are characterized by tension or conflict between opposed principles or by principles, such as filiation and residence, or, in medieval terminology, rights of 'race' and of election which are elsewhere mutually exclusive. Considerations limited to the rules of filiation and descent are unable to explain them for they tend to subvert the language of kinship that they utilize (1984: 189–91; 1987: 152).

Giving examples of the types of problems that such societies may confront, Lévi-Strauss mentions the integration of an agnatic lineage and a cognatic kindred (1984: 204), and the paradox that marriage only allies two groups when a woman is handed over to one group as a wife whilst maintaining her loyalty to the other group as a sister (1984: 215). These two examples are the reverse side of the Mẽbengokre case, with their uterine descent lines and cognatic kindreds, where men reside with their wives but belong to their natal Houses.

Lévi-Strauss considers that house-based societies have a historical dimension in the sense that they possess the mechanisms to create history from within. This could make sense of the Mẽbengokre tendency to appropriate names and *nekrets* via grandparents (MF, FM, FF) and/or inmarrying males (F or MF), whenever the opportunity arises.[24]

An important element of Mẽbengokre social organization is the fact that a large percentage of personal names and wealth is bestowed for life on individuals who are not members of the House that owns them, as in the case of the grandchildren of the true owners. Even someone who digs a grave single-handed acquires lifelong usufruct of one of the prerogatives of the deceased.

Consequently, the ideology of uterine descent does not always correspond to empirically observable reality in relation to property transmission. When someone from House X lends a name or *nekrets* to a member of House Y and, in the subsequent process of village fissions or of family migrations, there are no more members of House X residing in the village where the usufructuary of its name or *nekrets* lives, this House may appropriate (*amĩ nhòn*) the borrowed good, incorporating it into its own patrimony.

To take another example: if a woman does not know who her father's uterine descendants are, because her father died during her childhood and his House is absent from her village, she can save (*putà*) his name from extinction by giving it to a son (real or classificatory). If, subsequently, the legitimate owners of the name do not emigrate to this boy's village and demand their name back, the boy will consider himself to be the true owner, that is, able to pass it on to his ZS.

It is the possibility of finding a way round the rule which restricts the loan of goods outside the owners' House to lifelong usufruct that explains the transfer of certain goods from one House to another. The Mẽbengokre explain such cases as exceptions for they contradict their uterine ideology. In sum, amongst the Mẽbengokre, an affine can never become a member of his spouse's House, but his property can be incorporated into it if, upon his death, he does not leave behind him uterine relatives to reclaim their legitimate property.

Lévi-Strauss intended to introduce the concept of house-based societies in order to advance understanding of cognatic or undifferentiated systems. I have argued that although the Mẽbengokre possess cognatic kindreds, this does not entail a cognatic kinship system.

I have avoided classifying Mẽbengokre society as characterized by matrilineal descent for a number of reasons. Whilst in the field and before having access to Lévi-Strauss's work on house-based societies, following Mẽbengokre usage I differentiated between Houses (*kikre dzam dzà*) and houses (*kikre*). What appeared to be in question was matrilineal descent, though it was unclear what level of society would correspond to clans and which to lineages.

In one sense, a clan could correspond to the sum of dwellings distributed amongst the Mẽbengokre villages that are associated with a particular House. Nevertheless, before establishing permanent contact with national society, the normal pattern of inter-village relations was one of warfare, so such a clan could amount to no more than a reference to the ideal totality of society, that is, in terms of defining who were fellow Mẽbengokre through membership of the same set of Houses.

There are no founding ancestors of Houses or of their sub-divisions on an intra- or inter-village level, and groups of sisters and matrilateral parallel-cousins are the owners of the same stock of names and *nekrets*. Members of different abodes belonging to the same House, whether in one village or in various villages, stress that they belong to the same House, sharing an identical symbolic patrimony. In other words, the division of a House into a number of separate dwellings does not appear to entail a division into lineages in Mẽbengokre thought. The eldest members of any particular House are usually able to trace the genealogical link with their uterine relatives in the same or other villages, whilst they are unable to trace the genealogical links between them and their mythological ancestors. Genealogically distant members of a particular House attest to their links through the sharing of a series of personal names and prerogatives during the course of several generations.

In my view, the Houses are the key to Mẽbengokre social organization, despite functioning much like clans, as described in

223

chapter 4 of *La Pensée Sauvage* (Lévi-Strauss, 1962b). They produce men and women of different social species which justifies the exchange of men on the part of Houses, and simultaneously entails recognition of the fact that as members of the same natural species they are essentially all alike. Each House exercises specific ceremonial roles which are indispensable to the village community as a whole and which complement the roles attributed to the other Houses. Lévi-Strauss (1962b) treats clans and castes as variations on a single theme. It has long been recognized that the Jê and Bororo societies of Central Brazil constitute a system of transformations and this in turn implies that clan and house-based societies cannot be diametrically opposed; they are products of variation on a common theme.

In his discussion of house-based societies, Lévi-Strauss refers to 'pseudomorphs' (1983b: 1222) which appear to be patri- or matrilineal when in fact they are not. In my view, the Mẽbengokre matri-Houses[25] are closer to matrilineality than to a cognatic or undifferentiated system. Clans and lineages are defined primarily with reference to biological continuity (even though this may be largely fictitious), whereas the Mẽbengokre notion of House as a moral person is double-edged. It designates a uterine descent group; however, it also places emphasis not on people as such but on the House itself as the locus of a patrimony. A Mẽbengokre House is represented materially by one or more dwellings, yet in comparison with the majority of societies discussed in this volume, the symbolic significance of the House as a building is unimportant. Various of the papers on Indonesia mention the association of heirlooms with Houses. This term, though analogous, is not applicable in the Mẽbengokre case because individuals are buried along with their material goods. What survives them is the right to reproduce and display the patrimony associated with each House.

I disagree with Maybury-Lewis's statement that: 'The supposed matriliny of the Northern Gê is ... a misinterpretation based on the cumulative effects of uxorilocality' (1979: 304). I also diverge from Turner's portrayal of the Jê and Bororo cultural area (1979a) as one which is dominated by men, more specifically, where fathers-in-law dominate their sons-in-law by maintaining control of their daughters thanks to uxorilocality. It is naive to hear from an anthropologist the explanation that the women who constitute the core of the household, 'remain together by simple inertia ...' (1979a: 178).

Yanagisako (1979: 190) notes that the classical dichotomy between the domestic and the public spheres has recently been called into question. As far as I am aware, nobody but myself (1986) sees fit to challenge the consensus among researchers of the Jê and Bororo, concerning the dichotomy between the peripheral domestic female sphere and the central, public and ceremonial male sphere.

It might be suggested that my use of the term House does not correspond exactly to the use made by Lévi-Strauss and that not even this author has satisfactorily resolved the question of house-based societies. Mẽbengokre society, with its matri-Houses, cognatic kindreds and patrilines of formal friends, constitutes a no-man's-land, betwixt and between matrilineality, cognatic kinship and double descent. If I had not been inspired by Lévi-Strauss to analyze Mẽbengokre Houses as moral persons, I would have resigned myself (like Boas in his study of the Kwakiutl *numayma*[26]) to describing them as corresponding to no known type of structure in the ethnological records.

INSIDE-OUT AND BACK-TO-FRONT: THE ANDROGYNOUS HOUSE IN NORTHWEST AMAZONIA

11

Stephen Hugh-Jones

IN RECENT YEARS it has become increasingly evident that the small, fragmented tribes of Amazonian ethnography, twin products of colonial genocide and academic classificatory ethnogenesis, are poor guides for understanding an area once integrated by complex regional systems. If anthropologists have long recognized a fundamental unity beneath the manifest linguistic and cultural diversity of Amazonia, progress towards synthesis has been relatively slow. In studies of kinship, progress has often been hampered by the use of outmoded and alien theoretical models which delimit an artificially narrow field of study and square uneasily with local idioms.

Although there are a number of publications on architectural and spatial symbolism in different parts of lowland South America, many treat architecture as a sphere of analysis relatively independent from kinship and social structure. In this chapter[1] I want to extend previous explorations of the significance of Northwest Amazonian architecture[2] in a new direction by suggesting that their communal longhouses provide the eastern Tukanoan-speaking peoples with a way of conceptualizing their own social structure, one which is misrepresented and distorted when translated as unilineal descent. At the same time, I shall examine whether such native idioms are usefully included under Lévi-Strauss's (1983a, 1987) general rubric of 'house societies'.

My argument can be summarized as follows. Tukanoan social structure has typically been characterized in terms of patrilineal descent, virilocal residence, symmetric alliance, and a Dravidian relationship terminology, and described as an open-ended social system made up of a number of intermarrying exogamous language groups each internally divided into sets of ranked clans.[3] As against this received view, I shall argue that the Tukanoans themselves conceptualize social relationships in two different and complementary ways, each based on a different, gendered reading of the house as a building. One model, which emphasizes group autonomy and internal relations of hierarchy, is salient in mythological and ritual contexts, especially in male-dominated rituals of clanhood.[4] This model corresponds, in part, to the anthropologists' descent and also to the more lineage-like aspects of Lévi-Strauss's notion of house (see Introduction p. 18). The other model, emphasizing equality, inter-dependence and consanguinity, is especially pertinent to daily life but also receives ritual expression during ritual exchanges of food between neighbouring communities. Each of these two conceptualizations finds echoes elsewhere in Lowland South America, the former in Central Brazil, the latter in the Guianas.

THE MALOCA COMMUNITY

This is how Wallace first described a Tukanoan longhouse or maloca in the last century:

It was a large, substantial building, near a hundred feet long, by about forty wide and thirty high, very strongly constructed of round, smooth, barked timbers, and thatched with the fan-shaped leaves of the Caraná palm. One end was square, with a gable, the other circular; and the eaves, hanging over the low walls, reached nearly to the ground. In the middle was a broad aisle, formed by the two rows of principal columns supporting the roof, and between these and the sides were other rows of smaller and shorter timbers; the whole of them were firmly connected by longitudinal and transversal beams at the top, supporting the rafters, and were all bound together with much symmetry by sipós (vines).
   Projecting inwards from the walls on each side were short partitions of palm-thatch, exactly similar in arrangement to the boxes in a London eating-house, or those of a theatre. Each of these is the private apartment of a separate family, who thus live in a sort of patriarchal community. [...] The centre isle remains unoccupied and forms a fine walk through the house. At the circular end is a cross partition or railing about five feet high, cutting off

rather more than the semi-circle, but with a wide opening in the centre: this forms the residence of the chief or head of the malocca, with his wives and children; the more distant relations residing in the other part of the house. The door at the gable end is very wide and lofty, that at the circular end is smaller, and these are the only apertures to admit light and air.

(1889: 189–90)

Fitting exactly the few surviving malocas in Colombian territory, this sharply observed portrait needs but two finishing touches. Outside, on their front walls, many malocas are decorated with human figures and striking geometrical designs (Plate 8). Inside, suspended above the central space, hangs a large palm-leaf box containing feather head-dresses and other heirlooms; on the floor below lies a long wooden trough used to brew the manioc beer served at feasts. The significance of these details will become clear later.

The physical structure of the houses is identified with its inhabitants in several different ways. The men of the community, working together but usually without outside help, construct the wooden framework and they are identified, in particular, with the paired, hardwood central columns. The lengthy process of thatching typically involves outside labour; the men are helped by both their wives and their neighbours which gives thatching an affinal connotation. The completed house is inaugurated by a dance-feast which formally proclaims the establishment of a new community and allows the shamans to breathe life into the house and to protect it from harmful influences. The man who sponsors the construction is the owner of the house and the leader and representative of the community.[5] Building a house together implies recognition of the sponsor's leadership and acceptance of a particular social arrangement; the visual impact of the building – its size, decoration, upkeep and cleanliness – is an index of the leader's standing and of the cohesion of his group. When the leader dies, the house and community die with him; he is buried in the centre of the floor, the maloca is abandoned, and the community either reforms or divides.

The typical community, 'the people of one house' (*koho wiiãda*), consists of a group of brothers living with their wives, children and unmarried sisters, and perhaps with one or both of their parents.[6] Even long-term visitors such as men doing bride service are clearly distinguished from residents: visitors sleep in the front of the house

Plate 8   A Tukanoan (Makuna) longhouse with painted facade, Río Komeñya, 1990.

F–family compartments   C–manioc beer trough
G–communal hot plate   FB–feather box

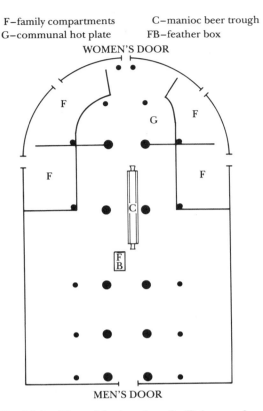

Fig. 11.1   Plan of the interior of a Tukanoan longhouse.

whilst residents sleep at the back. The community represents a compromise between unity and division, a compromise which is given spatial expression. The men, who all belong to the same group, are divided by their ties to wives from at least one other group; each family occupies a separate compartment towards the rear of the house. The men are also divided by differences in age: the headman, normally the father or eldest brother, is treated with a certain amount of deference and has his compartment on the right-hand side furthest to the rear; the compartments of his married younger brothers are further towards the front whilst unmarried youths sleep in the open near the front door (see Fig. 11.1). Each family, especially ones with grown male children, represents a potential household and, in the end, tensions between brothers (typically over food, sex and authority) lead to the break-up of the group, especially once both parents are dead.

In everyday life such lines of potential division are carefully downplayed. Instead, the emphasis is on the unity of the household as a group linked by co-residence, kinship, co-operation and, especially, by the sharing of food. Food is produced at a family level with men and women usually working alone, but both the preparation of manioc bread and the eating of meals serve to underwrite collective values. Each house has a communal hot-plate, situated in the intimate private space at the rear of the house, where bread is baked and where people sit warming themselves and gossiping. In shamanic discourse, this focal hearth is a womb which cooks the bread as a womb 'cooks' a child, the starch and fibre of manioc bread being compared to flesh and bones (see C. Hugh-Jones 1979).

If food production is individual and private, consumption should be public and collective. Sharing is crucial to the maintenance of group cohesion; when sharing stops this is a sure sign of tensions and divisions. Meals are eaten near the centre of the house, a public space reserved for unifying rituals which contrasts with the private compartments where wives cook their husbands' catch. Proper meals combine female-produced manioc products with male-produced fish or meat bound together with chilli-pepper, a substance with marked sexual connotations.[7] Men typically eat before women and children so that both ingredients and format combine to make of the communal meal an image of the household as a single family divided only by age and gender.[8] The ideal community, identified with the house it builds, is thus one that acts and thinks like a single family, an ideal underpinned by the images evoked by food and meals.

Each longhouse forms an autonomous and largely independent community but clusters of neighbouring malocas, belonging to two or more different exogamous groups, make up territorial groups with fluid, shifting boundaries defined by density of kinship ties, frequency of visiting and intermarriage, and by the areas of influence of shamans and other important men. If the maloca community is exogamous, symmetrical alliance and a preference for close marriage result in territorial groups which are relatively endogamous. Brothers and sisters usually live in neighbouring houses linked by longstanding ties of alliance so that their children tend to marry each other. *De facto* the territorial group is thus an extended endogamous kindred with a shaman or other leader as its focus, an arrangement similar to that found in the Guianas (see Overing Kaplan 1975). In the Guianas these territorial groups have a lower-level counterpart in the (ideally) endogamous settlement group (see Rivière this volume); despite its familial ethos the exogamous Tukanoan maloca community is structured according to quite different principles. However, at ritual dances where food is exchanged between affinally-related households, endogamous Tukanoan territorial groups do come together and, on such occasions, they marshal the connotations of co-residence, commensality and the gendered production of complementary foods to present themselves as if they formed a single community.

FOOD-GIVING HOUSE

A big maloca which holds many people is called a 'dance house' (*basaria wii*) and dance-feasts are called 'houses', the pretext of the dance qualifying the 'house' in question; by metonymy, 'house' also refers to the people gathered inside. At Food-giving House (*bare ekaria wii*) visiting men give their affines large amounts of smoked meat or fish and then dance in their hosts' maloca. In return, they are supplied with vast amounts of manioc beer which they must consume before leaving, even vomiting it out to make room for more. At the end of the dancing the hosts may provide a smaller, reciprocal gift of some complementary food – fish for meat, meat for fish – a foretaste of the gift they will give when they, in turn, go to dance in the house of their erstwhile guests.

The exchange of complementary foods reflects the opposed, complementary and egalitarian relationship between affinally-related groups who are represented, in the context of the ritual, primarily by men. Many aspects of the ritual serve to underline the fact that affinal relations between maloca communities are here represented in terms of gender. Male donor-guests provide male-produced fish or meat and remain in the front, men's end of the house. As the food is brought in, they shout obscene jokes which leave no doubt about their implied relationship with their hosts. In the mythological charter for this dance, the food is given by an ancestor to his father-in-law in return for his wife. The hosts give the visitors female-produced

232

manioc beer and remain towards the women's end where they receive the fish or meat like women receiving their husband's catch.

To emphasize their status as outsider-affines, the visitors spend the first night camped outside and, to begin with, their hosts keep separate from them and treat them very formally. Initially only guests dance but, by the end, hosts and guests sit together, dance together and progress from formal chanting between opposed groups to informal banter and raucous laughter between undifferentiated individuals. This progressive effacement of formality and separation between hosts and guests, kin and affines, culminates in a communal meal. The smoked meat or fish is served up with home-baked manioc bread to everyone present so that the territorial group, made up of neighbouring houses, now presents itself as a single commensal 'family', the guests acting like a meat-providing 'husband' and the hosts as a bread-baking, meat-cooking 'wife'.

The image of a food-exchanging, commensal couple living with their children in a single residential space thus generates a nested series extending from family compartment through maloca community to the territorial group, a series whose connecting thread is marriage and reproduction. Marriage between a man and woman creates a family in a compartment; their married sons build a house and create a community which celebrates its affinal relations with neighbouring communities in food-exchanges which provide the context for further liaisons and marriages. As the sons have children of their own, the community dissolves and replicates itself anew. Like daughters of women who become mothers in their turn, each compartment contains within it the germ of a future house. Not surprisingly, the house itself is sometimes spoken about as a woman: its rounded rear end is her head, the front entrance is her vagina, and the cavernous interior is her womb.

THE WORLD HOUSE

In myth and shamanism, the nested imagery of womb and child, compartment and family, longhouse and community, territory and neighbourhood group, extends outwards to embrace the cosmos and humanity. The longhouse itself replicates and models the structure of the cosmos: its floor is the earth and its posts are mountains which

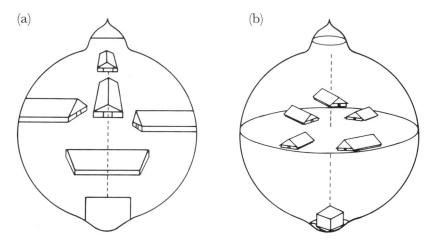

Fig. 11.2a   The Universe House (from Umúsin Panlõn Kumu and Tolamãn Kenhíri 1980:194).
Fig. 11.2b   The Universe House redrawn according to the accompanying text (Umúsin Panlõn Kumu and Tolamãn Kenhíri 1980:51–4)

support the roof or sky above. Down the centre of the maloca, from rear to front, West to East, runs an invisible river on whose banks and tributaries the people live. At rituals, human time merges with timeless myth and the maloca assumes the proportions and significance of the cosmos.

According to a Desana creation myth,[9] the universe was created by a female deity who covered her body with feather ornaments to form a protective house. Inside this 'universe-house' or 'universe-womb', the deity created five Thunders, each in his own compartment, four at the cardinal points and a fifth suspended above the centre space (see Figs 11.2a, 11.2b and 11.3). Like its analogue the feather-box, this compartment in the sky contained feather ornaments in male-female pairs; the ornaments were a semen-like generative principle associated with the light of the sun (see also Reichel-Dolmatoff 1971: 48). The Thunder at the zenith vomited up the feather ornaments which became proto-men and women who travelled up river from the East inside an anaconda-canoe, the Thunder's transformed body. The name of this vessel, 'fermentation-anaconda/canoe', evokes the beer-trough which lies beneath the feather-box, floating on the waters of the cosmic river.

As they travelled, the feather-people stopped, went up onto the

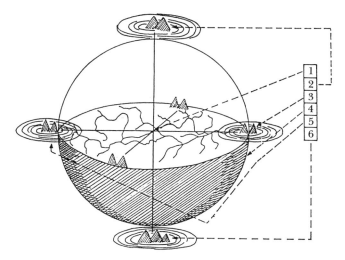

Fig. 11.3 The world according to a Tukano shaman (from Béksta 1988:47): (1) Our house in the centre; (2) House of the Sky Thunder; the shaman's safest refuge; (3) Milk River House at the mouth of the Amazon; (4) Protective sphere; (5) House of Night at the headwaters; (6) Underworld House; the shaman's alternative refuge.

banks and danced. The anaconda's journey gave rise to the river and its stopping places, the rapids and rock outcrops along the river, are 'transformation-houses', sacred sites and ancestral dwellings created by the dances of the feather-people (see Fig. 11.4). This journey and dancing are likened to a gestation; by the time the anaconda-canoe had reached the Vaupés region, the centre of the world, the feather-people were now fully human. At the 'house of emergence' the ancestors disembarked, each emerging through a different hole in the rocks, carrying the ornaments from which they were born. The ancestors of the different Tukanoan groups, each with his own language, dispersed to ancestral houses in their respective territories whilst the anaconda-canoe returned to its original form, the Thunder in the sky.

Told as an account of the origins of all Tukanoan groups, this myth downplays the potential hierarchy implied by an order of emergence and stresses an equality of difference marked by each group's different, emblematic language. As we shall see, this contrasts with an emphasis on rank and hierarchy when versions of the myth relate the origins of one specific group.

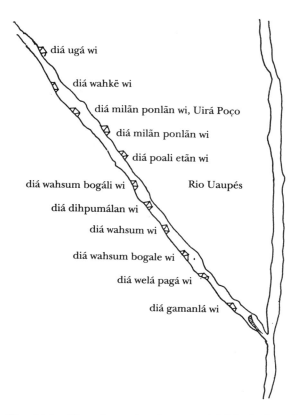

diá ugá wi

diá wahkẽ wi

diá milãn ponlãn wi, Uirá Poço

diá milãn ponlãn wi

diá poali etãn wi

diá wahsum bogáli wi

Rio Uaupés

diá dihpumálan wi

diá wahsum wi

diá wahsum bogale wi

diá welá pagá wi

diá gamanlá wi

Fig. 11.4   Transformation houses established along the Río Tiquié by the ancestral anaconda (from Umúsin Panlõn Kumu and Tolamãn Kenhíri 1980:209).

This myth confirms the suggestion of the nesting series – (womb + child) ↔ (compartment + family) ↔ (maloca + community) ↔ (territory + neighbourhood) ↔ (cosmos + humanity) – mentioned earlier. In addition, it either states or implies further equivalences between various house-like containers: between the feather-box, anaconda-canoe and beer-trough; between anacondas and rivers; and between rocks, rapids, mountains and ancestral houses. Gestation-like processes, portrayed as travelling and dancing, take place inside these containers and culminate in movements between container and contained, inseminations and parturitions via female vaginas and male mouths. These movements are replicated during rituals: as the feather ornaments are taken from their box and placed on the heads of the dancers inside the house, the dancers return to their ancestral proto-human state in a wider cosmos. Shouting jokes charged with sexual imagery, they bring 'male' meat and fish in through the door of their host's 'female' house later emerging to vomit out the beer they are given in exchange.

Thus far we can conclude that although the usual characterization of Tukanoan social structure in terms of unilineal descent, hierarchy, exogamy, virilocality and agnatic residential groups reflects local views, it also overshadows an equally important indigenous emphasis on equality, endogamy and on the consanguineal character of residential and territorial groupings. These two complementary models both receive expression at ritual gatherings known as 'houses'. The latter model is dominant at Food-giving House, a gathering which stresses the equal-but-different status of affinally-related maloca communities and which presents the house as a commensal, consanguineal group or extended family. The former model comes to the fore at *He* House, a rite of clanhood which reaffirms ties to the group's founding ancestor and presents an image of the house as made up of a ranked set of male siblings (see below).

Århem (1981: 196–7) comes to a similar conclusion with respect to the Tukanoan Makuna but undermines its significance by confusing the co-existence of two different models with a 'dichotomy between categorical ideal and social practice' which he sees as evidence of a 'Makuna anomaly' (1989: 16). Far from deviating from some ideal, close marriage, local endogamy, a stress on consanguinity, and an ethos of family and kinship are part of an alternative idiom which receives expression in the final, feeding stage of Food-giving House. Affinity, highlighted in the early stages, blurs into co-resident consanguinity in a meal which represents the gathering as a single family and house.

We are thus left with two different conceptualizations of social relationships which correspond to the anthropologists' 'descent' and 'consanguinity'. Affinity, as a between relationship, is expressed in relational terms: in the relative placing of individuals within the house or of houses within a given area. Consanguinity, as a within relationship, receives concrete expression in the womb-like interior of the maloca. Depending on context, the family contained in this womb may be the nuclear family in its compartment, the community in the maloca, the territorial group at a dance house, or the whole of humanity inside the house-as-cosmos. It remains to be seen how descent is expressed.

HOUSE OF AWAKENING

Attempts to apply the notion of descent in lowland South America have met with many problems.[10] Common substance is rarely seen as a significant attribute of clans or lineages, the idea of corporateness hardly applies, and people often seem to express little interest in genealogies extending much beyond the realm of the living (genealogical reckoning may also be rendered difficult by taboos on the names of the dead or by the recycling of names between generations). In this recalcitrant analytic sea, Northwest Amazonia has sometimes seemed like a haven of calm for here, at least, 'patriliny ... presents enough of the classic and familiar features of descent, including a segmentary and hierarchical ordering of descent units, for the use of these concepts to be relatively unproblematic' (Shapiro 1987: 303).

Though not without some foundation, this secure view of North-west Amazonian social structure also has its problems. I have already suggested that it is one-sided and tends to overshadow an ethos of consanguinity which is more pertinent to everyday life. A second problem is that the very familiarity of the received notion of descent sometimes obscures, rather than clarifies, what it is supposed to explain. The conventional or descent view of the Tukanoans might be summarized as follows. Exogamous, patrilineal groups such as the Tukano, Desana, Barasana or Makuna each descended from an eponymous anaconda ancestor, speak their own languages and own territories centred on a particular river or river section. Each group is divided into one or more sets of clans internally ranked as elder or younger brothers as if they were a group of male siblings, the sons of the anaconda father. Within each set, members of any particular clan are fairly clear as to what they think is their relative status *vis-à-vis* the others; they are less certain, and less concerned, about the ranking of their own clans with respect to those in other, more distant sets.

Sets of clans, ideally numbering five (like the compartments in the primal house), claim specialized roles as their ritual prerogatives: the top clan are chiefs followed by chanter-dancers, warriors, shamans and servants in that order. In any given area, not all these roles are necessarily represented by extant clans. In ritual this caste-like division is symbolically expressed at the level of the clan but in daily practice it operates only at an individual level. Male children should be given a name, appropriate to their birth order, which is linked with the ritual role which they should adopt in adult life. Despite variations in practice, the eldest brother is indeed usually the maloca headman and younger siblings quite often specialize as dancers, chanters and shamans according to their birth order.

It should now be clear that the lowest-order unit, a group of co-resident, male agnates, replicates the highest-order, ancestral group of brothers born of the same anaconda father. In theory, all members of one clan should live in the same house and perhaps did so in the past; in ideal terms it matters little whether they do or not for there is a sense in which this replication of the ancestral state means that they do so by definition. The counterpart of the nested series of family–household–territorial group–humanity is the reduplication of a basic structure consisting of a father and his ranked sons which applies at any level from house though clan-segment, clan, clan-set, to whole exogamous group. In myth, these are all one and the same and are rendered equivalent to one another by the transmission of names and by other ritual devices. They are all derived from a five-from-one blueprint represented, in different contexts, by a house with five compartments, a settlement with five malocas, the segmented body of an anaconda, a hand with five fingers, the head and limbs of the human body, plants stemming from a common stock, a river and its affluents, the gable and ribs of the roof-frame, or a vertebral column and ribs.

Although Tukanoan genealogical knowledge extends much further than is sometimes thought, its relevance is strictly contextual. Consistent with the father-and-sons image, shallow, branching genealogies are used to determine relationships between closely related people, both living and recently dead, and more extended genealogies may be used to structure historical narratives. Beyond this, genealogies in the sense of a succession of father–son links, are but one of several 'lines' (*bã*) which serve as umbilical links between the present and the ancestral past.

We have already met such lines in the form of journeys along rivers with houses strung out along their banks (see Fig. 11.4). These correspond to real-life displacements as succeeding generations move to different sites along the rivers, leaving their dead, buried in abandoned house-sites, behind them. Vegetable lines – coca and manioc cuttings placed end to end, or vines with nodes or fruits at regular intervals – evoke the distinctive clones of different cultivars which are transmitted across the generation as group patrimony whilst the contrast between stock and tip is used to express that between senior and junior. Such plant metaphors recall the sweet-potato vine matrilines of the central Brazilian Jê (W. H. Crocker 1990: 266–7; Lea pers. commun.) and similar images in island Indonesia (see McKinnon and Waterson this volume). Complementing the image of a nesting, englobing house, such lines figure much more prominently than genealogies as an idiom of descent. Despite what is sometimes implied (e.g. Århem 1981: 101), genealogies do not appear to be used as a more general way of specifying orders of segmentation, a quite inappropriate rendering of the nesting image of hierarchy which slips in all too easily under the umbrella of 'descent'.

To complete this picture of hierarchy it is necessary to refer back to myth. When versions of the myth recounted above are used to describe the origins of a single group, they present the anaconda-canoe as that group's particular ancestor-father. The myths describe how, on their journey up river, the ancestors concerned obtained various ceremonial goods, songs and spells. These stories of acquisition are themselves a component of the group's patrimony which serve to validate its ritual prerogatives and claim to a given territory. The anaconda ends its journey in the group's ancestral river. It swims to the top and turns round to lie with its head at the river mouth: the river is the anaconda transformed. The rapids or 'houses' which divide up the river are the stopping places of the anaconda, the preferred sites for the malocas of the different clans. The rapid nearest the mouth is the group's 'house of awakening', the place where the anaconda vomited the clan ancestors from its body, and the place to which the souls of group members return at death.[11] The ancestors' birth order determines both clan rank and also their placement along the river: the top-ranking clan or 'head' lives at the mouth and the 'tail' lives at the headwaters. Names of Tukanoan language groups often derive from the name of a top-ranking clan: just as the builder and owner of a maloca represents his people, so too does the 'head' clan stand for and encompass the rest.

The architectural imagery of a 'house of awakening', mediating between group and territory, extends to include various other landmarks. Mountains owned by the group are its 'house posts' and other rocky ridges and rapids are its 'beams'; the entire territory, defined and structured by these posts and beams, is thus a house with an ancestral river running down the middle. Whole exogamous language groups may be referred to as the 'people of one house' but this time the house is no englobing feminine womb but rather a very masculine, linear anaconda. His backbone and ribs, the river and its side-streams, are the gable and ribs of the roof, his body patterns adorn the front walls, and his image is painted on the main house-posts, the counterparts of his own slender form (see Fig. 11.5).

Lévi-Strauss defines his notion of the 'house' as a group of people or 'moral person', owning a domain consisting of both material and non-material property – wealth, names and titles – transmitted along a real or fictive line which is held to be legitimate so long as its continuity can be expressed in the language of filiation or marriage or, more usually, both together (1987: 152). In addition to the Tukanoans' use of 'house' to refer to and represent patrilineal groups, each group owns the following prerogatives and items of wealth which comprise its identity and ancestral powers: (1) feather head-dresses and ceremonial goods kept inside the feather-box; (2) a set of sacred musical instruments; (3) rights to make particular items of material culture such as baskets, stools and canoes which are exchanged at rituals analogous to ceremonial exchanges of food; (4) non-material, linguistic and musical property comprising the names of people and ritual objects, a language, chants, spells, songs, instrumental melodies, musical styles, and a body of myths which identify and legitimate ancestral powers which are activated in ritual. It would seem then that there is some overlap between Lévi-Strauss's generalized notion of 'house' and the Tukanoans' own use of 'house' as an idiom for social groupings.

I have deliberately left 'group' ill-defined for, given the hierarchical system described above, there is room for considerable ambiguity as to precisely at what level – longhouse, clan, exogamous language group – the notion of house applies and ambiguity too concerning who represents whom and owns what. In one sense this is a non-issue for the house is an idealized, ritual construct – which is why it has

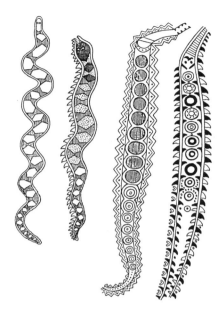

Fig. 11.5   Anacondas painted on the main columns of Tukanoan long-houses (redrawn from Koch-Grünberg 1910: 243).

been necessary to explicate the idea of 'descent' though reference to ritual, shamanism and myth. On a more practical level, these issues, and the related one of relative clan ranking, are the very essence of traditional Tukanoan politics. The capture of dance ornaments was once a main objective of warfare and bitter arguments still rage over questions of relative rank and over the headship of malocas, clans and wider groupings.[12] Demographic fluctuations, the adoption of individuals and sometimes whole clans from one group to another, and transfers of ritual wealth by ceremonial exchange, borrowings and illicit theft, have left a situation in which, though all subscribe to the same ideal picture, not everyone agrees as to how this ideal maps onto current reality.

Despite my doubts about the generalized use of descent as a rendering of the Tukanoan idiom of house, it is here that we do need to hang on to the more restricted notion of clan to talk about the down-to-earth reality of the groups of people (mainly men) who negotiate marriages and sponsor food-exchanges and other rituals.

If the house as group is primarily an ancestor-focused, generalized, collective and ritual construct, real malocas and territorial groups, the latter made up of both agnatically- and affinally-related maloca communities, are focused upon specific individuals. Men who build large houses, count on the co-operation of many male kin, who know much mythology, are good orators and who control a box of feathers and a set of sacred musical instruments, are clearly at an advantage. The malocas of such men become ceremonial centres for the surrounding population and the rituals they stage serve as switch points between the maloca and the 'house', arenas for demonstrating powers and prerogatives, and set an official seal on the current constitution of political groups and on current claims to status.

HE HOUSE

The most important of these validatory rituals is *He* House (*he wii*), a secret initiation cult from which women are excluded (see S. Hugh-Jones 1979). In a general sense, *he* refers to the ancestral state and its powers; more specifically it refers to paired flutes and trumpets, made from polished black palm-wood, which represent ancestral qualities in their most condensed form. These instruments, the bones of the anaconda ancestor, are also referred to as *bota*, a nominal classifier applied also to house posts and to the surrounding mountains. The names of the instruments are those of the anaconda ancestor and his sons, the same personal names which are owned by the group and conferred on living individuals, each name being also linked with a different central column of the maloca (Béksta 1988: 51).

The flutes and trumpets are kept underwater like dormant anacondas lying in the river. At *He* House, they are taken from their hiding place and brought to the house. Assembled together, decked out in feather ornaments, and blown to give them breath and voice, these dry, black bones return to life as the ancestor-father who adopts each new generation of initiates as his sons. In this ritual context, the house itself assumes the human guise of this same anaconda ancestor: the front door is his mouth, the painted walls are his painted cheeks and the leaves of the roof are the feathers on his head. His heart is the feather-box, his stomach the rounded rear where food is processed, and from his cavernous thorax, the interior of the house, his breath issues forth in the booming of trumpets and melody of flutes. In one grand fusion body, house and cosmos coincide, the present becomes the past, individuals become whole clans, and the group becomes one with its ancestor.

Food-giving House is the very antithesis of *He* House. The former is a co-operative, egalitarian and intergroup affair; the latter (ideally) brings together the whole clan, a single, male-only unit with its own particular interests, asserting its independence as it presents its painted face to world. It is vertically oriented towards the ancestors and also intrinsically hierarchical, employing a number of ritual devices to mark out the relative standing of the people involved. The ethos of complementary nurturing which characterizes Food-giving House is likewise far removed from that of *He* House. No fires must be lit, no beer is served, and normal food is far from mind. During preliminary rites, forest fruits, often supplied as tribute by dependent (and, by implication, lower-ranking) agnatic communities, are brought into the house accompanied by flutes and trumpets referred to as 'birds'. Instead of acting as predatory fish- or meat-eaters – with the inevitable implications of exchange in trade, war or marriage – the community now adopts an avian mode, feasting on the ripe fruits which are redistributed at the end of the rite. Fruit has connotations of independence and incompleteness: unlike fish and meat which are always eaten in company accompanied by manioc bread, fruit is typically a snack food to be eaten alone and on its own (see Hugh-Jones 1994a).

At *He* House no food of any kind enters the maloca and its aftermath is characterized by a two-month-long fast during which men avoid all contact with women. The fast is broken by a dance called The House of Manioc Bread (*dāhu kitiria wii*) at which the missing, female element is restored. Neighbours and affines come to a feast where the men dance with the women and huge amounts of snowy-white bread made from pure manioc starch are distributed. People throw bits of this bread, tied together with strips of bast, up into the rafters of the house till the interior is festooned in white. If the men of the clan are the bones and framework of the house, their wives and affines give this framework substance, restoring its flesh in the bread they throw. This rite marks the resumption of normal meals, a return to the consanguineal mode of daily life.

THE ANDROGYNOUS HOUSE

As observers we look out from inside a warm familiar body; others see us as those bodies. There is a similar, inherent ambiguity in our houses, an ambiguity which corresponds to lived experience. A reversible topography, the house is an entity which is at once both an inside and an outside, a contained and a container, a backstage and a frontstage, a home and a facade, a place where we live and where others visit us. Seen from without, the maloca is a single building and community, represented by men in its dealings with outsiders, and with a slightly hard but imposing feel about it which recalls the way these men like to present themselves in public. Experienced from within, it is divided into family compartments surrounding an open communal space towards the middle and front. On a normal day, the interior of the house, especially the domestic space at the rear, has a relaxed, informal, slightly unkempt air about it like that of the residents at home. On ritual occasions, rules of etiquette mark a clear division between the rear women's section and that of the men in the front. This linear, gendered division corresponds to the two gendered, anthropomorphic readings of the maloca, one, focused on the interior womb, which sees it as a woman with her head to the rear, the other, focused on its external appearance and face, which sees it as a man with his head to the front.[13]

I have argued earlier that these two readings relate to two different conceptualizations of social relations ritually expressed as different kinds of 'houses'. One, setting individuals and groups apart, combines internal hierarchy with outwardly directed self-interest and represents the community as a male-dominated unit identical in structure and essence to its ancestral counterpart. The other integrates individuals and groups, combines equality with accommodation and mutual identification, and represents the community as a nurturing womb-like family. The former corresponds to the anthropologists' descent, the latter to consanguinity. Alliance, theoretically an equal and balanced relation between houses or communities, contains an inherent ambiguity. Conceptualized in terms of gender, its male side may appear either as generous givers – the case in food-giving between friendly affines – or as predatory takers – the case in bride-capture between strangers. This ambivalence, together with the fact that the loyalties of any group of brothers are threatened and divided by their ties to their wives, means that alliance often gets disguised as consanguinity.

All this would appear to fit with Lévi-Strauss's suggestion that the house serves to integrate contradictory notions which anthropologists normally use to distinguish between different social types (1983a: 187). It would also seem to fit with his argument that the house has a fetishistic quality which serves to mask the contradictions and tensions inherent in the alliance relation (1987: 155ff.). As building and as group, Tukanoan house is inherently ambiguous, an ambiguity exemplified in the maloca's linear, front-to-back androgyny and reduplicated in a multitude of ambivalent lower-level pairs. Paired central columns, paired flutes and trumpets, and paired feather ornaments can each be described as both male and female and as elder and younger brother. This 'diametric' ambiguity is given an added, 'concentric' dimension by representing the relation between the house, its contents and its setting as a reduplicative nested series: each male inside is englobed by a female outside which is male with respect to a yet more inclusive encompassment. On a cosmic scale, the female universe house englobes the houses of the male Thunders; on a more human scale, like the maloca community surrounded by its affines, the central space with its ritual, masculine connotations is surrounded by a more domestic, feminine periphery. In myth, births are represented as transitions between inside and outside and in ritual the return to an ancestral state is also a shift from microcosm to macrocosm.

This brings me to a final point about bodily imagery which relates back to my discussion of descent, consanguinity and affinity. An important component of the Tukanoan conceptualization of 'descent' involves ideas concerning the differing parental contributions to the bodies of children. A child is said to derive bone from its father's semen; both semen and name also contribute to the child's soul (*isî*). Like the house posts, rocks and mountains with which they are associated, these male-derived components are hard and durable; they contrast with the more ephemeral, maternally derived flesh and blood which surrounds the bone. Initiation severs a young man's childhood ties to his mother and he begins to assert adult independence. He wears feather ornaments for the first time. These feathers, also aspects of soul, are like visible counterparts of his names: as he begins to wear them, the names of his childhood are no longer used in public. Though they are derived from his father's house, names and feathers are conferred by people other than his father – a shaman in the case of names, shamans assisted by affinal 'god-fathers' in the case of feathers. Bone and blood have to do with physical being; names and feathers with a man's social being. Secret names represent an inner strength whilst the feathers and other ornaments he wears are his public face.

In marriage, men and women from affinally-related groups become more like kin via children created from their complementary substances. Family and kinship is the daily ethos of the maloca community. At initiation, the prelude to their politico-ritual life, male children are incorporated into an ancestral house through a ritual process of adoption; at death their souls return to this house, embodied in a stone 'house of awakening'. The maloca itself undergoes a similar kind of process. Its columns and frame, the bones of the house, are erected by the men. They are given substance by the residents and clothed in a roof of feather-like leaves contributed by wives and affines. Abandoned by its people, the maloca dies along with its owner. Roof and walls rot away leaving the heavy hardwood columns, standing like bleached bones on a site full of memories, the histories of its residents.

CONCLUSION

The reason why Lévi-Strauss has not applied his house concept of South America appears to relate to his earlier thinking about elementary kinship structures. For him, the house applies, in particular, to cognatic systems like those in Southeast Asia (1987: 153ff.). Whereas these systems lack positive marriage rules and thus lie 'beyond' the elementary structures, positive marriage rules are integral to Amazonian Dravidian systems. The cognatic systems of Amazonia are of a quite different order from their Southeast Asian counterparts. Without lineages or sections to provide a global logic, they represent the internal limits of restricted exchange, truly elementary structures reduced to cousin-marriage within the kindred and ordered by a logic of ego-centred kin terms. By definition they cannot be 'house societies' in Lévi-Strauss's terms (see Viveiros de Castro 1993). As Rivière concludes in his contribution to this volume, for the cognatic Guiana Caribs the notion of house seems to add little to that of co-residence, the significance of which was appreciated long ago. It is only in their mythical stone houses that we find some approximation to the 'real thing'.

Given the above, we are thus left in a quandary. On the one hand, there is an apparent incompatibility between Lévi-Strauss's notion of house as a social type and a type of social structure widespread in Amazonia; on the other hand, we have ethnographic evidence, from Northwest Amazonia and elsewhere (see Lea this volume), of the use of a notion of house as a local idiom for lineage-like groupings whose identity is defined principally in terms of the ownership of sacra and other ritual prerogatives, a feature also emphasized in Lévi-Strauss's original characterization (1983a). The solution is not to follow him to the letter by expanding yet further the already heterogeneous and over-stretched category of 'house societies' in order to accommodate these new data, but rather to follow him in spirit by recognizing the significance of his more general insight concerning the widespread use of buildings as an idiom for various kinds of social groupings.

Errington (1987: 403–5) has already shown the value of a focus on the house as idiom in comparing different forms of social organization within a single cultural area. With reference to Southeast Asia, she uses it to explore the relationship between the preferentially endogamous cognatic societies of the Centrist Archipelago and the lineal, asymmetric alliance systems of Eastern Indonesia. An Amazonian parallel might be drawn in the relationship between the preferentially endogamous cognatic systems of the Guiana Caribs and the lineal Tukanoan systems of Northwest Amazonia, although in this latter case both systems involve symmetric alliance. Viewing the Tukanoans, their Arawakan neighbours, and the semi-nomadic Makú as making up a common system, we can also find a parallel with the Tanimbarese case in which contrastive forms of affiliation, residence and marriage coexist within the same society (see McKinnon this volume). Within this wider Northwest Amazonian system, we find differences in the degree to which people conform to the ideals of isogamy, virilocality and exogamy, differences which, as in Tanimbar, are related to a status hierarchy. The Makú, whom Tukanoans treat as servants, share their 'master's' vision of group exogamy and clan ranking but in practice they show a marked statistical tendency towards both settlement and group endogamy. This feature, reminiscent of endogamy amongst the Guiana Caribs, is also found, to a much lesser extent, amongst some Tukanoan groups (see also Århem 1989).

Lévi-Strauss's observation that the house may serve as an ambiguous projection of descent, property or residence which serves to mask the contradictions and tensions inherent in the alliance relation (1987: 155–6) is also suggestive in the context of regional comparison in lowland South America. Affinity, involving as it does the contradiction between self-sufficiency and dependence on others, might be described as *the* problem underlying the Dravidian systems of Amazonia. By adopting an endogamous solution and 'doing away with' affinity by disguising it as consanguineal co-residence, the Guiana Caribs have opted for a peaceful life. The cost is a weakly integrated, atomistic society made up of small, inward-looking and impermanent communities, each housed in a single communal dwelling. Here there is no room for more than one projection of the house – a building which is at once family, hearth and home. But in the house of the ancestral spirits, cold, hard mountains looming through the clouds above the forest canopy, we can find ancestral clans and moieties, shadowy reflections of their Tukanoan counterparts (Overing Kaplan 1981: 162).

The Tukanoans have opted for a less restful but more powerful alternative. Exploiting the possibilities of lineage and hierarchy, they have generated what are potentially relatively large, internally differentiated groupings, formed round hierarchically organized agnatic cores linked together into an open-ended regional system based on the exchange of women, goods and ritual services. The cost is to bring the problem of affinity right to the forefront. The solution consists of a number of differing ceremonial gatherings or 'houses', each reinforcing a different facet of the system and each refracting a partial image of the constitution of society onto the buildings in which they take place. Here affinity is both a relation between houses and disguised as consanguinity within an encompassing house.

The organic solidarity of the Tukanoans, though highly ritualized, nonetheless rests upon down-to-earth alliance. Amongst the Mẽbengokre, and even more so amongst the Bororo (see Crocker 1985), affinity all but disappears. Solidarity between houses gets shifted further towards the symbolic realm, a shift reflected in a shift in the significance of architecture. In many ways, features of the Mẽbengokre seem to correspond, in an inverted term-by-term fashion, to those of the Tukanoans. Here I will focus only on those that relate buildings to social groups and categories. In both cases houses own very similar kinds of material and immaterial wealth – prerogatives, ornaments and names. All Tukanoan houses have free access to raw materials and their ornament repertoire is virtually identical: the ornaments of different houses are distinguished primarily at the verbal level of myth. Amongst the Mẽbe...ɔkre and Bororo, raw materials are owned by different houses and there is a proliferation of different ornament types which seems to correspond to a proliferation of personal names.

In the Tukanoan case, each individual has a 'spirit name' and one or two nicknames; though spirit names are conferred by living members of the proximal generation, the names themselves are those of dead parental grandparents who are replaced by their grand-children. In the Mẽbengokre case, names are conferred by a name-giver and pass typically from maternal uncle to nephew or from father's sister to niece, but the relation between eponym and name-receiver is assimilated to that between grandparent and grandchild (see Lea this volume).

The Mẽbengokre live in nucleated, circular settlements made up of uxorilocal extended-family houses built, originally, by women alone, in fixed places round a central plaza and men's house. Each Tukanoan language-group lives in a number of virilocal, extended-family houses, constructed by men and 'clothed' by women and affines, arranged in dispersed, linear settlements with places fixed according to clan rank along the banks of a single river. In each case, correspondence between ideal and actual settlement is always incomplete but all settlements represent an ideal in which all the houses, each in a fixed position, are there by definition.

Though superficially quite distinct, the overall plan of Mẽbengokre or other Northern Jê villages shows some interesting parallels with the interior of a Tukanoan maloca. Inside the maloca we find a semi-circular arrangement of nuclear family compartments behind a central, ritual forefront and a more general concentric dualism which opposes a 'masculine' ritual centre to a 'feminine' domestic periphery. In Jê villages, the concentric predominates over the linear; in the Tukanoan case, though a few malocas are also circular (see S. Hugh-Jones 1985), most represent a compromise between the concentric and the linear, a rectangular structure with a rounded apse (see C. Hugh-Jones 1979). However, the Jê exploit linear features in various forms of diametric dualism and the Tukanoans also represent their ideal settlement in concentric terms as four malocas surrounding a fifth shamanic and ritual centre (see Fig. 11.3). The Tukanoan dwelling represents a human body and allows for several different symbolic readings; amongst the Mêbengokre, the dwelling itself appears to lack symbolic elaboration but it reappears one level up in a village which also represents a human body. In some Jê groups, concentric and linear readings of the village are associated with different moiety groupings which combine to generate an intense organic solidarity in which affinity, the mainstay of Tukanoan organic solidarity, plays no part (see also Melatti 1979).[14]

In this essay I have tried to show how a focus on a native idiom of the house might throw new light on Tukanoan social organization and provide fresh comparative insight for lowland South America. Rather than use this concept to construct 'house society' as a new, hybrid and over-stretched social type, I would use it as a heuristic device which, along with others, may allow us to get away from such types altogether. If categories such as 'Dravidian' and 'Crow-Omaha', 'cognatic' and 'descent', appear to separate and to fragment, a focus on houses and the house reaffirms that the Guiana Caribs, the Tukanoans and the Jê all inhabit the same geographic and cultural space. In each case the house may serve as an idiom of one or more social groupings but it is given a different nuance in each one. Although architecture itself plays only a minor role in Lévi-Strauss's discussion of 'house societies', I have tried to show that his concept of the house may fruitfully redirect our attention to the relation between buildings, groups and categories. The insights this brings are not merely about space and category but also about time and process, for house and hearth encode ideas about biological and social reproduction. The transformational relation between space and time is a recurrent theme in South American culture and architecture – the round of dances held in Tukanoan houses are stages on the journey from past to present, from foetus to adult, and from one season to another.

Although there appears to be no necessary link between houses and hierarchy (see Waterson this volume), Lévi-Strauss (1983a) sees hierarchy as a characteristic feature of 'house societies', one related to competition over emblems, titles and prerogatives. The connection between the Tukanoan house and hierarchy is very clear in their ranked clans. At a higher level, the whole of Tukanoan society may be divided into senior, junior and servant classes. Each class refers to the others in terms of kinship: seniors are 'grandchildren', juniors are 'father's brothers' and servants are 'grandfathers' (see Chernela 1993). The Tukanoan *kubu* or priest, distinguished from the more typical Amazonian shaman as the keeper of an elaborate mythological canon, adds a further dimension to this hierarchy. Tantalizing historical accounts suggest that these priests once acted in consort with powerful chiefs as the leaders of quite large political groupings (see Hugh-Jones 1994c).

Without necessarily accepting its more general evolutionary implications, in this context it is tempting to link Lévi-Strauss's suggestion that the institution of the house is related to the emergence of groups based around political and economic interests which are expressed in the language of kinship (1983a: 186), with his earlier suggestion that the myths of Northwest Amazonia represent remnants of a genuine civilization with a much higher level of religious, social and political organization than anything that has been observed since (1973: 272). Recent archaeological research in Amazonia has uncovered the existence of large, urbanized populations which require a complete re-evaluation of our view of the region as a whole (Roosevelt 1991). The origin myths of the Tukanoans speak of their migration from the Milk River located downstream in the East. Their notion of house is always contextually defined; like the reflections in a mirrored hall, its nested imagery can recede outwards to encompass ever wider goupings. Despite Lévi-Strauss's warning that 'cracked bell(s), alone surviving the work of time, will never give forth the ring of bygone harmonies' (1963: 117), it is still possible that, in tarnished silvering, we may yet glimpse the shadows of a past grandeur.

NOTES

1: Introduction

1 Thanks are due to Michael Stewart for initial inspiration, to the University of Cambridge's Evans Fund for a grant which made the workshop possible, to King's College, Cambridge for the generous extension of their facilities, and to Jonathan Spencer for moral support, substantive comments and editorial advice.

   We are grateful to Tim Ingold, to the contributors to this volume, and to readers for Cambridge University Press for comments on an earlier draft of this introduction.

2 A modest workshop and a normal-sized book cannot cover all continents. Our intensive comparative focus on two regions allows only superficial coverage of Europe, Japan and Africa. Feudal Europe and Japan figure prominently in Lévi-Strauss's discussions of house societies whilst a long-term awareness of the ethnographic significance of houses in Africa has recently begun to crystallize into a subversive critique of descent theory.

   Japan is covered by Waterson in her comparative survey of the house in Southeast Asia whilst we as editors include a brief discussion of both Europe and Africa in this introduction. In our treatment of Europe, we have drawn on two papers by Frances Pine and João de Pina Cabral which were reluctantly dropped from this volume for reasons of space.

3 Exceptions include R. and S. Levine (1991) on the Gusii and Willis's (1974) brief discussion of the Fipa.

4 See, for example, Arnold 1992; Barraud 1979; Caiuby Novaes 1983; Cunningham 1964; Errington 1989; Griaule and Dieterlen 1954; C. Hugh-Jones 1979; Moore 1986; and Waterson 1990.

5 See, for example, Prussin 1969; Rapoport 1969; Guidoni 1975; Blier 1987; Oliver 1987; Lawrence 1987; Lawrence and Low 1990.

6 See Sabean (1990) for a useful critical overview of the extensive literature on

family and household in studies of kinship, economics and historical demography and see also the works to which he refers.

7　Two notable exceptions are Waterson's (1990) regional survey of Southeast Asian architecture and Cuisenier's (1991) work on rural architecture in France.

8　The original translation gives 'corporate body' for 'personne morale'. As much hinges on the precise meaning of this phrase we have kept as close as possible to the original.

9　For a discussion of European noble houses see Bullough (1969); Duby (1972; 1977); Martindale (1977); Flandrin (1979); and Goody (1983: 223–39). The relation between house, lineage and *lignage* is discussed below. It appears that in the early modern period the house in Europe becomes a significant category both for the state (partly for reasons of taxation and property regulation) and for the non-aristocratic population but is replaced by 'family' in reference to bourgeois domestic groups by the nineteenth century. 'House' is then reserved for the product of aristocratic alliances (Sabean 1990: 92–4). Sabean discusses the changing significance of the house in Neckerhausen in the early modern period as well as the flaws in the approaches of many social scientists and historians which exclude the content of social relations entailed by the house from their analysis.

10　See the exchange between Leach (1977) and Lévi-Strauss (1977) for an example of the ambiguities surrounding the translation of this word.

11　See Sabean (1990) for a discussion of the relation between the aristocratic house and its peasant counterpart in early modern Europe.

12　See, for example Yalman (1967) and Rivière (1984).

13　We are aware, of course, of the differences in relative emphasis given to continuity, authority, rights and duties, and property-holding by different Anglo-Saxon authors. As the whole topic of 'alliance and descent' involves such well-worn debates within kinship theory, about which there is already an extensive literature, we have decided to keep our text free of cluttering references. Interested readers might consult Kuper 1988 for a recent, if polemical, exposition of these issues.

14　The Batak are of course not geographically situated in Eastern Indonesia but have been described as falling in this type of society (Errington 1990; Rodgers 1990).

15　Given the ambiguities discussed above it would be imprudent to translate this term here.

16　Classic instances would include Leach 1958, 1961, and Strathern 1973. See also Rivière this volume.

17　This section briefly summarizes some of the issues raised by a focus on the house in the context of Southeast Asia. For a fuller discussion of these and other issues, readers should refer to Waterson (1990) (see also Dumarçay 1987).

18　See Barraud 1979; Traube 1986; Errington 1989; McKinnon 1991.

19　Freeman's (1958; 1970) work on the Iban *bilek* is something of an exception in this regard.

20　See also Barnes (1974); Milner ed. (1978); Fox ed. (1980); Izikowitz and Sorensen eds. (1982).

21 In this collection the chapters by Lundstrom (1982) and Wulff (1982) stand out as devoting considerable attention to the people who live in houses and what they do there.

22 *Semangat* 'life-essence' or 'vital force' is a key notion in Southeast Aia. It can be described as a pervasive life-force common to living things – plants, animals and humans – but also present in certain other kinds of material entity, including houses, mountains, boats and heirlooms (see Endicott 1970; Anderson 1972; Benjamin 1979; Errington 1983).

23 The house's importance as a kin group emerges from studies of many other societies in Southeast Asia. See Clamagirand 1975; 1980 (Ema of Timor); van Wouden 1956 (West Sumba); Kana 1980 (Savu); Schulte Nordholt 1971 (Atoni); Waterson 1986; 1990 (Sa'dan Toraja). Waterson (1990: 138–66) discusses these and other examples.

24 This distinction does not operate within strictly defined geographic boundaries (Errington 1987: 404); Errington (1990) adopts the term 'Exchange Archipelago' rather than 'Eastern Indonesia'.

25 See also de Barandiarán 1966; S. Hugh-Jones 1979; Wilbert 1981; von Hildebrand 1983; Reichel and von Hildebrand 1985; Fénelon Costa and Botelho Malhano 1987; Price 1987; Guss 1989; W. Crocker 1990; S. Hugh-Jones in press.

26 See Bamberger 1967, 1974; J. C. Crocker 1969, 1977a, 1977b, 1985; Da Matta 1976a, 1976b; Maybury-Lewis ed. 1979; Seeger 1980, 1981.

27 See, for example, the papers by Da Matta, Lave and Melatti in Maybury-Lewis ed. (1979).

28 See Hugh-Jones 1982; Fabian 1992 for two South American examples.

29 See Hodder 1990 for a discussion of the semantic and other links between 'focus' and 'hearth'.

30 For Lea's Mẽbengokre the literal translation of 'house' (*kikre*) is 'oven' (*ki*) 'hole' (*kre*); the stone ovens which stand outside each house are identical to grave mounds.

2: Houses and hierarchies in island Southeast Asia

1 Compare Fox (1988) for a transformative approach to models of early Austronesian social organization based upon the reconstruction of kin terms.

2 By the same token, it is problematic to apply the concept of 'house society' in the absence of any corresponding indigenous category, as Digard (1987) does to the segmentary lineage organization of the Bakhtiari nomads of Iran. Bakhtiari kinship is unequivocally patrilineal, and the 'tent', as the smallest domestic unit of the society, does not correspond to anything which could be called a 'house' grouping in Lévi-Strauss's sense. Digard sees 'irresistible' parallels with Lévi-Strauss's description of feudal European society, in the political manipulations of kinship ties by the grand khans of the Bakhtiari. From the mid-nineteenth century, these chiefs were attempting to create a centralized polity out of a segmentary system – an enterprise in which they were sufficiently successful, at moments, even to threaten the Iranian state within which they were situated (Digard 1987: 13, 32). But the manipulation of kinship ties can (and no doubt

does) occur in any system; in itself this feature would scarcely seem to justify the introduction of the 'house' concept. While the question of the transformation of segmentary systems into states remains a highly important one, there is no reason to suppose that 'house' organization must of necessity play a part in such processes. In fact Digard does not really supply enough detail about the khans' manipulation of the kinship system – for example, the exploiting of ties traced through females – for us to decide how far he is justified in pushing the 'house' analogy. I am grateful to Charles Macdonald for drawing my attention to this article.

3 Clearly, not all indigenous concepts relating to household organization need have anything to do with 'house societies'. The Balkan *zadruga*, for example, according to Hammel, can be entirely adequately explained in terms of more conventional kinship categories, as a product of 'a combination ... of lineage organization, virifocality, patrilocality, and agnatic bias', which, combined with 'certain demographic rates and particular external constraints ... will produce the complex households of the Balkans' (Hammel 1972: 337).

4 On the shaping role of the Church in the development of modern European kinship institutions, see Duby (1983) and Goody (1983).

5 Both the Iban and the Kwakiutl are classic examples of redistributive economies in which surpluses are regularly dispersed in communal feasting. Among the Kayapó, the intense importance attached to the passing on of names, and their accompanying ritual prerogatives and decorations, is not accompanied by any marked degree of social stratification.

6 At least in principle, the chief can demand a fine from a household wishing to leave, and will also claim their apartment, fruit trees and cleared lands.

7 It is clear from the work of Sather (1993) and others that the lack of longhouse unity which Freeman describes for the pioneer Iban whom he studied in the Third Division of Sarawak is not typical of Iban in other Divisions, where there is a far greater degree of unity, particularly in the contexts of warfare and ritual. Studies of other groups such as the Gerai of Kalimantan (Helliwell 1993) and the Kenyah Badeng (Armstrong n.d.) also stress the intensity of interactions *between* apartment groups within the longhouse. On the other hand, Sellato (1987a: 42) cautions that 'house societies' appear more dominant in Sarawak than in other parts of Borneo.

8 James Fox (personal communication).

9 Illuminating perspectives on the 'feudalism' debate are to be found in Leach, Mukherjee and Ward (1975).

10 See Waterson (1990, 1993, n.d.a.) for a fuller exposition of these shared features. Fox (1993b) also discusses the distribution of some important Austronesian terms and concepts.

11 This contrasts with the situation among the Iban, for example, where one temporarily surrenders all rights in the *bilek* household of one's birth when one takes up residence in the *bilek* of one's spouse.

12 History itself has been closely bound up with houses and their genealogies and founding myths (see Waterson 1992).

13 Nobles often took women of lower ranks as wives and their children claimed a

half share of noble substance (*rara buku* or 'blood and bone' in the Toraja phrase). Other ranks were also bound by noble claims on their co-operation and labour on ceremonial occasions. This included providing an entourage for nobles attending other people's ceremonies. For this they had to be rewarded with meat from sacrificial animals. While potentially promoting a sense of shared glory, these relationships were (and are) open to a variable amount of abuse by the nobility.

14 I have discussed this more fully in Waterson (n.d.b.).
15 James Fox (personal communication).
16 See Bigalke (1981).
17 Hamonic (1987) reconstructs the process by which Buginese *bissu* or transvestite shamans became guardians of the cult of royal regalia, stored in attics and used to make contact with the deities. As such they also served as instruments of legitimation for the ruling noble families.
18 Merchants formed part of the remaining percentage, their households too being organized as *ie*, while *samurai*, the highest status group, constituted only 6 per cent.
19 Even landowners with their own clients might deliberately lease a piece of land from a more powerful landlord in order to enter into clientage relations with him, such ties being ceremonially established in the mould of the 'parent–child' (*oya–ko*) relationship, and creating a lasting bond between the two *ie* (Fukutake 1967: 69).

3: The resurrection of the house amongst the Zafimaniry of Madagascar

1 The term they use is *Belefona*, *lit*. 'the many spears'. The avoided term is the normal term for rebel, *fahavalo*, which means, literally, the eighth people. The number eight has strongly negative connotations for the Zafimaniry.
2 I cannot be completely sure exactly the length of this period since the accounts I was given varied somewhat.
3 An exception to this are the beliefs concerning standing stones.
4 This statement is only true if we forget about the existence of a group of descendants of slaves whom the Zafimaniry consider 'beyond the pale', and therefore not an organic part of society.
5 One could argue that the only 'real' symbolic house among the Merina is the royal palace while the tomb gradually replaces the house the lower one goes down in the social hierarchy (Bloch 1981).
6 See Turton 1972.
7 *Efa Nahazo Toko trano ve?*
8 Spouses are chosen for children on the basis of Zafimaniry calculations of compatibility, which are quite complex. I hope to discuss these and other aspects of arranged marriage in more detail in future publications.
9 In fact the Zafimaniry find it very odd that spouses without living children can continue to get on well together. When this happens, as was the case for a couple in my village, this becomes a subject of puzzled speculation.
10 The term *ala fady* is usually explained in the ethnography of Madagascar as the removal of the incest relation which might exist between the spouses (Rakoto 1965). This is probably right in many cases but the Zafimaniry emphatically denied that the phrase had this meaning for them.

11 The double affiliation of both spouses to each other's parents is similar to what I discussed in Bloch 1978.

12 The wood of the hot post should be Nato (*Imbricaria Madagascariensis*). The wood of the cold posts should be Tamboneka (*Hediocaryopsis Madagascariensis*). For descriptions of the structure of Zafimaniry houses see Vérin 1964 and Couland 1973.

13 *Omena vonahitra amin' ny teza ny hazo*. The concept of *Teza* is further discussed in Bloch 1993b and 1994.

14 The expansion of the bilateral group of descendants is severely restricted by the fact that marriages tend to be exchanges between two moieties. This is a subject I discuss to some extent in Bloch (1975), and which I also hope to address in future publications.

15 At a meeting where a youth was accused of hitting the central post with a bottle he was told: 'This is not wood but the old gentleman (*Rangahy*).'

16 Zafimaniry blessings often occur at dawn so that the rays of the sun can enter through the eastern windows of the house and shine on the descendants sitting to the west. The new light coming through the house in this way seems to represent this continuing life of the house although I was never told so explicitly. It is for this blessing that Zafimaniry houses have windows to the east while most Malagasy houses do not.

17 This moiety system is mainly operated by a strong preference for pairs of cross-sex siblings marrying other pairs of cross-sex siblings rather than by a rule of cross-cousin marriage, though the result is similar.

18 When one rebuilds a holy house one should make a sacrifice to ask for forgiveness for the inevitable harm one does to the old structure.

19 The fact that many people, especially elders, have died there makes the house more holy.

4: The hearth-group, the conjugal couple and the symbolism of the rice meal among the Kelabit of Sarawak

1 The PhD research on which this paper is based was supported by an award from the Economic and Social Research Council. Fieldwork was conducted in the Kelabit Highlands, Sarawak in 1986–8 under the auspices of the Sarawak Museum, which I would like to thank for its support. Additional financial support was provided by the Malinowski Memorial Fund of the Royal Anthropological Institute. I am grateful to my PhD supervisor, Maurice Bloch, for comments on the ideas presented in this paper. I am also grateful to participants in the writing-up seminar at the London School of Economics for their comments, particularly to Elvira Belaunde. Work on the final version of the paper continued during the period of tenure of an Evans Fellowship at the University of Cambridge, and I am grateful to the Evans Fund for this help.

2 Carsten (1987) argues that, in Langkawi, the larger community is similarly conceived of as an enlarged house which consumes rice meals together in certain circumstances. The presence of an entity founded on the notion of house (*rumaq* in Proto-Malayo-Polynesian – Blust 1980a: 211) but operating at different levels has been suggested for a number of insular Southeast Asian societies (Fox

1980: 11, 1987; Barraud 1979; Sellato 1987a: 39–41). Hanks (1972: 80–92, 116) gives an interesting discussion of the nature of kinship and the household in Thailand and suggests that the kingdom is equivalent to the household in the way it attracts dependants.

3 See also Janowski 1991, chs 7, 8 and 10 for a more detailed discussion.

4 Nowadays, events described as *irau*, 'naming feasts', are also held once a year in association with the Christian Easter. Such *irau* are rotated around the major population centres associated with the church to which the Kelabit belong, the Sidang Injil Borneo, and are hosted by the host community rather than by one hearth-group.

5 According to Rousseau (1990: 211–14), the Kelabit and other 'Kelabitic' groups represent a weakened version of the basic Central Bornean system. He sees Kelabit competitive feasting as aberrant and characteristic of this weakening (1990: 209).

In order to legitimate their position, Kelabit leaders must host frequent and lavish feasts. I would argue that these feasts display the essential nature both of leadership and of the prestige upon which it is based. Instead of being proof of the weakening of a system of differential prestige, as Rousseau argues, competitive feasting would thus rather appear to be the core of that system.

6 Rice eaten at the rice meal is described as *nuba'*. This appears to refer to the physical form it most often takes at such meals, cooked to a soft paste and packed in leaves; although not eaten at rice meals, corn and roots cooked in this way are also described as (maize) *nuba'* and (root) *nuba'*.

However, *nuba'* also refers to rice cooked in such a way that the grains remain separate; to differentiate between the two forms in which rice is eaten at the rice meal, one is described as 'soft' (*laya'*) and the other as 'hard' (*to'a*). *Nuba'* is not the only form in which rice is eaten. *Senape*, rice grains or rice flour steamed in leaves, are distributed outside the hearth-group on certain occasions, including feasts. Thus, in the context of rice meals, the term *nuba'* refers both to the characteristic *forms* of rice eaten and to the rice itself.

7 Like the Berawan Creator (Metcalf 1989: 60–1), this deity is of uncertain gender. Kelabit, Berawan, and all other Malayo-Polynesian languages allow gender to remain unspecified. Metcalf (1989: 60–2) points out that many Bornean peoples have a couple as their creator deities. It seems possible that where there are single creator deities, as among the Berawan and Kelabit, their gender is ambiguous.

8 Meat consumed on an everyday basis is always wild, at least in Pa' Dalih where game is still abundant, but meat consumed at feasts is always from domestic animals (pigs and buffaloes nowadays; I was told that sambhur deer were used in the past). This means that the meat *belongs* to the host hearth-group which is thus very explicitly providing both components of the rice meal, each with a distinct value. Although meat at feasts is from domestic animals, these share the ability of all living things other than rice to 'live on their own' (*mulun sebulang*). The contrast between rice and the meat eaten with rice thus pertains both to everyday rice meals and to *irau* feasts.

9   Meat eaten at the rice meal is almost always boiled, while it is always roasted when eaten as a snack food.

10 Fat appears to be very closely associated both with the forest itself and with the powers residing in primary forest. Women say that they are afraid to enter such forest for fear of spirits (*ada'*). *Ada'* control powers which can be used malevolently towards humans or which can be tapped so that they become benevolent. Men who have relationships with *ada'* can harness their powers for both good and evil. These powers are dangerous to both men and women but men must enter the primary forest, deal with its dangers, and show no fear. Although the mother mentioned may have feared for her son too, she could not appropriately express this.

11 The contrast between what the Kelabit themselves assert – that there is no specific association of men and women with different parts of the longhouse and hearth-group apartment – and what appears to be the case – a greater association of women with the 'inside', the *dalim*, and of men with 'non-inside', the *tawa'* – is echoed in Langkawi (Carsten, this volume).

5: Houses in Langkawi: stable structures or mobile homes?

The fieldwork on which this paper is based was conducted between 1980 and 1982 and was funded by a grant from the Social Science Research Council (ESRC) with additional funds from the Central Research Fund of the University of London. Subsequent fieldwork in 1988–89 was funded by the British Academy, the Wenner-Gren Foundation and the Evans Fund of the University of Cambridge. I thank Maurice Bloch and participants in anthropology seminars at the University of Manchester, Universiti Sains Malaysia, the National University of Singapore, the University of Rochester, and the workshop on *Houses: Buildings, Groups and Categories* for comments on earlier drafts.

1   See Macdonald (ed.) 1987; Errington 1987; 1989.

2   See also Macdonald (1987a: 5) on the difficulty of applying Lévi-Strauss's criteria to highly different societies and (1987a: 7–10) on the correlation between more prominent 'houses' with more hierarchized societies.

3   Elsewhere in Malaysia this part of the house is often called the *anjung* or the *rumah tangga* and the term *ibu rumah* refers to the main body of the house (Hilton 1956).

4   See Provencher 1971: 164–7.

5   See Douglas (1975: 256ff.).

6   See also Lundstrom (1982: 131).

7   See also Lundstrom-Burghoorn (1981: 72).

8   See McKinley (1981) for a full account of siblingship in Malay kinship.

9   The prohibition on marriage between 'milk siblings' is an Islamic one but the elaboration of these ideas is, I would argue, specific and local.

10 These rituals are described in detail by Laderman (1983: 174–207).

11 Errington (1987: 404) notes that this distinction does not operate within strictly defined geographic boundaries.

12 See also Barraud (1979: 39–54, 87–94) for elaborations of similar ideas in Tanebar-Evav.

13 Errington distinguishes between the hierarchical states and the more egalitarian societies of the Centrist Archipelago. It follows from her analysis and that presented in this volume that houses in the more hierarchical societies, especially those of the aristocracy and royalty, would have more complex spatial divisions which reflect and express this hierarchy. (See also Introduction and McKinnon and Waterson in this volume.)

14 See Headley's (1987b) comparative discussion of siblingship and the house in Southeast Asia. Where the house resembles Lévi-Strauss's model more weakly (e.g. Malaysia and Java), Headley suggests it is 'vehiculed by the idiom of siblingship' (p. 209).

15 This idea is itself suggested by Lévi-Strauss: 'it is not the individuals or families that act, it is the houses, which are the only subject of rights and duties' (1983a: 173).

6: Having your house and eating it: houses and siblings in Ara, South Sulawesi

1 Fieldwork was carried out in Ara in 1988 and 1989 with the financial support of the Harry Frank Guggenheim Foundation and the institutional support of the Universitas Hasanuddin. I wish to thank, in particular, Professor Abu Hamid of the Faculty of Social and Political Sciences and Abdul Hakim Dg. Paca of Ara, both of whom provided me with many stimulating leads into the nature of Bugis-Makassar society. The interpretations contained in this paper are mine alone.

2 It should be understood that I am writing in the 'ethnographic present' and that some of these practices have been abandoned in the last generation. For an eye-witness account of them in Bira in the 1930s, see Collins 1937: 148–462.

7: The Lio House: building, category, idea, value

1 For a long time I was confused by Lévi-Strauss's definitions of 'house', especially in the chapter on Indonesia. I now feel that my confusion might mirror his own. His insistence on 'houses' as mediating a universal conflict of relations between descent and affinity arose, perhaps, not so much out of the ethnographic material on the Kwakiutl, or even the Iban and other Borneo societies, but out of his own lifelong concern with elementary structures.

2 Of course, not all non-differentiated societies can be found to have Houses in the sense that he outlines. This remains an empirical question to ascertain in each case. Lévi-Strauss does not address this point.

3 Several studies in this volume, which draw upon empirical data from non-differentiated societies, make the point that while the concept of the House has proved a useful one, Lévi-Strauss's insistence upon it being a hypostatization of the unstable relation of descent and affinity is not always borne out. Similar conclusions emerged in a previous study (Macdonald (ed.) 1987).

4 In the Indonesian context, the ethnographic examples chosen exemplify the former type. His model of the House as a reification of conflicting relations is substantiated because wife-givers and wife-takers live within the same house. However, this does not suffice since there are many other societies in the region

where this is not the case, but where Houses nevertheless are of major importance.

5   Since I first began to work among the Lio, several other anthropologists have been conducting fieldwork in different regions of Lioland. Research so far demonstrates both a uniformity and diversity of ideas and practices, hence I have found it necessary to specify the particular region that I know.

6   Fieldwork with the Northern Lio was initiated in 1982, and carried out in 1984, 1986 and 1989 under the auspices of the Indonesian Institute of Sciences, and with sponsorship from Universitas Nusa Tengana, Timor. It has been supported by the British Academy, the Centre for African Studies, the University of Edinburgh, and by the Norwegian Institute for Comparative Cultural Studies. On Flores, Father J. Smeets, SVD, has been of invaluable support both practically and intellectually throughout this period. I am very grateful to him. An earlier version of the paper was presented to the Department of Social Anthropology, University of Gothenberg, and to a graduate discussion group at my own Department in Oslo. The manuscript has been read and commented upon by Ada Engebrigtsen, Janet Hoskins, Olaf Smedal, Valerio Valeri and by the joint editors of this volume. It has been a difficult paper to get into shape and their comments have been extremely helpful. Whatever muddles remain are, of course, due to my own limitations.

7   Although people tend to emphasize the men who first settled the land, and to describe these as brothers, I nevertheless wish to suggest that there is enough evidence in myth, invocations and rituals to maintain that the first settlers were in fact brother–sister pairs. I was never told that these early siblings were twins (see Errington 1987 for a discussion of opposite-sex twins in Eastern Indonesia), but it is explicitly forbidden (*piré*) for opposite-sex twins to be born. They have committed incest in the womb and I was told that they never survive. If mythic brother–sister pairs were in fact twins, the enforced separation of them through subsequent marriage rules becomes even more poignant. See the discussion of MBD marriages of the Lio priest-leaders below.

8   It is usual in anthropological literature dealing with kinship systems of the matrilateral cross-cousin kind to place the analytic emphasis on the relationship between a male ego and his maternal uncle. Thus one speaks of 'mother's brother's daughter' marriage. Such a phrasing is misleading in the Lio case. My argument is that Lio alliances are to be understood as transformations of brother–sister unions. Thus, to designate them as marriages between children of 'uncles' and 'aunts' would create a wrong impression. In a sense there is no single ego in marriage, but that of the brother and sister. Most commonly, Lio express their marriage system as one of marriage between 'child (implicit daughter) of the brother' and 'child (implicit son) of the sister'. Hence, I will drop the customary M and F (of MBD/FZS) and talk simply in terms of BD and ZS marriage.

9   I have been informed that the person to be placed in the hole under the main house pillar of the temple should be a son of a trunk priest-leader. If this was the case, it would affirm graphically the close link perceived between this role and the original ancestors and major deities. It would also be an instance of sacrificial substitute, bridging the gap between the sacrificer and sacrificed.

262

10   This personification of the ancestors in the persons of the priest-leaders is not
just a fanciful idea on my part. During the rebuilding of a *kéda*, the council of
priest-leaders sat together on the newly erected platform for the building, eating
the special cuts of a sacrificed pig. The rest of the Lio stood some distance away
watching, waiting for the remainder of the meat to be distributed to them on the
dance-burial place. 'There sit the great ancestors', some people said to me,
pointing to the priest-leaders and adding that, although all we could see were
people we knew, in reality it was the ancestors who were there eating.

11   The Lio are explicit on this point. A wife whose descent group does not accept
that sufficient goods have been transferred will not be 'brought' by them in
order to 'enter' her husband's House. This is only applicable to wives of priest-
leaders. Such a ceremony frequently takes place long after the marriage has
been consummated. The event graphically marks the relinquishing of ultimate
rights to the wife-takers. The woman leaves her natal group as sister and
daughter and enters her husband's House as a true wife (*tu'a pu'u*) who, as such,
is also the sister of the House.

8: Houses and hierarchy: the view from a South Moluccan society

1   Portions of this chapter have been adapted from McKinnon (1991). I would like
to thank Joel Robbins and Jos Platenkamp for their critical readings of earlier
drafts of this chapter, and also Marilyn Strathern for her thoughtful commentary
on a book manuscript that inspired me to develop some of the ideas presented
here.

2   For other early attempts to come to terms with the various forms of kinship and
marriage in Indonesia, see, for example, van Ossenbruggen (1930, 1935) and
Fischer (1935, 1936). Remarkably, van Wouden's model continues to be
replicated in the historical reconstructions formulated more recently by Blust
(1980a, 1980b), van Dijk and de Jonge (1987), and others.

3   Most of the commentators on the Nuer, for instance, have been unable to free
themselves from this particular straitjacket. Having defined the structural ideal
in terms of patrilineality, all the other seemingly contradictory social practices
engaged in by the Nuer end up being characterized as failure of the real to
accord with the ideal or of practice to accord with structure. Such commentators
do not appear to recognize that the source of this disjunction is located in their
own formulation. Rather, they locate the disjunction in Nuer life – between
Nuer ideals and action (see, for example, Glickman 1971; Karp and Maynard
1983; Southall 1986; and Evens 1989 for different sides of this issue).

4   Yet, if one looks at the number of societies that, by their own formulation,
declare themselves to be house societies, there remain precious few that can be
described in the 'elementary' terms of an exclusive form of descent or marriage.
In fact, the word that has been glossed as 'patrilineage' in many of the
ethnographies that provide the classic models for unilineal descent turns out to
be the word for 'house'. Thus, to take just a few examples, the Nuer *thok dwiel*
means 'the entrance to the hut', the Tikopia *paito* and the Tallensi *yir* mean
'house', and the Yapese *tabinau* means either 'house' or 'landed estate' (Evans-
Pritchard 1940: 247; Firth 1963: 300; Fortes 1949: 10; Schneider 1984: 21;

Labby 1976: 15; see also Geertz and Geertz 1975 on the Balinese *dadia*; Lévi-Strauss 1983a and 1987 on the Kwakiutl *numayma*; and Parmentier 1984 on the Balauan *blai*).

5   For several anthropological works that use the concepts of objectification and personification in various ways, see Gregory (1982), Thomas (1985) and Strathern (1988).

6   The importance, in Indonesia, of the ideology of the generation of life, conceived as the relation between source and issue or trunk and tip, has been well documented (see, for example, Fox 1971, 1980; Traube 1980, 1986).

7   While there are four distinct language groups in the Tanimbar Islands (Yamdenan, Fordatan, Selaruan and Selwasan), the speakers of these languages share a common cultural framework. Nevertheless, my own work was carried out primarily among speakers of the Fordatan language on the islands of Fordata, Larat and Sera and should not be generalized to the whole of the archipelago (see Pauwels 1990). The indigenous terms used throughout this paper are Fordatan.

8   Rows of allied houses are named and can connect anywhere from six to twelve houses, but one row may feed into another, thereby forming longer pathways that link up to twenty houses. The entire system is such that the 'sisters and aunts' pathways feed into 'small rows' (*lolat ko'u*), which feed into 'big rows' (*lolat dawan*), which in turn feed into a double cycle of asymmetric alliance, called the 'Great Row' (*Lolat Ila'a*) that stands at the very top of the entire network of exchange pathways.

9   See Mauss (1967: 39–41), who clearly understood the nature of this tension between the forces of encompassment and separation and its relation to the dynamics of hierarchy and equality (McKinnon 1991: 163–98).

10 Elsewhere I have explored the iconic nature of the male and female valuables involved in this process (McKinnon 1989; 1991). Thus, not only are the different portions of the bridewealth referred to in terms of weapons ('bow', 'spear' and 'sword') but the male valuables given by the wife-takers speak of hardness, penetration, severance, killing and death, whereas the female valuables given by the wife-givers speak of softness, encompassment, and qualities that encircle, tie, and bind together.

9: Houses, places and people: community and continuity in Guiana

1   I wish to acknowledge the helpful comments of the participants at the workshop 'Houses: Buildings, Groups and Categories' held at Cambridge on 6–7 April, 1991. I am also very grateful to Audrey Colson, Paul Henley and Joanna Overing who provided invaluable comments on a later draft.

2   The Yanoama, by far the largest group in the region, are excluded from consideration here since they are sufficiently different to warrant separate treatment. Although reference is made at points to the Piaroa, they also differ in certain ways from the Carib-speakers and some of the conclusions do not apply to them.

3   Butt Colson states that a 'true village has a large communally built house for dancing and feasting' (1970: 37). In a letter dated 1 January 1991 she further

stated 'The visible mark of a village, as opposed to just a large settlement (i.e. a cluster of houses) is the presence of a communal, festival building'. This parallels almost exactly the situation among the Tukanoan Cubeo among whom the presence of a dancefloor is a crucial marker of a proper house and social and ceremonial autonomy (Goldman 1963: 39–41).

4　The main ethnographic examples used in this paper are the Trio and the Ye'cuana. They provide a useful contrast, having respectively single- and multi-house settlements. Furthermore, the ethnography of the Ye'cuana house is particularly rich (see Koch-Grünberg 1923; de Barandiarán 1966; Arvelo-Jiminez 1971; Wilbert 1981; and Guss 1989). Except where it is a matter of direct citation I have drawn indiscriminately from these various sources. I rely on my own field data and Frikel (1973) for information on the Trio.

5　Interestingly enough Dumont continues 'Although in the Western tradition we think of ourselves as coextensive to time and base our being on our historicity, we are not totally unable to think of ourselves in terms similar to those of the Panare. Do we not speak of Charles V as being "of the *house*" of the Hapsburgs?'

6　See Frikel (1973) for descriptions and drawings of the various type of houses. The number of different types may well be further evidence for the claim that the modern Trio are an assorted group whose constituent parts, coming from various directions, took refuge in the area (Rivière 1969: 27–8). On the question of whether the Trio ever had communal houses see Bos (1973). The answer to this would seem to depend on how 'communal' is defined. I can find no evidence to suggest that their settlements, like those of the Ye'cuana, were once composed of single large longhouses in which the whole community lived. On the other hand there is no doubt that dwellings often house extended families.

7　There has been considerable debate on whether the rectangular house is a recent, post-conquest, introduction. This is not an important question for the present purposes and will not be considered.

8　The Trio term for this area is *wïrïpëhtao*, about the meaning of which there is some uncertainty. The word *wïrïpë* means 'spirit' and the suffix *-htao* means 'in'. The problem is what connotation surrounds that word *wïrïpë*. The missionaries have argued that it has the unequivocal sense of 'bad', whereas I have always maintained it involves the notion of 'ambiguity'. I would, therefore, translate *wïrïpëhtao* as an ambiguous area, the betwixt-and-between of village and forest.

9　The word *pata* occurs in a number of Carib languages, and it has the literal meaning of 'place'. It is not only people who have a *pata*. One refers to an armadillo's hole as *kapai pata*, and to a garden site as *wïi pata*, literally 'manioc place' or 'village'.

10　An exception to this are the Piaroa among whom the association of the centre with men and the periphery with women is not obvious. However, the association of the centre with communal activities and the periphery with family concerns is there (see Overing Kaplan 1975: 31). However, the Piaroa shaman chants all night in his compartment, located on the periphery, and not in the centre (Overing: pers. commun.). Overing has also expressed to me some doubt about the front/back opposition with reference to the Piaroa.

265

11   The Waiyana, the eastern neighbours of the Trio, secure in the ceiling of the house in which communal events take place a wooden disc decorated with mythic creatures. Audrey Colson tells me that all the senior men of the village are involved in painting the disc and suggests that this activity is an expression of their collectivity. I would like to speculate that the disc is made from hard wood and that it is transported to a new village as and when the old village is abandoned, thus symbolizing continuity as well as collectivity.

12   An example of where the option to repair the existing house rather than to build a new one is preferred is afforded by the groups of the Upper Xingu. It might be added that the size of the house has no apparent bearing on whether the preference is to repair or to relocate. The Xinguano house is similar in size to those of the Tukanoans and of the Ye'cuana, both of whom prefer to relocate.

13   Among the Kapon and Pemon a village leader is also known as the 'village owner', the term being *pata esak*. *Esak* has a semantic range which is similar to but not identical with that of *entu*. Whereas both words mean 'owner', the former also means 'body' and has the general sense of 'incorporation' (Butt Colson 1989: 54–5).

14   The term *ebu/epu* is found in a number of Carib languages and everywhere has the connotations of shaft, axis, handle, support and pillar. Thus, in Trio, the term for 'cotton spindle' is *maru epu*, literally 'cotton shaft'. One also finds elsewhere in Lowland South America a terminological relationship between a structural part of the house and the village leader. For example, Rosengren (1987: 159) reports that the Matsigenka term for the beams which support the house roof is also used for leader.

15   I would still stand by most of what I wrote in that article although I am now able to elaborate on certain aspects of the question, in particular the political tension between brothers-in-law.

16   Analogies are dangerous, but the best I can think of to help understand this case is to liken it to an underground railway system in which the tracks are permanent but the stations temporary and shifting. An observer at surface level can see the station entrances (settlements) but not the tracks (the invisible world). Because the stations are shifting the observer will note them in different places at different times, whereas the unseen 'permanent way' will remain constant.

10: The Houses of the Mẽbengokre (Kayapó) of Central Brazil – a new door to their social organization

1   All translations are my own.

2   The Mẽbengokre are better known as the (Northern) Kayapó, who number some 3,600 individuals. For details of the other Jê groups see footnote 6 below.

3   I wish to thank the Coordenação de Aperfeiçoamento de Pessoal de Nivel Superior (CAPES) for enabling me to participate in the workshop that led to the creation of this book in 1990. I also acknowledge support for fieldwork from the Conselho Nacional de Desenvolvimento Científico e Tecnológico (CNPq) and the Financiadora de Estudos e Projetos (FINEP).

4   These villages are Bàù, Pùkanù, Kubẽkàkre and Kapòto to the west of the
    Xingu river and Gorotire, Kubẽkrãkeyn, Kokraymoro, Kikre-tum and Aùkre to
    the east. Kapòto, which united the members of the former Mẽtùktire villages of
    Kretire and Jarina, was itself later renamed as Mẽtùktire, reserving the name
    Kapòto for a new, inland village to which some of the inhabitants of Mẽtùktire
    are presently moving.
        Between 1978 and 1987, I spent sixteen months with the Mẽbengokre, mostly
    in the village of Kretire.
5   The term patrimony would be better rendered 'matrimony' if the latter did not
    already refer to marriage, since the Mẽbengokre patrimony passes along the
    uterine line.
6   For comparative purposes, the Bororo are often included in the same cultural
    area as the Jê-speaking societies of Central Brazil. This paper focuses on the
    Northern and Central Jê amongst whom the study of social organization has
    been concentrated. The relations between their various sub-groupings are
    shown in the following table:
    Northern Jê
        Eastern Timbira
            Apaniekra
            Ramkokamekra
            Krĩkatí
            Krahó
            Gavião
        Western Timbira
            Apinayé
        Northern Kayapó
            Mẽbengokre
            Xicrin
        Southern Kayapó
            Panara
        Suya
    Central Jê
        Xerente
        Xavante
    Bororo
    Southern Jê
        Kiangang
        Xocleng
    (See Maybury-Lewis 1979: 4 from which this table was adapted.)
7   See Lea 1986, for further details on *nekrets*, and 1992 concerning onomastics.
8   *Mùt apoy dzà*, 'sun come out place'.
9   Further details of such myths are given in Lea 1993.
10 The Mẽbengokre say that in the old days the men had to remain assembled in
    the men's house in readiness to defend the village from the attacks of external
    enemies. Young boys used to be sent off to live in the men's house in the centre
    of the village. Nowadays they tend to remain in their mothers' homes until

267

marriage. Turner (1966 and 1979b) discusses the fact that the Mẽbengokre used to have two men's houses.

11 The word eponym is used, rather than homonym, for the latter is a reciprocal term. What is in question here is the relation between someone in an ascending generation, whose name is transmitted to a relative of a descending generation, who is thereby the latter's eponym.

12 As in the case of the mother's mother in relation to her daughters' children.

13 This, ideally, is the case of the mother's father in relation to his daughters' children.

14 As in the case of the father's mother and father's father in relation to their sons' children.

15 Cf. Ladeira: 'Data collected by me among the Timbira indicate that the terms for cross-cousins vary depending on ego's sex, as a result of the influence of naming' (1982: 100).

16 They are also found among other Native Amazonians. See, for example, Viveiros de Castro (1986: 439), concerning the Araweté (Tupi-Guarani).

17 Verswijver, for instance, writes in English of matrilines (1983) but in Portuguese he uses the term matrilineage (1984). W. H. Crocker (1977; 1979; 1990) also uses an assortment of terms – uterine lines, matrilines, ritual matrilineages etc.

18 After last leaving the field I deduced a hypothetical system of generalized exchange (cf. Lea, in press). It has to be checked, for as yet it is merely an exercise in the formal analysis of extrapolation based on a possible principle of matrimonial alliance. Its plausibility is suggested here because it would be relevant to the understanding of Mẽbengokre social organization and transformations throughout the Jê area. See also Viveiros de Castro (1990), concerning Jê and Bororo spouse preferences.

19 Cf. Carneiro da Cunha, 1978, Ch. V.

20 Cf. Overing (1975) for the first discussion of Dravidian systems in the context of lowland South America.

21 In the literature, the Xicrin are classified as a Kayapó sub-group. Since the Mẽtùktire consider them as a separate people (Dzore), this usage is adopted here.

22 The name Southern Kayapó is deceptive; linguistically the Mẽbengokre (Northern Kayapó) appear to be closer to the Timbira and Suya.

23 Cf. Müller, 1976: 178–9 and 189.

24 In order to assess the extent to which this happens, further research on the patrimony of Mẽbengokre Houses would be necessary, to allow the comparison of any House's heritable wealth on an inter-village level, on both sides of the Xingu river.

25 A neologism suggested to me by Eduardo Viveiros de Castro.

26 See Lévi-Strauss 1983a: Ch. 13.

11: Inside-out and back-to-front: the androgynous house in Northwest Amazonia

1 Based on some 30 months of field research, carried out between 1968 and 1991 by C. and S. Hugh-Jones, and variously supported by the Social Science

Research Council (now ESRC), King's College, Cambridge, and the British Museum. This support is gratefully acknowledged.

2   See especially C. Hugh-Jones 1979 and Béksta 1988.

3   Principal ethnographic sources include Goldman 1963; Reichel-Dolmatoff 1971; C. Hugh-Jones 1979; S. Hugh-Jones 1979; Århem 1981; and Jackson 1983. Local ethnography refers to 'sibs'; here I employ the more usual 'clan'.

4   S. Hugh-Jones 1979 provides detailed discussion of these rituals.

5   *Wiiogi*, a Tukano word usually translated as 'headman' or 'chief', actually means 'house builder'.

6   Historical records speak of malocas with up to 100 individuals and of several malocas in a single settlement. Though most contemporary malocas stand alone and communities rarely exceed 30 individuals, mission-inspired settlements may combine nuclear family dwellings with one or more adjacent malocas.

7   See also C. Hugh-Jones 1979 and S. Hugh-Jones 1994a.

8   Men and women call the children of co-resident adults 'son' and 'daughter' and treat them more or less as their own.

9   Condensed from Umúsin Panlõn Kumu and Tolamãn Kenhíri 1980: 51–70.

10   See Shapiro 1987 and the works she cites.

11   In other versions, the anaconda becomes a slit-gong which is beaten to 'awaken' (i.e. bring into being) the people. At certain dances, young men pummel the beer-trough (= anaconda-canoe = slit-gong) with their fists to 'awaken' the people at the dance.

12   See Bidou 1976 for an account of such politics-in-the-mode-of-myth amongst the Tatuyo.

13   This two-headed house calls to mind the ancestral anaconda which heads upstream on its journey but comes to rest with its head downstream (see p. 234).

14   To take these suggestions further would require a systematic comparison of naming and hierarchy among the Jê and Tukano; data on naming are sorely lacking for the Tukano as are data on hierarchy for the Jê.

BIBLIOGRAPHY

Anderson, B. R. O'G. 1972. 'The idea of power in Javanese culture', in C. Holt (ed.), *Culture and Politics in Indonesia*, Ithaca: Cornell University Press.

Århem, K. 1981. *Makuna Social Organisation*, Stockholm: Almqvist and Wiksell International.

—— 1989. 'The Makú, the Makuna and the Guiana system: transformations of social structure in northern lowland South America', *Ethnos* 54(I–II): 5–21.

Armstrong, R. n.d. 'The Kenyah Badeng longhouse', Paper presented at the Comparative Austronesia Project's Seminar on House and Household, ANU, May 1989.

Arnold, D. 1992. 'La casa de adobes y piedras del Inka: genero, memoria y cosmos en Qaqachaka', in D. Arnold (ed.), *Hacía un Orden Andino de las Cosas: Tres Pistas de los Andes Meridionales*, HISBOL, La Paz.

Arvelo-Jimenez, N. 1971. *Political Relations in a Tribal Society: a Study of the Ye'cuana Indians of Venezuela. Cornell University Latin American Program Dissertation Series, 31*, Ithaca: Cornell University.

—— 1973. 'The dynamics of the Ye'cuana ("Maquiritare") political system: stability and crises', *International Work Group for Indigenous Affairs (Copenhagen) Document*, 12.

Bachelard, G. 1964. *The Poetics of Space*, New York: Orion Press.

Bachnik, J. 1983. 'Recruitment strategies for household succession: rethinking Japanese household organisation', *Man* 18: 160–82.

Bamberger, J. 1967. 'Environment and Cultural Classification: A Study of the Northern Kayapó', Ph.D. thesis, Harvard University.

—— 1974. 'Naming and the transmission of status in a Central Brazilian society', *Ethnology* 13(4): 363–78.

Banks, D. J. 1983. *Malay Kinship*, Philadelphia: Institute for the Study of Human Issues.

Barandiarán, D. de 1966. 'El habitado entre los indios Yekuana', *Antropológica* 16: 3–95.

Barnes, R. H. 1973. 'Two terminologies of symmetric prescriptive alliance from Pantar and Alor in eastern Indonesia', *Sociologus* 23: 71–89.

1974. *Kédang: a Study of the Collective Thought of an Eastern Indonesian People*, Oxford: Clarendon Press.

1977. 'Alliance and categories in Wailolong, East Flores', *Sociologus* 27: 133–57.

1978. 'Injunction and illusion: segmentation and choice in prescriptive systems', *Anthropology* 2(1): 19–30.

1980a. 'Concordance, structure, and variation: considerations of alliance in Kédang', in J. J. Fox (ed.), *The Flow of Life: Essays on Eastern Indonesia*, Cambridge, Mass.: Harvard University Press.

1980b. 'Marriage, exchange and meaning of corporations in Eastern Indonesia', in J. L. Comaroff (ed.), *The Meaning of Marriage Payments*, New York: Academic Press.

Barnes, R., de Coppet, D. and Parkin, R. (eds.) 1985. *Contexts and Levels: Anthropological Essays on Hierarchy*, Oxford: JASO.

Barraud, C. 1979. *Tanebar-Evav: une société de maisons tournée vers le large*, Paris: Cambridge University Press.

Beaujard, P. 1983. *Princes et paysans: les Tanala de l'Ikongo*, Paris: L'Harmattan.

Béksta, C. 1988. *A maloca tukano-dessana e seu simbolismo*, Manaus: SEDUC/AM.

Benjamin, G. 1979. 'Indigenous religious systems of the Malay peninsula', in A. Becker and A. Yengoyan (eds.), *The Imagination of Reality: Essays in Southeast Asian Coherence Systems*, Norwood: Abbex.

Benveniste, E. 1973 [1969]. *Indo-European Language and Society*, London: Faber and Faber.

Bidou, P. 1976. 'Les fils de l'anaconda céleste (les Tatuyo): étude de la structure socio-politique', thèse de troisième cycle, University of Paris.

Bigalke, T. 1981. 'A Social History of "Tana Toraja", 1870–1965', Ph.D. thesis, University of Wisconsin.

Blier, S. 1987. *The Anatomy of Architecture: Ontology and Metaphor in Batammaliba Architectural Expression*, Cambridge: Cambridge University Press.

Bloch, M. 1971. *Placing the Dead: Tombs, Ancestral Villages and Kinship Organisation in Madagascar*, London: Seminar Press.

1975. 'Property and the end of affinity', in M. Bloch (ed.), *Marxist Analyses and Social Anthropology*, London: Malaby Press.

1977. 'The disconnection between rank and power as a process: an outline of the development of kingdoms in central Madagascar', in J. Friedman and M. Rowlands (eds.), *The Evolution of Social Systems*, London: Duckworth.

1978. 'Marriage amongst equals: an analysis of Merina marriage rituals', *Man* 13(1): 21–33.

1981. 'Tombs and states', in S. C. Humphries and H. King (eds.), *Mortality and Immortality: The Anthropology of Death*, London and New York: Academic Press.

1986. *From Blessing to Violence: History and Ideology in the Circumcision Ritual of the Merina of Madagascar*, Cambridge: Cambridge University Press.

1991. 'Language, anthropology, and cognitive science', *Man* 26(2): 183–98.

1993a. 'What goes without saying: the conceptualization of Zafimaniry society', in A. Kuper (ed.), *Conceptualising Society*, London: Routledge.

1993b. 'Domain specificity, living kinds and symbolism', in P. Boyer (ed.), *Cognitive Aspects of Religious Symbolism*, Cambridge: Cambridge University Press.

1994. 'People into places: Zafimaniry concepts of clarity', in E. Hirsch and M. O'Hanlon (eds.), *The Anthropology of Landscape*, Oxford: Oxford University Press.

Blust, R. 1980a. 'Early Austronesian social organization: the evidence of language', *Current Anthropology* 21(2): 205–26.

1980b. 'Notes on proto-Malayo-Polynesian phratry dualism', *Bijdragen tot de Taal-, Land- en Volkenkunde* 136: 215–47.

Boon, J. 1977. *The Anthropological Romance of Bali, 1597–1972: Dynamic Perspectives in Marriage and Caste, Politics and Religion*, Cambridge: Cambridge University Press.

Bos, G. 1973. 'Communale hutten bij de Trio Indianen', *Nieuwe West-Indische Gids* 49: 143–62.

Bourdieu, P. 1977. *Outline of a Theory of Practice*, Cambridge: Cambridge University Press.

1990. *The Logic of Practice*, Oxford: Polity.

1990 [1970]. 'The Kabyle house or the world reversed', in *The Logic of Practice*, Cambridge: Polity Press.

Bullough, D. 1969. 'Early medieval social groupings: the terminology of kinship', *Past and Present* 45: 3–18.

Butt Colson, A. J. 1970. 'Land use and social organisation of tropical forest peoples of the Guianas', in J. P. Garlick (ed.), *Human Ecology in the Tropics*, Oxford and New York: Pergamon Press.

1971. 'Comparative studies of the social structure of Guiana Indians and the problem of acculturation', in F. M. Salzano (ed.), *The Ongoing Evolution of Latin American Populations*, Springfield, Illinois: Charles C. Thomas.

1989. 'La naturaleza del ser. Conceptos fundamentales de los Kapón y Pemón', in *Las Religiones Amerindias: 500 años Despues. Colección 500 años 4*, Quito: Ediciónes Abya-Yala.

Caiger, J. 1968. 'The aims and content of school courses in Japanese history, 1872–1945', in E. Skrzypczak (ed.), *Japan's Modern Century*, Tokyo: Sophia University Press.

Caiuby Novaes, S. (ed.) 1983. *Habitações Indígenas*, São Paulo: Livraria Nobel.

Carneiro da Cunha, M. 1978. *Os Mortos e os Otros*, São Paulo: Hucitec.

Carsten, J. 1987a. 'Analogues or opposites: household and community in Pulau Langkawi, Malaysia', in C. Macdonald (ed.), *De la hutte au palais: sociétés "à maisons" en Asie du Sud-Est insulaire*, Paris: Editions du CNRS.

1987b. 'Women, Kinship and Community in a Malay Fishing Village on Pulau Langkawi, Kedah, Malaysia', Ph.D. Thesis, University of London.

1989. 'Cooking money: gender and the symbolic transformation of means of exchange in a Malay fishing community', in J. Parry and M. Bloch (eds.), *Money and the Morality of Exchange*, Cambridge: Cambridge University Press.

1990. 'Women, men, and the long and the short term of inheritance in Pulau Langkawi, Malaysia', *Bijdragen tot de Taal-, Land- en Volkenkunde* 146(II/III): 270–88.

1991. 'Children in between: fostering and the process of kinship on Pulau Langkawi, Malaysia', *Man* 26(3): 425–48.

Chernela, J. 1993. *The Wanano Indians of the Brazilian Amazon: a Sense of Space*, Austin: University of Texas Press.

Clamagirand, B. 1975. 'La maison Ema (Timor Portugais)', *Asie du Sud-Est et Monde Insulindien* 6(2–3): 35–60.

1980. 'The social organisation of the Ema of Timor', in J. J. Fox (ed.), *The Flow of Life: Essays on Eastern Indonesia*, Cambridge, Mass.: Harvard University Press.

Collins, G. E. P. 1937. *Makassar Sailing*, London: Jonathan Cape.

Conklin, H. 1964. 'Ethnogenealogical method', in W. H. Goodenough (ed.), *Explorations in Cultural Anthropology*, New York: McGraw-Hill.

Coulaud, D. 1973. *Les Zafimaniry: un groupe ethnique de Madagascar à la poursuite de la forêt*, Tananarive: Fonontan-Boky.

Crocker, J. C. 1969. 'Reciprocity and hierarchy among the Eastern Bororo', *Man* 4(1): 44–58.

1977a. 'Why are the Bororo matrilineal?', in J. Overing (ed.), *Social Time and Social Space in Lowland South America* (*Actes du XLIIe Congrès International des Américanistes*, Vol. 2), Paris.

1977b. 'My Brother the Parrot', in D. Sapir and C. Crocker (eds.), *The Social Use of Metaphor*, Pennsylvania: University of Pennsylvania Press.

1985. *Vital Souls: Bororo Cosmology, Natural Symbolism, and Shamanism*, Tucson: University of Arizona Press.

Crocker, W. H. 1977. 'Canela "group" recruitment and perpetuity; incipient "unilinearity"?' in J. Overing (ed.), *Social Time and Social Space in Lowland South America* (*Actes du XLIIe Congrès International des Américanistes*, Vol. 2), Paris.

1979. 'Canela kinship and the question of matrilineality', in W. E. Margolis and W. E. Carter (eds.), *Brazil*, New York: Columbia University Press.

1990. *The Canela (Eastern Timbira), I: an Ethnographic Introduction*, Washington D.C.: Smithsonian Institution Press.

Cuisenier, J. 1991. *La maison rustique: logique sociale et composition architecturale*, Paris: PUF.

Cunningham, C. 1964. 'Order in the Atoni house', *Bijdragen tot de Taal- Land- en Volkenkunde*, 120: 34–68.

Da Matta, R. 1976a. *Um Mundo Dividido: a Estrutura Social dos Indios Apinayé*, Petrópolis: Editora Vozes Ltda.

1976b. 'Uma reconsideração da morfologia social Apinayé', in E. Schaden (ed.), *Leituras de Etnologia Brasileira*, São Paulo: Companhia Editora Nacional.

Digard, J-P. 1987. ' "Jeux de structures": segmentarité et pouvoir chez les nomades Baxtyari d'Iran', *L'Homme* 102, XXVII/2: 12–53.

Dijk, T. van and de Jonge, N. 1987. 'The house on the hill: moieties and double descent in Babar', *Bijdragen tot de Taal-, Land- en Volkenkunde* 11: 67–101.

Douglas, M. 1975. 'Deciphering a meal', in *Implicit Meanings*, London: Routledge and Kegan Paul.

Dreyfus, S. 1963. *Les Kayapo du Nord*, Paris: Mouton and Co.

(ed.) 1972. *Etudes sur le territoire et l'habitat dans l'ouest amazonien.* (*Journal de la Société des Américanistes de Paris*. Vol. 61).

Duby, G. 1972. 'Lignage, noblesse et chevalerie au XIIe siècle dans la région mâconnaise: une révision', *Annales E.S.C.* 27: 803–23.

1977. 'Présentation de l'enquête sur famille et sexualité au moyen âge', in G. Duby and J. LeGoff (eds.), *Famille et parenté dans l'occident médiéval*, Rome.

1983. *The Knight, the Lady and the Priest: the Making of Modern Marriage in Medieval France*, New York: Pantheon.

Dumaray, J. 1987. *The House in South-East Asia* (trans. and ed. M. Smithies), Singapore: Oxford University Press.

Dumont, J-P. 1976. *Under the Rainbow: Nature and Supernature among the Panare Indians*, Austin: University of Texas Press.

1977. 'Le sens de l'éspace chez les Panare', in J. Overing (ed.), *Social Time and Social Space in Lowland South America (Actes du XLIIe Congrès International des Américanistes,* Vol. 2), Paris.

Dumont, L. 1970. *Homo Hierarchicus: the Caste System and its Implications*, London: Weidenfeld and Nicolson.

Egenter, N. 1992. *Architectural Anthropology 1*, Lausanne: Structura Mundi.

Ellen, R. 1986. 'Microcosm, macrocosm and the Nuaulu house: concerning the reductionist fallacy as applied to metaphorical levels', *Bijdragen tot de Taal-, Land-en Volkenkunde* 142(1): 2–30.

Embree, J. F. 1950. 'Thailand: a loosely structured social system', *American Anthropologist* 52(2): 181–92.

Endicott, K. 1970. *An Analysis of Malay Magic*, London: Cambridge University Press; reprinted Kuala Lumpur: Oxford University Press, 1981.

Errington, S. 1983. 'Embodied *sumange* in Luwu', *Journal of Asian Studies* 42(3): 545–70.

1987. 'Incestuous twins and the house societies of insular Southeast Asia', *Cultural Anthropology* 2(4): 403–44.

1989. *Meaning and Power in a Southeast Asian Realm*, Princeton: Princeton University Press.

1990. 'Recasting sex, gender and power: a theoretical and regional overview', in S. Atkinson and J. M. Errington (eds.), *Power and Difference: Gender in Island Southeast Asia*, Stanford: Cambridge: Stanford University Press.

Evans-Pritchard, E. 1940. *The Nuer: a Description of the Modes of Livelihood and Political Institutions of a Nilotic People*, Oxford: Oxford University Press.

1951. *Kinship and Marriage among the Nuer*, Oxford: Oxford University Press.

Evens, T. M. S. 1989. 'An illusory illusion: Nuer agnation and first principles', *Comparative Social Research* 11: 301–18.

Fabian, S. M. 1992. *Space–Time of the Bororo of Brazil*, Gainesville: University of Florida Press.

Feldman, J. 1984. 'Dutch galleons and South Nias palaces', *Res* 7/8: 21–32.

Fénelon Costa, M. H. and Botelho Malhano, H. 1987. 'Habitação indígena brasileira', in B. Ribeiro (ed.), *Suma Etnológica Brasileira*, Petrópolis: Vozes.

Firth, R. 1963. *We, The Tikopia: A Sociological Study of Kinship in Primitive Polynesia*, Boston: Beacon Press.

1966 (2nd edn). *Housekeeping among Malay Peasants*, London: Athlone Press.

Fischer, H. T. 1935. 'De aanverwantschap bij enige volken van de Nederlands-Indische archipel', *Mensch en maatschappij* 11: 285–97; 365–78.

1936. 'Het asymmetrisch cross-cousin huwelijk in Nederlandsch Indië', *Tijdschrift voor den Indische Taal-, Land- en Volkenkunde* 76: 359–72.

1957. 'Some notes on kinship systems and relationship terms of Sumba, Manggarai and South Timor', *Internationales Archiv für Ethnographie* 48: 1–31.

Flandrin. 1979 [1976]. *Families in Former Times*, Cambridge: Cambridge University Press.

Fock, N. 1963. *Waiwai: Religion and Society of an Amazonian Tribe*, Copenhagen: National Museum of Denmark, Ethnographic Series, 8.

Forde, D. 1970 [1950]. 'Double descent among the Yakö', in A. R. Radcliffe-Brown and D. Forde (eds.), *African Systems of Kinship and Marriage*, London: Oxford University Press.

Forge, A. 1973. 'Style and meaning in Sepik art', in A. Forge (ed.), *Primitive Art and Society*, London: Oxford University Press.

Fortes, M. 1949. *The Web of Kinship among the Tallensi; the Second Part of an Analysis of the Social Structure of a Trans-Volta Tribe*, London: Oxford University Press.

   1958. 'Introduction', in J. Goody (ed.), *The Developmental Cycle in Domestic Groups*, Cambridge: Cambridge University Press.

Forth, G. 1981. *Rindi: an Ethnographic Study of a Traditional Domain in Eastern Sumba*, The Hague: Nijhoff.

Fox, J. J. 1971. 'Sister's child as plant: metaphors in an idiom of consanguinity', in R. Needham (ed.), *Rethinking Kinship and Marriage*, London: Tavistock.

   (ed.) 1980. *The Flow of Life: Essays on Eastern Indonesia*, Cambridge, Mass.: Harvard University Press.

   1987. 'The house as a type of social organisation on the island of Roti', in C. Macdonald (ed.), *De la Hutte au Palais: sociétés 'à Maison' en Asie du Sud-est Insulaire*, Paris: Editions du CNRS.

   1988. 'Possible models of early Austronesian social organization', *Asian Perspectives* 24/1, IPPA Proceedings Issue, (ed.) P. Bellwood and W. G. Solheim, pp. 34–44.

   (ed.) 1993a. *Inside Austronesian Houses: Perspectives on Domestic Designs for Living*, Canberra: Australian National University.

   1993b. 'Origin structures and systems of precedence in the comparative study of Austronesian societies', in P. Li *et al.* (eds.), *Austronesian Studies Relating to Taiwan*, Taipei: Acedemia Sinica.

   n.d. 'Possible models of early Austronesian social organization'. Paper presented at the 12th Congress of the Indo-Pacific Prehistory Association, Peñablanca, Philippines, 1985.

Freeland, F. 1986. 'The search for sense; dance in Yogyakarta'. Ph.D. thesis, School of Oriental and African Studies, University of London.

Freeman, D. 1958. 'The family system of the Iban of Borneo', in J. Goody (ed.), *The Developmental Cycle in Domestic Groups*, Cambridge: Cambridge University Press.

   1970. *Report on the Iban*, London: Athlone Press.

Frikel, P. 1973. *Os Tiriyó: seu Sistema Adaptativo*, Hanover: Kommissionsverlag Munstermann-Druck.

Fukutake. 1967. *Japanese Rural Society*, Tokyo: Oxford University Press.

Geertz, C. 1960. *The Religion of Java*, Chicago: Chicago University Press.

   1980. *Negara: The Theatre State in Nineteenth-Century Bali*, Princeton, New Jersey: Princeton University Press.

Bibliography

Geertz, H. 1961. *The Javanese Family: a Study of Kinship and Socialization*, Glencoe, Ill.: The Free Press.

Geertz, H. and Geertz, C. 1975. *Kinship in Bali*, Chicago: University of Chicago Press.

Gibson, T. 1986. *Sacrifice and Sharing in the Philippine Highlands*, London: Athlone Press.

Glickman, M. 1971. 'Kinship and credit among the Nuer', *Africa* 41(4): 306–19.

Gluckman, M. 1950. 'Kinship and marriage among the Lozi of Northern Rhodesia and the Zulu of Natal', in A. R. Radcliffe-Brown and D. Forde (eds.), *African Systems of Kinship and Marriage*, London: Oxford University Press.

Goldman, I. 1963. *The Cubeo: Indians of the Northwest Amazon*, Urbana: University of Illinois Press.

Goody, J. (ed.) 1958. *The Developmental Cycle in Domestic Groups*, Cambridge: Cambridge University Press.

  1983. *The Development of the Family and Marriage in Europe*, Cambridge: Cambridge University Press.

Gose, P. 1992. 'House rethatching in an Andean annual cycle: practice, meaning, and contradiction', *American Ethnologist* 18(1): 39–66.

Gray, R. F. and Gulliver, P. H. (eds.) 1964. *The Family Estate in Africa: Studies in the Role of Property in Family Structure and Lineage Continuity*, London: Routledge and Kegan Paul.

Gregory, C. A. 1982. *Gifts and Commodities*, London: Academic Press.

Griaule, M. and Dieterlen, G. 1954. 'The Dogon', in D. Forde (ed.), *African Worlds*, London: Oxford University Press.

Gudeman, S. 1992. 'Remodelling the house of economics: culture and innovation', *American Ethnologist* 19(1): 141–54.

Gudeman, S. and Rivera, A. 1990. *Conversations in Colombia*, Cambridge: Cambridge University Press.

Guerreiro, A. 1987. ' "Longue maison" et "grande maison": considérations sur l'ordre social dans le centre de Bornéo', in C. Macdonald (ed.), *De la hutte au palais: sociétés "à maisons" en Asie du Sud-Est insulaire*, Paris: Editions du CNRS.

Guidoni, E. 1975. *Primitive Architecture*, New York: Harry N. Abrams.

Gulliver, P. H. 1955. *The Family Herds: a Study of Two Pastoral Tribes in East Africa – the Jie and Turkana*, London: Routledge and Kegan Paul.

Guss, D. M. 1989. *To Weave and Sing: Art, Symbol and Narrative in the South American Rain Forest*, Berkeley: University of California Press.

Hall, E. T. 1959. *The Silent Language*, Greenwich: Conn.: Fawcett Publications.

Hammel, E. 1972. 'The zadruga as process', in P. Laslett (ed.), *Household and Family in Past Time*, Cambridge: Cambridge University Press.

Hamonic, G. 1987. *Le langage des dieux: cultes et pouvoirs pré-islamiques en pays Bugis, Célèbes-Sud, Indonésie*, Paris: Editions du CNRS.

Hanks, L. M. 1972. Rice and Man: Agricultural Ecology in Southeast Asia, Chicago: Aldine.

Harrison, S. J. 1990. *Stealing People's Names: History and Politics in a Sepik River Cosmology*, Cambridge: Cambridge University Press.

Headley, S. 1987a. 'The body as a house in Javanese society', in C. Macdonald (ed.), *De la hutte au palais: sociétés "à maisons" en Asie du Sud-Est insulaire*, Paris: Editions du CNRS.

1987b. 'The idiom of siblingship: one definition of "house" societies in Southeast Asia', in C. Macdonald (ed.), *De la hutte au palais: sociétés "à maisons" en Asie du Sud-Est insulaire*, Paris: Editions du CNRS.

n.d. 'Houses in Java: the missing kin', Paper presented at the seminar on Cognatic Forms of Social Organisation in Southeast Asia, University of Amsterdam, 1983.

Heelas, R. 1979. 'The Social Organization of the Panara, a Gê Tribe of Central Brazil', D.Phil. thesis, Oxford University.

Heidegger, M. 1971. 'Building, dwelling and thinking', in *Poetry, Language and Thought* (trans. A. Hofstader), New York: Harper Row.

Helliwell, C. 1993. 'Good walls make bad neighbours: the Dayak longhouse as a community of voices', in J. J. Fox (ed.), *Inside Austronesian Houses: Perspectives on Domestic Designs for Living*, Canberra: Australian National University.

Henley, P. S. 1982. *The Panare: Tradition and Change on the Amazonian Frontier*, New Haven: Yale University Press.

Héritier, F. 1981. *L'Exercise de la parenté*, Paris: Gallimard.

Héritier-Augé, F. and Copet-Rougier, E. 1990. *Les complexités de l'alliance: les systèmes semi-complexes*, Montreux: Gordon and Breach.

Hildebrand, M. von 1983. 'Vivienda indígena, Amazonas', *Proa (Bogotá)*, 323: 12–21.

Hilton, R. N. 1956. 'The basic Malay house', *Journal of the Malay Branch of the Royal Asiatic Society* 29 Part 3: 134–55.

Hodder, I. 1990. *The Domestication of Europe*, Oxford: Blackwell.

Howe, L. 1983. 'An introduction to the cultural study of traditional Balinese architecture', *Archipel* 25: 137–58.

Howell, S. 1989. 'Of persons and things; exchange and valuables among the Lio of eastern Indonesia', *Man* 24(3): 419–38.

1990. 'Husband/wife or brother/sister as the key relationship in Lio kinship and sociosymbolic relations', *Ethnos* 55: 248–59.

1991. 'Access to the ancestors: re-constructions of the past in a non-literate society', in R. Grønhaug *et al.* (eds.), *The Ecology of Choice: Festschrift in Honour of Fredrik Barth*, Bergen: Alma Mater.

1992. 'Time past, time present, time future: contrasting temporal values in two Southeast Asian societies', in S. Wallman (ed.), *Contemporary Futures*, London: Routledge.

Hugh-Jones, C. 1979. *From the Milk River: Spatial and Temporal Processes in Northwest Amazonia*, Cambridge: Cambridge University Press.

Hugh-Jones, S. 1977. 'Like the leaves on the forest floor: ritual and social structure amongst the Barasana', in J. Overing (ed.): *Social Time and Social Space in Lowland South America (Actes du XLIIe Congrès International des Américanistes*, Vol. 2). Paris, 205–15.

1979. *The Palm and the Pleiades: Initiation and Cosmology in Northwest Amazonia*, Cambridge: Cambridge University Press.

1982. 'The pleiades and scorpius in Barasana cosmology', in A. Aveni and G. Urton (eds.), *Ethnoastronomy and Archaeoastronomy in the American Tropics, Annals of the New York Academy of Sciences*, Vol. 385, New York: New York Academy of Sciences.

1985. 'The maloca: a world in a house', in E. Carmichael, S. Hugh-Jones and B. Moser (eds.), *The Hidden Peoples of the Amazon*, London: British Museum Publications, pp. 77–93.

1994a. 'Indian drugs? Coca, tobacco and other peculiar substances in Northwest Amazonia', in P. Lovejoy (ed.), *Peculiar Substances: Essays in the History and Anthropology of Addictive Substances*, London: Routledge.

1994b. 'Amazonian architecture', in P. Oliver (ed.), *Encyclopaedia of Vernacular Architecture*, Oxford: Blackwell.

1994c. 'Shamans, prophets, priests and pastors', in C. Humphrey and N. Thomas (eds.), *Shamanism and the State*, Ann Arbor: University of Michigan Press.

Humphrey, C. 1988. 'No place like home in anthropology: the neglect of architecture', *Anthropology Today* 4(1): 16–18.

Ingold, T. n.d. 'Building, dwelling, and living: how animals and people make themselves at home in the world', Paper delivered at the ASA IV Decennial Conference, Oxford, 1993, m.s.

Ito, T. and Reid, A. 1975. 'From harbour autocracies to "feudal" diffusion in seventeenth century Indonesia: the case of Aceh', in E. Leach, S. Mukherjee and J. Ward (eds.), *Feudalism: Comparative Studies*, Sydney: Pathfinder.

Ivanoff, J. 1987. 'Les Moken et la "Maison" ', in C. Macdonald (ed.), *De la Hutte au Palais: Sociétés "à Maisons" en Asie du Sud-Est Insulaire*, Paris: Editions du CNRS.

Izikowitz, K. G. and Sorensen, P. (eds.) 1982. *The House in East and Southeast Asia: Anthropological and Architectural Aspects*, London: Curzon Press.

Jackson, J. 1975. 'Recent ethnography of indigenous northern lowland South America', *Annual Review of Anthropology* 4: 307–40.

1983. *The Fish People*, Cambridge: Cambridge University Press.

Janowski, M. R. H. 1991. 'Rice, Work and Community among the Kelabit of Sarawak', Ph.D. Thesis, London School of Economics.

Jordaan, R. E. and Niehof, A. 1988. '*Sirih pinang* and symbolic dualism in Indonesia', in D. S. Moyer and H. M. Claessen (eds.), *Time Past, Time Present, Time Future. Essays in Honour of P. E. de Josselin de Jong*, Dordrecht: Foris Publications.

Josselin de Jong, P. E. de 1951. *Minangkabau and Negri Sembilan: Socio-Political Structure in Indonesia*, Leiden: Ijdo.

Kana, N. 1980. 'The order and significance of the Savunese house', in J. J. Fox (ed.), *The Flow of Life: Essays on Eastern Indonesia*, Cambridge, Mass.: Harvard University of Press.

Karp, I. and Maynard, K. 1983. 'Reading the Nuer', *Current Anthropology* 24, 481–503.

King, V. T. (ed.) 1978. *Essays on Borneo societies*, Oxford: Oxford University Press.

Kis-Jovak, J., Nooy-Palm, H. Schefold, R. and Dornburg, U. 1988. *Banua Toraja: Changing Patterns in Architecture and Symbolism among the Sa'dan Toraja, Sulawesi, Indonesia*, Amsterdam: Royal Tropical Institute.

Ko, T. H. J. 1987. 'Minor indigenous groups in Sarawak', *Sarawak Gazette* 113(1501): 31–3.

Koch-Grünberg, T. 1910. *Zwei Jahre unter den Indianern: Reisen in Nordwest-Brasilien*, Berlin: Wasmuth.

1923. *Vom Roraima zum Orinoco*, vol. III, Stuttgart: Strecker and Schröder.

Koelewijn, C. with Rivière, P. G. 1987. *Oral Literature of the Trio Indians of Surinam*, Dordrecht: Foris Publications.

Kroeber, A. 1925. *Handbook of the Indians of California*. Bureau of American Ethnology, Bulletin 78. Washington D.C.

1938. 'Basic and secondary patterns of social structure', *Journal of the Royal Anthropological Institute* 68: 299–309.

1985. *Handbook of the Indians of California*, Washington: Smithsonian Institution.

Kuper, A. 1982a. *Wives for Cattle*, London: Routledge.

1982b. 'Lineage theory: a critical retrospect', *Annual Review of Anthropology* 11: 71–95.

1982c. 'African-Omaha: a review article', *Bijdragen tot de Taal-, Land- en Volkenkunde* 138: 152–60.

1988. *The Invention of Primitive Society*, London: Routledge.

1993. 'The "house" and Zulu political structure in the nineteenth century', Journal of African History 34: 469–87.

Labby, D. 1976. *The Demystification of Yap: Dialectics of Culture on a Micronesian Island*, Chicago: University of Chicago Press.

Ladeira, M. E. 1982. 'A troca de nomes e a troca de cônjuges: uma contribuição ao estudo do parentesco Timbira', M.A. thesis, São Paulo University.

Laderman, C. 1983. *Wives and Midwives; Childbirth and Nutrition in Rural Malaysia*, Berkeley: University of California Press.

Laslett, P. (ed.) 1972. *Household and Family in Past Time*, Cambridge: Cambridge University Press.

Lave, J. C. 1967. 'Social Taxonomy among the Krĩkàti (Gê) of Central Brazil', Ph.D. thesis, Harvard University.

Lawrence, D. L. 1987. 'What makes a house a home?', *Environmental Behaviour* 19: 154–68.

Lawrence, D. L. and Low, S. M. 1990. 'The built environment and spatial form', *Annual Review of Anthropology* 19: 154–68.

Lea, V. 1986. 'Nomes e *nekrets* Kayapó: uma concepčão de riqueza', Ph.D. thesis, Federal University of Rio de Janeiro.

1992. 'Mẽbengokre (Kayapó) onomastics: a facet of Houses as total social facts in Central Brazil', *Man* 27(1): 129–53.

1993. 'Casas e casas Mẽbengokre (Jê)', in E. Viveiros de Castro and M. Carneiro de Cunha (eds.), *Amazônia: Etnologia e História Indígena*, São Paulo: NHII-USP/FAPESP.

in press. 'Casa–se do outro lado: un sistema simulado de aliança referente aos Mẽbengokre (Jê)', in E. Viveiros de Castro (ed.), *Parentesco Amazônico*, Rio de Janeiro: Editora da UFRJ.

Leach, E. R. 1951. 'The structural implications of matrilateral cross-cousin marriage', *Journal of the Royal Anthropological Institute* 81: 54–104.

1954. *Political Systems of Highland Burma*, London: Athlone.

1958. 'Concerning Trobriand clans and the kinship category *tabu*', in J. R. Goody (ed.), *The Development Cycle in Domestic Groups*, Cambridge: Cambridge University Press.

1961. *Pul Eliya, a Village in Ceylon: a Study of Land Tenure*, Cambridge: Cambridge University Press.

1977. 'The atom of kinship, filiation and descent: error in translation or confusion of ideas?', *L'Homme* 17(2–3): 127–9.

Leach, E. R., Mukherjee, S. and Ward, J. (eds.) 1975. *Feudalism: Comparative Studies*, Sydney: Pathfinder.

Levine, R. and Levine S. 1991. 'House design and the self in an African culture', in A. Jacobson-Widding (ed.), *Body and Space: Symbolic Models of Unity and Division in African Cosmology and Experience*, Uppsala: Almqvist and Wiksell.

Lévi-Strauss, C. 1962a [1980]. *Le totémisme aujourd'hui*, Paris: Plon.

1962b. *La pensée sauvage*, Paris: Plon.

1963 [1956]. 'Do dual organisations exist?', in *Structural Anthropology*, Vol. I, New York: Basic Books.

1965. 'The future of kinship studies', *Proceedings of the Royal Anthropological Institute for 1965*: 13–22.

1969 [1949]. *The Elementary Structures of Kinship*, Boston: Beacon Press.

1973. *From Honey to Ashes*, London: Jonathan Cape.

1973a [1955]. *Tristes tropiques*, London: Cape.

1977. 'Réponse à Edmund Leach', *L'Homme* 17(2–3): 131–3.

1979. *La voie des masques*, Paris: Plon.

1983a. *The Way of the Masks* (trans. S. Modelski), London: Jonathan Cape.

1983b. 'Histoire et ethnologie', *Annales* 38(2): 1217–31.

1984. *Paroles données*, Paris: Plon.

1987. *Anthropology and Myth: Lectures 1951–1982*, Oxford: Blackwell.

1989. *Des symboles et leurs doubles*, Paris: Plon.

1991. 'Maison', in P. Bonte and M. Izard (eds.), *Dictionnaire de l'ethnologie et de l'anthropologie*, Paris: Presses Universitaires de France.

Lim, J. Y. 1987. *The Malay House: Rediscovering Malaysia's Indigenous Shelter System*, Pulau Pinang: Institut Masyarakat.

Littlejohn, J. 1967 [1960]. 'The Temne house', in J. Middleton (ed.), *Myth and Cosmos: Readings in Mythology and Symbolism*, New York: American Museum of Natural History.

Loyré, G. 1987. 'Les maisons de Mindanao', in C. Macdonald (ed.), *De la Hutte au Palais: Sociétés "à Maisons" en Asie du Sud-Est Insulaire*, Paris: Editions du CNRS.

Lundstrom, W. 1982. 'The group of people living in a house', in K. Izikowitz and P. Sorensen (eds.), *The House in East and Southeast Asia: Anthropological and Architectural Aspects*, London: Curzon Press.

Lundstrom-Burghoorn, W. 1981. *Minahasa Civilization: a Tradition of Change*, Gothenburg: University of Gothenburg.

Macdonald, C. (ed.) 1987. *De la hutte au palais: sociétés "à maisons" en Asie du Sud-Est insulaire*, Paris: Editions du CNRS.

1987a. 'Histoire du projet: de la notion de "maison" chez Lévi-Strauss à la comparaison des sociétés en Asie du Sud-est insulaire', in C. Macdonald (ed.), *De la hutte au palais: sociétés "à maisons" en Asie du Sud-Est insulaire*, Paris: Editions du CNRS.

1987b. 'Sociétés "à maisons" et types d'organisation sociale aux Philippines', in C. Macdonald (ed.), *De la hutte au palais: sociétés "à maisons" en Asie du Sud-Est insulaire*, Paris: Editions du CNRS.

Macfarlane, A. 1978. *The Origins of English Individualism: the Family, Property and Social Transition*, Oxford: Blackwell.

Marshall, M. (ed.) 1981. *Siblingship in Oceania: Studies in the Meaning of Kin Relations*, Lanham, MD: University Press of America.

Martindale. 1977. 'The French aristocracy in the early middle ages: a reappraisal', *Past and Present* 75: 5–45.

Mattéi-Muller, M. and Henley, P. S. 1990. *Los Tamanaku: su lengua, su vida*, Caracas: Editorial Arte.

Mauss, M. 1954. *The Gift: Forms and Functions of Exchange in Archaic Societies*, London: Cohen and West.

Mauss, M. with Beuchat, H. 1979 [1904–5]. *Seasonal Variations of the Eskimo: a Study in Social Morphology*, London: Routledge and Kegan Paul.

Maybury-Lewis, D. (ed.) 1979. *Dialectical Societies: the Gê and Bororo of Central Brazil*, Cambridge, Mass.: Harvard University Press.

McKinley, R. 1981. 'Cain and Abel on the Malay peninsula', in M. Marshall (ed.), *Siblingship in Oceania: Studies in the Meaning of Kin Relations*, Lanham, MD: University Press of America.

McKinnon, S. 1983. 'Hierarchy, Alliance and Exchange in the Tanimbar Islands', Ph.D. thesis, University of Chicago.

1987. 'The house altars of Tanimbar: abstraction and ancestral presence', *Tribal Art (Bulletin of the Barbier-Mueller Museum*, Geneva) 1: 3–16.

1989. 'Flags and half-moons: Tanimbarese textiles in an "engendered" system of valuables', in M. Gittinger (ed.), *To Speak with Cloth: Studies in Indonesian Textiles*, Los Angeles: University of California Cultural History Museum.

1991. *From a Shattered Sun: Hierarchy, Gender and Alliance in the Tanimbar Islands*, Madison, Wisconsin: University of Wisconsin Press.

Melatti, J. C. 1979. 'The Relationship System of the Krahó', in D. Maybury-Lewis (ed.), *Dialectical Societies: the Gê and Bororo of Central Brazil*, Cambridge, Mass.: Harvard University Press.

Metcalf, P. 1974. 'The Baram district: a survey of Kenyah, Kayan and Penan peoples', in J. Rousseau (ed.): *The Peoples of Central Borneo. Sarawak Museum Journal Special Issue* 22(43): 29–43.

1989. *Where Are You Spirits? Style and Theme in Berawan Prayer*. Washington and London: Smithsonian Institution Press.

Milner, G. B. (ed.) 1978. *Natural Symbols in Southeast Asia*, London: School of Oriental and African Studies, University of London.

Moore, H. 1986. *Space, Text and Gender*, Cambridge: Cambridge University Press.

Morgan, L. H. 1965 [1981]. *Houses and House-Life of the American Aborigines*, Chicago: University of Chicago Press.

Morris, H. S. 1953. *Report on a Melanau Sago Producing Community in Sarawak*, London: HMSO (for the Colonial Office).

Morton, J. A. 1979. 'Conceptions of Fertility and Mortality Among the Waiwai Indians of Southern Guiana', M.Litt. thesis, University of Oxford.

Moyer, D. S. 1983. 'Cultural constraints on marriage: anti-exchange behaviour in nineteenth century South Sumatra', *Bijdragen tot de Taal-, Land- en Volkenkunde* 139: 247–58.

Bibliography

Murakami, Y. 1984. 'Ie society as a pattern of civilization', *Journal of Japanese Society* 10(2): 279–363.

Murdock, G. 1960. 'Cognatic forms of social organization', in G. P. Murdock (ed.), *Social Structure in Southeast Asia*, Chicago: Quadrangle Books.

———— 1965. *Social Structure*, New York: Free Press.

Murphy, R. 1979. 'Lineage and lineality in lowland South America', in M. Margolis and W. Carter (eds.), *Brazil: Anthropological Perspectives*, New York: Columbia University Press.

Müller, R. 1976. 'A pintura do corpo e os ornamentos Xavante: arte visual e comunicação social', M.A. thesis, State University of Campinas (UNICAMP).

Nakane, C. 1970. *Japanese Society*, Harmondsworth: Penguin.

Needham, R. 1956. 'A note of kinship and marriage on Pantara', *Bijdragen tot de Taal-, Land- en Volkenkunde* 112: 285–90.

———— 1957. 'Circulating connubium in Eastern Sumba: a literary analysis', *Bijdragen tot de Taal-, Land- en Volkenkunde* 113: 168–78.

———— 1962. *Structure and Sentiment*, Chicago: University of Chicago Press.

———— 1966. 'Terminology and alliance, I: Garo, Manggarai', *Sociologus* 16: 141–57.

———— 1967. 'Terminology and alliance, II: Mapuche, conclusions', *Sociologus* 17: 39–53.

———— 1968. 'Endeh: terminology, alliance and analysis', *Bijdragen tot de Taal-, Land- en Volkenkunde* 124: 305–35.

———— 1970. 'Endeh, II: test and confirmation', *Bijdragen tot de Taal-, Land- en Volkenkunde* 126: 246–58.

———— 1980. 'Principles and variations in the structure of Sumbanese society', in J. J. Fox (ed.), *The Flow of Life: Essays on Eastern Indonesia*, Cambridge, Mass.: Harvard University of Press.

Nimuendajú, C. 1971 [1946]. *The Eastern Timbira*, New York: Berkeley and Los Angeles University of California Press, Kraus Reprint Co.

———— 1983 [1939]. *Os Apinayé*, Belém, Pará: Museu Paranense Emílio Goeldi.

Norbeck, E. 1954. *Takashima: A Japanese Fishing Community*, Salt Lake City: University of Utah Press.

Oliver, P. 1987. *Dwellings: the House Across the World*, Oxford: Phaidon.

Onvlee, L. 1980. 'Mannelik en vrouwelijk in de sociale organisatie van Soemba', in R. Schefold, J. W. Schoorl and J. Tennekes (eds.), *Man, Meaning and History. Essays in honour of H. G. Schulte Nordholt*, The Hague: Martinus Nijhoff.

Ossenbruggen, F. D. en van 1930. 'Verwantschaps- en huwelijksvormen in den Indischen archipel', *Tijdschrift van het Aardrijkskundig Genootschap* 47: 212–29.

———— 1935. 'Het oeconomisch-magische element in Tobasche verwantschapsverhoudingen', *Mededeelingen der Koninklijke Akademie van Wetenschappen, Afd. Letterkunde* 80: 63–125.

Overing Kaplan, J. 1975. *The Piaroa: a People of the Orinoco basin*, Oxford: Clarendon Press.

———— 1981. 'Review article: Amazonian anthropology', *Journal of Latin American Studies* 13: 151–65.

Parmentier, R. J. 1984. 'House affiliation systems in Belau', *American Ethnologist* 11: 656–76.

Parry, J. and Bloch, M. (eds.) 1989. *Money and the Morality of Exchange*, Cambridge: Cambridge University Press.

Pauwels, S. 1990. 'From Hursu Ribun's "three hearth stones" to Metanleru's "sailing boat"; a ritual after the harvest', *Bijdragen tot de Taal-, Land- en Volkenkunde* 146(1): 21–34.

Pina-Cabral, J. de 1986. *Sons of Adam, Daughters of Eve: the Peasant Worldview of the Alto Minho*, Oxford: Clarendon Press.

1990. 'L'héritage de Maine: repenser les catégories déscriptives dans l'étude de la famille en Europe', *Ethnologie Française* 29(4): 292–340.

Price, D. 1987. 'Nambiquara geopolitical organization', *Man* 22(1): 1–24.

Prior, J. M. 1988. *Church and Marriage in an Indonesian Village*, Frankfurt: Peter Lang.

Provencher, R. 1971. *Two Malay Worlds: Interaction in Urban and Rural Settings*, Berkeley: Center for South and Southeast Asian Studies.

Prussin, L. 1969. *Architecture in Northern Ghana*, Berkeley: University of California Press.

Radcliffe-Brown, A. R. 1950. 'Introduction', in A. R. Radcliffe-Brown and D. Forde (eds.), *African Systems of Kinship and Marriage*, London: Oxford University Press.

Rakoto, I. 1965. *Le Fafy est-il une simple levée d'empêchement au marriage*, Cahier du Centre des Études des Coutumes, Université de Madagascar.

Rapoport, A. 1969. *House Form and Culture*, New Jersey: Prentice Hall.

Reichel, E. and von Hildebrand, M. 1985. 'Vivienda indĩgena. Grupo Ufaina, Amazonas. Función socio-polĩtica de la maloca', *Proa (Bogotá)* 372: 16–23.

Reichel-Dolmatoff, G. 1971. *Amazonian Cosmos: the Sexual and Religious Symbolism of the Tukano Indians*, Chicago: Chicago University Press.

Rivière, P. G. 1969. *Marriage Among the Trio*, Oxford: Clarendon Press.

1970. 'Factions and exclusions in two South American village systems', in M. Douglas (ed.), *Witchcraft Confessions and Accusations*, London: Tavistock.

1981. 'A report on the Trio Indians of Surinam', *Nieuwe West-Indische Gids* 55: 1–38.

1984. *Individual and Society in Guiana: a Comparative Study of Amerindian Social Organisation*, Cambridge: Cambridge University Press.

Rodgers, S. 1990. 'The symbolic representation of women in a changing Batak culture', in J. M. Atkinson and S. Errington (eds.), *Power and Difference: Gender in Island Southeast Asia*, Stanford: Stanford University Press.

Rodman, M. C. 1985. 'Moving houses: residential mobility and the mobility of residence in Longana, Vanuatu', *American Anthropologist* 87: 56–72.

Roosevelt, A. 1991. *Moundbuilders of the Amazon*, London–New York: Academic Press.

Rosengren, D. 1987. *In the Eyes of the Beholder. Ethnological Studies* 39, Göteborg: Etnografiska Museum.

Roth, W. E. 1924. *An Introductory Study of the Arts, Crafts, and Customs of the Guiana Indians. 38th Annual Report of the Bureau of American Ethnology*, Washington: Government Printing Office.

Rousseau, J. 1990. *Central Borneo: Ethnic Identity and Social Life in a Stratified Society*, Oxford: Clarendon Press.

Sabean, D. 1990. *Property, Production, and Family in Neckarhausen, 1700–1870*, Cambridge: Cambridge University Press.

Bibliography

Sahlins, M. D. 1965. 'On the ideology and composition of descent groups', *Man* 65: 104–7.

——— 1974. *Stone Age Economics*, London: Tavistock.

Sather, C. 1993. 'Posts, hearths and thresholds; the Iban longhouse as a ritual structure', in J. Fox (ed.), *Inside Austronesian Houses: Perspectives on Domestic Designs for Living*, Canberra: Department of Anthropology, Research School of Pacific Studies.

Schneider, D. M. 1984. *A Critique of the Study of Kinship*, Ann Arbor: University of Michigan Press.

Schulte Nordholt, H. G. 1971. *The Political System of the Atoni of Timor*, The Hague: Nijhof.

——— 1980. 'The symbolic classification of the Atoni of Timor', in J. J. Fox (ed.), *The Flow of Life: Essays on Eastern Indonesia*, Cambridge, Mass.: Harvard University Press.

Schwartzman, S. 1987. 'The Panara of the Xingu National Park', Ph.D. thesis, Chicago University.

Seeger, A. 1980. *Os Indios e Nós*, Rio de Janeiro: Campus.

——— 1981. *Nature and Society in Central Brazil: the Suya Indians of Matto Grosso*, Cambridge: Harvard University Press.

Sellato, B. 1987a. 'Note préliminaire sur les sociétés "à maisons" à Bornéo', in C. Macdonald (ed.), *De la hutte au palais: sociétés "à maisons" en Asie du Sud-Est insulaire*, Paris: Editions du CNRS.

——— 1987b. ' "Maisons" et organisation sociale en Asie du Sud-Est', in C. Macdonald (ed.), *De la hutte au palais: sociétés "à maisons" en Asie du Sud-Est insulaire*, Paris: Editions du CNRS.

Seymour-Smith, C. 1991. 'Women have no affines and men no kin: the politics of the Jivaroan gender relation', *Man* 26(4): 629–49.

Shapiro, J. 1987. 'Men in groups: a re-examination of patriliny in Lowland South America', in J. Collier and S. Yanagisako (eds.), *Gender and Kinship: Essays Towards a Unified Analysis*, Stanford: Stanford University Press.

Smith, R. 1983. *Japanese Society: Tradition, Self and the Social Order*, Cambridge: Cambridge University Press.

Southall, A. 1986. 'The illusion of Nath agnation', *Ethnology* 25(1): 1–20.

Strathern, A. 1973. 'Kinship, descent and locality: some New Guinea examples', in J. R. Goody (ed.), *The Character of Kinship*, Cambridge: Cambridge University Press.

Strathern, M. 1988. *The Gender of the Gift: Problems with Women and Problems with Society in Melanesia*, Berkeley: University of California Press.

Tambiah, S. J. 1969. 'Animals are good to think and good to prohibit', *Ethnology* 8: 423–59.

Thomas, D. J. 1982. *Order Without Government: the Society of the Pemon Indians of Venezuela*. Illinois Studies in Anthropology, 13, Urbana: Illinois University Press.

Thomas, N. 1985. 'Forms of personification and prestations', *Mankind* 15(3): 223–30.

Traube, E. G. 1980. 'Mambai rituals of black and white', in J. J. Fox (ed.), *The Flow of Life: Essays on Eastern Indonesia*, Cambridge, Mass.: Harvard University Press.

1986. *Cosmology and Social Life: Ritual Exchange among the Mambai of East Timor*, Chicago: University of Chicago Press.

Tronchon, J. 1974. *L'Insurrection Malgache de 1947*, Paris: Maspéro.

Turner, T. 1966. 'Social Structure and Political Organization among the Northern Kayapó', Ph.D. thesis, Harvard University.

1979a. 'The Gê and Bororo societies as dialectical systems: a general model', in D. Maybury-Lewis (ed.), *Dialectical Societies: the Gê and Bororo of Central Brazil*, Cambridge, Mass.: Harvard University Press.

1979b. 'Kinship, household and community structure among the Kayapó', in D. Maybury-Lewis (ed.), *Dialectical Societies: the Gê and Bororo of Central Brazil*, Cambridge, Mass.: Harvard University Press.

Turton, A. 1972. 'Matrilineal descent groups and spirit cults of the Thai-Yuan in Northern Thailand', *Journal of the Siam Society* 60(2): 217–56.

1978. 'Architectural and political space in Thailand', in G. Milner (ed.), *Natural Symbols in Southeast Asia*, London: School of Oriental and African Studies.

Umúsin Panlõn Kumu and Tolamãn Kenhíri 1980. Antes o mundo não existia. São Paulo: Livraria Cultura.

Valeri, V. 1975–76. 'Alliances et échanges matrimoniaux à Seram Central (Moluques)', *L'Homme* 15(3–4): 83–107; 16(1): 125–49.

1980. 'Notes on the meaning of marriage prestations among the Huaulu of Seram', in J. Fox (ed.), *The Flow of Life: Essays on Eastern Indonesia*, Cambridge, Mass.: Harvard University Press.

Vansina, J. 1973. *The Tio Kingdom of the Middle Congo 1880–1892*, London: Oxford University Press.

Vérin, P. 1964. 'Les Zafimaniry et leur art. Un groupe forestier continuateur d'une tradition ésthétique malgache méconnue', *Revue de Madagascar* 27: 1–16.

Verswijver, G. 1983. 'Cycles in Kaiapo naming practices', *Communication and Cognition* 16(3): 301–23.

1984. 'Ciclos nas práticas de nominacão Kaiapó', *Revista do Museu Paulista* 29: 97–124.

Vidal, L. 1977. *Morte e Vida de uma Sociedade Indígena Brasileira*, São Paulo: Hucitec.

Viveiros de Castro, E. 1986. *Araweté: os Deuses Canibais*, Rio de Janeiro: Zahar/ANPOCS.

1990. 'Princípios e Parâmetros: um comentário a L'Exercise de la Parenté. Programa de Pós-graduacão em Antropologia Social, Museu Nacional, UFRJ', *Comunicação* no. 17.

1993. 'Alguns aspectos da afinidade no dravidianato amazonico', in E. Viveiros de Castro and M. Carneiro da Cunha (eds.), *Amazônia: Etnologia e História Indígena*, São Paulo: Núcleo de História Indígena.

Wagner, R. 1967. *The Curse of Souw: Principles of Daribi Clan Definition and Alliance*, Chicago: University of Chicago Press.

1975. *The Invention of Culture*, Englewood Cliffs, New Jersey: Prentice-Hall.

1977. 'Analogic kinship: a Daribi example', *American Ethnologist* 4: 623–42.

Wallace, A. R. 1889. *Travels on the Amazon and the Rio Negro*, London: Ward Lock.

Waterson, R. 1984. 'Ritual and Belief among the Sa'dan Toraja', *Occasional Paper No. 2, University of Kent Centre of Southeast Asian Studies*.

285

1986. 'The ideology and terminology of kinship among the Sa'dan Toraja', *Bijdragen tot de Taal-, Land- en Volkenkunde* 142(1): 87–112.

1990. *The Living House: an Anthropology of Architecture in Southeast Asia*, Kuala Lumpur: Oxford University Press.

1992. 'Using houses as history in Tana Toraja, Sulawesi (Indonesia)', *People and Physical Environment Research* 39–40: 15–21.

1993. 'Houss and built environment in island South-East Asia', in J. Fox (ed.), *Inside Austronesian Houses: Perspectives on Domestic Designs for Living*, Canberra: Department of Anthropology, Research School of Pacific Studies.

n.d.a. 'Houses and life processes in island South-East Asia: the notion of *semangat* and the living house', Paper presented at the Seminar on Architectural Research in Small-Scale Societies of South-East Asia, Centre of Non-Western Studies, University of Leiden, 2–3 Dec. 1993.

n.d.b. 'Houses, graves and the limits of family among the Sa'dan Toraja of Sulawesi (Indonesia)', Paper presented at the First Asean Inter-University Seminar on Social Development, at the Universiti Kebangsaan Malaysia, Sabah Campus, Kota Kinabalu, 12–15 Nov. 1993.

Whittier, H. L. 1973. 'Social Organisation and Symbols of Social Differentiation: an Ethnographic Study of the Kenyah Dayak of East Kalimantan (Borneo)', Ph.D. thesis, Michigan State University.

Wilbert, J. 1981. 'Warao cosmology and Yekuana roundhouse symbolism', *Journal of Latin American Lore* 7(1): 37–72.

Willis, R. 1974. *Man and Beast*, St Albans: Palladin.

Wilson, P. 1988. *The Domestication of the Human Species*, New Haven: Yale University Press.

Wouden, F. A. E. van. 1968 [1935]. *Types of Social Structure in Eastern Indonesia*, The Hague: Nijhoff.

1977 [1956]. 'Local groups and double descent in Kodi, West Sumba', in P. E. de Josselin de Jong (ed.), *Structural Anthropology in the Netherlands*, The Hague: Nijhoff.

Wulff, I. 1982. 'Habitation among the Yakan, a Muslim people in the Southern Philippines', in K. Izikowitz and P. Sorensen (eds.), *The House in East and Southeast Asia: Anthropological and Architectural Aspects*, London: Curzon Press.

Yalman, N. 1967. *Under the Bo Tree*, Berkeley and Los Angeles: University of California Press.

Yamaguchi, M. 1989. 'Nai Keu, a ritual of the Lio in Central Flores', *Bijdragen tot de Taal-, Land- en Volkenkunde* 145(4): 478–89.

Yanagisako, S. J. 1979. 'Family and household: the analysis of domestic groups', *Annual Review of Anthropology* 8: 161–205.

Yde, J. 1965. *Material Culture of the Waiwai, Ethnographic Series*, 10, Copenhagen: National Museum of Denmark.

INDEX

Page numbers in *italics* refer to illustrations

abandonment of house, 40, 197, 198, 228, 247
above–below symbolism, 22, 123, 124, 158
abstract category, house as, 32, 50, 68
Aceh, 53–4
affines, affinity, 8, 22, 131, 218, 251
    affinal relations, 150, 175–7, 181–3, 232–3
    and consanguinity, resolution of opposition between, 199–200, 204, 211, 237, 249–50
    and siblingship, 38–9, 115, 116, 127, 144
    transformation into kin, 38–9, 119, 120--1, *122*, 132, 144--5
    see also alliance; wife-givers and wife-takers
African societies, 13, 15, 16–17, 18, 217, 253 n.2
agnatic descent, *see* patrilineality
Akawaio Indians, 189, 194, 198
alliance, 166–7, 246, 254 n.13
    asymmetric, 22, 24, 26, 33, 122, 124, 155, 163, 248
    and descent, house's role in resolving antagonisms between, 8, 29, 84–6, 105–6, 126–7, 149–51, 249, 261nn.1 & 3
    symmetric, 33, 227, 231
    theory, Lévi-Strauss's formulation of, 8, 13–15, 18, 84, 106, 126–7, 130–1, 165

Amazonia, 21, 37, 40, 226, 248, 249
    Northwest, 33, 200, 203, 219, 238, 248–9
    see also ancestors; mountain symbolism; myth; river symbolism; shaman; Tukanoans
anaconda, 234–6, 238–41 *passim*, *242*, 243–4, 269 nn.11 & 13
ancestors, 54, 56
    Amazonian, 37, 40, 232, 234–6, 238–41 *passim*, 243–4, 249
    Lio, 154–5, 157, 159, 161, 163, 165, 166, 167, 263 n.10
    Makassarese, 137–8
    Malagasy, 71, 80, 83
    Mêbengokre, 209, 223
    Tanimbarese, 177–8
    see also genealogies
Andean societies, 3, 5
'androgynous house', 44, 178–9, 241, 245–7
animate being, house as, 23, 37, 40, 42
    see also body imagery
antagonisms, house's role in resolution of, *see* opposing principles
Apinayé, 219, 267 n.6
Ara, ritual cycle in, 132–48
    see also Makassarese
architectural features, 20–1, 26, 27, 43, 78–9, 228, 241
    and rank, relationship between, 11–12, 58–60
    see also doors; hearth; houseposts; thatch(ing); structure of house
architecture, in anthropological analysis, 2–6, 20–1, 226

Southeast Asian categories, 22, 24,
28–9, 55, 153, 161–8 *passim*, 246
see also alliance; matrilineality;
patrilineality; unilineality
'domestic cluster', 33, 219, 220, 221
domestic domain, 32, 35, 193, 216
associated with women, 210, 225, 246
domestic group, 4, 17, 22
doors, entrances, 193, 228, 233
Dravidian systems, 30, 33, 218, 227,
248, 249, 251, 268 n.20
Dreyfus, S., 31, 211
dualism, 24–5, 125, 131
concentric, 24–5, 31, 122–3, 194, 251
Dumont, J-P., 190, 202
Dumont, L., 56
Durkheim, E., 130

east–west symbolism, 32, 124, 125, 207,
211
economy, house as, 5, 20, 39, 42
egalitarianism, 10, 11, 34, 60, 67, 71,
125
in Tukanoan social relations, 227,
237, 244
elementary structures, Lévi-Strauss's
concept of, 9–10, 12–13, 14–15,
18, 31
Ellen, R., 23, 24
encompassment, image of, 25, 60–1,
123, 180, 194, 246, 250, 264, n.10
endogamy, 7, 24, 123, 125, 131
in Guiana, 198–9, 204, 248
Langkawi, 116, 119
Tukanoan, 231, 237, 249
English aristocratic houses, 63
Errington, S., 50, 131, 154
characterization of Southeast Asian
societies, 24–5, 28, 122–5 *passim*,
128, 151–2, 248
Europe, feudal, 49, 50–1, 54, 61, 254
n.9
Lévi-Strauss's analysis of noble
houses, 6–7, 11, 15, 28, 47, 62–3,
152
Evans-Pritchard, E., 6, 15, 16, 170, 171

exchange
Langkawi, 118–19, 120, 126
Lio, 166–7
Tanimbarese, 175–8, *179*, 264 n.8
Tukanoan, 232–3
see also food
exogamy, 7, 219, 220
Tukanoan, 227, 231, 237, 238, 249

fasting, 244–5
feasts, Langkawi, 118, 121
see also dance-feasts; naming-feasts;
rice meals
feather symbolism, Tukanoan
feather-box, 228, *230*, 234, 236–7,
241, 244
head-dresses and ornaments, 228,
234, 236–7, 241, 247
myth of feather-people, 234–5
'fetishization' of house, 25, 79
Lévi-Strauss's formulation of, 8, 12,
50, 106, 174, 246
feudalism, 50–1, 52–4, 56, 61, 67, 148
Japanese, 63–6
see also Europe
Firth, R., 22, 107
fish, fishing, 99, 101, 120, 211, 231, 237
'five' symbolism, 234, 238, 239, 251
Flores, 26, 152, 154
food
consumption, 27, 42, 97, *122*, 211
displays, 133, 141–2
exchange, 117, 119, 227, 232–3, 237
gender associations, 27, 95, 100–2,
103, 114, 231, 232–3, 237
production, provision, 87, 95, 96–7,
98, 100–2, 114
restrictions, 101, 215–16
sharing, 93–4, 99–100, 114, 231
see also cooking symbolism; feasts; fish;
fruit; hearth; meat; rice
Food-giving House, Tukanoan, 232–3,
237, 244
forest, 86–7, 100, 101, 102, 193
'forest estates', Tanimbarese, 175, 177
Fortes, M., 15

Makuna, *229*, 237, 238
Malaysia, 25, 41, 44, 107, 123, 124
  social structures, 22, 38, 125
  see also Langkawi
maloca, Tukanoan, 12, 226, 227–47,
  249–52 *passim*
  plan of interior, *230*
Mambai, 24, 57
manioc beer, 232–3
  trough, 228, 234, 236
manioc bread, 231, 244–5
Maranao sultanate, 53
marriage, 105, 170–1
  and creation of Zafimaniry house, 26,
   71, 72–9, 81
  cross-cousin, 155, 162, 163, 168,
   182–3, 184, 214, 248
  in 'elementary' and 'complex'
   structures, Lévi-Strauss's discussion
   of, 9, 12–13, 14–15, 31, 130, 247–8
  Guianese, 198–200, 204, 248
  Langkawi, 119, 121, 126, 127
  Lévi-Strauss's emphasis on conjugal
   couple as core of house, 26–7, 71,
   72, 84, 103–4, 131
  Lio, 155, 162, 163, 168
  Makassarese, 134–5, 138, 141
  Mẽbengokre, 214, 217
  relationship of conjugal pair to
   Kelabit house, 26–7, 84–6, 94–8,
   103–4
  Tanimbarese, 29–30, 179, 182–3,
   184–6, 187
  Tukanoan, 227, 231–2, 233, 237,
   247, 249
  see also endogamy; exogamy;
   uxorilocality; virilocality; wife-
   givers and wife-takers
Marx, Karl, 8
Mato Grosso, Brazil, 208
matrilateral affiliation, 29, 175, 179,
  180–1, 199
matrilineality, 32, 33, 125, 173, 218,
  219, 220, 240
  Mẽbengokre, 34, 221, 222, 223, 224
Mauss, M., 5, 14

Maybury-Lewis, D., 210, 224
meat, 42, 93, 99, 101, 102, 209, 211,
  231, 237
Mẽbengokre (Kayapó), 10, 41, 206–25,
  255 n.30
  compared with Tukanoans, 34, 36,
   43, 250–1
  see also Bororo; clan; friendship;
   marriage, matrilineality; moral
   persons; myth; names; *nekrets*;
   patrilineality; patrimony; ritual;
   siblings; structure of house;
   uxorilocality; village
Melanau tribe, Borneo, 87
Melatti, J. C., 215, 219
men,
  men's houses, 32, 43, 211, 250
  relations between, 112, 120
  see also ceremonial domain; food;
   gender
Merina, Madagascar, 37, 69, 71, 73
Mẽtùktire (Txukarramãe), 208
microcosm, house as, 23, 42, 60, 160,
  194–5, 196
  see also cosmology
Minahasan, 123, 124, 125
Minangkabau, 61
miñe' (Trio beehive-shaped house), 191,
  192, 196
mobility of houses, 40, 107–9, 126, 128,
  198–9
Moken sea nomads, 50, 68
Moluccas, 24, 26
  see also Tanimbarese
Moore, H., 36, 41
moral persons, 14
  in Lévi-Strauss's notion of the house,
   6–7, 149–50, 169, 201, 202, 241
  Lio houses as, 152, 160, 163, 164,
   166
  Mẽbengokre houses as, 206, 210, 224
Morgan, L. H., 5
Morton, J. A., 202
mountain symbolism
  Amazonian, 233–4, 241, 247, 249
  Guianese, 35, 194, 196, 201, 202